CONTENTS

List of Illustrations   vii
Preface   ix
Introduction   1

1 Transportation and the Effective Occupation of Australia   5
2 The First Governor and his People   29
3 The Years of Struggle 1788–1860   48
4 Trials of 'the Tyrants'   58
5 The 'Dark People'   73
6 Pastures, Progress and Gold 1850–1900   90
7 'A Radiant Land'   107
8 The Ethnic Origins of the Australians   127
9 Views and Prospects of Australia in the Eighties   142
10 An Evolving Relationship 1900–18   166
11 Credits, Crises and Cricket 1918–39   177
12 Mr Curtin Moves Over   194
13 Windows on the World   208
14 Australia Today; Australia Tomorrow   236

Map of Australia   260
Further Reading   262
Index   267

AUSTRALIA
1788–1988
THE CREATION OF A NATION

Charles Wilson

BARNES & NOBLE BOOKS
Totowa, New Jersey

First published in the USA 1988 by
Barnes & Noble Books
81 Adams Drive
Totowa, New Jersey, 07512

ISBN 0-389-20768-3

Library of Congress Cataloging-in-Publication Data

Wilson, Charles, 1914–
     Australia, 1788–1988

     Includes bibliographical references and index.
     1. Australia – History.   I. Title.
DU108.W55   1988   994   87-17487
ISBN 0-389-20768-3

Printed in Great Britain

ILLUSTRATIONS

Arthur Phillip by Francis Wheatley (by courtesy of the National Portrait Gallery)

The Captain Matthew Flinders memorial window (by kind permission of A. K. James)

The ruins of the former penal colony at Port Arthur, Tasmania (Promotion Australia, London)

A family of New South Wales natives, engraved by William Blake after a sketch by Governor King (Weidenfeld & Nicolson archive)

Governor Lachlan Macquarie by John Opie (Max Dupain and Associates, Sydney)

St Matthew's Church, Windsor (Weidenfeld & Nicolson archive)

Gold Diggings near Mount Alexander, 1874 by Samuel Thomas Gill (Sotheby's Australia)

Nellie Melba (Royal Opera House archive)

Percy Grainger (E. T. Archive)

Eugene Goossens with Arturo Toscanini (author's photo)

Steve Fairbairn by D. B. Quinn (by kind permission of the Master and Fellows of Jesus College, Cambridge)

Nineteenth-century terrace with cast-ironwork (Promotion Australia, London)

Sir Henry Parkes by Tom Roberts (Art Gallery of New South Wales)

A View of Sydney Harbour by Conrad Martens (Mitchell Library, Sydney)

Spring's Innocence by Norman Lindsay (Sotheby's Australia)

Melbourne Burning by Arthur Boyd (Sotheby's Australia)

Sydney today (Weidenfeld & Nicolson archive)

PREFACE

This book makes no claim to be a definitive history of Australia. It simply explores a selection of episodes which seem to me important and sometimes misunderstood.

The venture originated in my birthplace, Market Rasen, Lincolnshire, where my family have farmed and traded for at least two centuries. It lies at the foot of the Wolds, on the perimeter of a small triangle of country from which came some of the greatest names in early Australian history. From Revesby Abbey came Sir Joseph Banks and his two sturdy tenants, Biscoe and Roberts, who all accompanied James Cook in 1770; from Donington, a little to the south, Matthew Flinders and his brother Samuel, respectively skipper and first lieutenant of the *Investigator*. Five miles west is Aswarby, home of Flinders' closest collaborator and discoverer of the Bass Strait, George Bass: probably also a relation of Flinders. The coast of South Australia pays nostalgic tribute to their efforts – Cape Donington, Spalding Cove, Sleaford Mere, Boston Island and a dozen other echoes of fen, marsh and wold. For years the coast of South Australia was to be known as Flinders' Land.

Flinders and Bass were what, in local parlance, were known as 'yellow-bellies' – fenmen. Flinders' midshipman, John Franklin, and second lieutenant, Robert Fowler, came from a little further north, Spilsby and Horncastle, small towns in the wold country.

Franklin was related by marriage to Flinders. He was also the link between the explorers and the Tennyson family. His two nieces married Tennysons: Emily became the wife of Alfred, Poet Laureate; Louisa married Charles, Alfred's brother. This brings us back to Market Rasen, where Michael Tennyson, surgeon and physician, and his son George, attorney (1750–1835) had founded the Tennyson fortunes. Even in my childhood, George, grandfather of the Poet Laureate, was still remembered in village folk lore as a shrewd, acquisitive, domineering lawyer. As children we would sit on the wall by the mill stream and watch the kingfishers flash, blue and green, over the sunlit water as they dived after the sticklebacks. The stream ran down past the pleasant house where old George had lived before he moved out, and up, to grander country properties on the Wolds.

George split his fortune, and his family. To his second son, Charles, he entrusted most of his money; his eldest, George Clayton, disinherited as eccentric and unreliable, became the penurious incumbent of the tiny Wolds village of Somersby, surrounded by a brood of eleven wild, gifted children as eccentric as their father. They included Alfred, future Poet Laureate, and his brother Charles, whose first joint book of verse was published by my great-grandmother's family at Louth, Jacksons, the printers and publishers, in 1827.

When Alfred finally married, after years of hypochondriac self-doubt, he chose as his bride Emily Sellwood, niece of Sir John Franklin, who was later to become Lieutenant Governor of Tasmania and martyred hero of the search for the North West Passage. It took an hour or so to drive in my cousin's pony and trap across the Wolds to gaze at his impressive bronze statue by Charles Bacon opposite Spilsby Church. His epitaph in Westminster Abbey was composed by Tennyson.

The bond that held together this remarkable group was Banks of Revesby, imperious President of the Royal Society for nearly half a century and Privy Counsellor from 1798. It was Banks who, on their behalf, prodded torpid ministers and ungrateful Admiralty mandarins, and comforted and guided them through their problems with wise advice.

The Lincolnshire connection did not end with Franklin. In the 1880s Henry Parkes was on close and friendly terms with Alfred Tennyson, who read him *The Northern Farmer* in the strong Somersby dialect he had spoken since childhood.*

The Poet Laureate's son, Hallam, Second Baron, became Governor of South Australia in 1899, then, in 1903, second Governor General of the new Commonwealth of Australia. Thus continued the Lincolnshire connection into the twentieth century.

It has taken a long time, much travel†, research, and talk, to collect the material and ideas of this book, and is impossible therefore to make individual acknowledgements of gratitude, deeply felt though they are.

---

* See my 'Mirror of a Shire: Tennyson's Dialect Poems': BBC Third Programme broadcast August 2nd, 1959; reprinted in the *Durham University Journal*, 1959.
† I would like to thank the Small Grants Fund of the British Academy for a contribution towards travel costs.

Nearly a century ago Francis Adams, an English visitor to Australia who faced the same problem, dedicated his book, *The Australians*, as follows: 'To my Australian friends – so many, so dear.' I cannot do better than to repeat his dedication.

Charles Wilson
April 1987

Visit of Hope to Sydney Cove near Botany-Bay

Where Sydney Cove her lucid bosom swells,
Courts her young navies, and the storm repels;
High on a rock amid the troubled air
HOPE stood sublime, and wav'd her golden hair;
Calm'd with her rosy smile the tossing deep,
and with sweet accents charm'd the winds to sleep;
To each wild plain she stretch'd her snowy hand,
High-waving wood, and sea-encircled strand.
'Hear me', she cried, 'ye rising Realms! record
'Time's opening scenes, and Truth's unerring word.—
'There shall broad streets their stately walls extend,
The circus widen, and the crescent bend;
'There, ray'd from cities o'er 'the cultur'd land,
'Shall bright canals, and solid roads expand.—
'There the proud arch, Colossus-like, bestride
'You glittering streams, and bound the chafing tide;
'Embellish'd villas crown the landscape-scene,
'Farms wave the gold, and orchards blush between.—
'There shall tall spires, and dome-capt towers ascend,
'And piers and quays their massy structures blend;
'While with each breeze approaching vessels glide,
'And northern treasures dance on every tide!'—
Then ceas'd the nymph-tumultuous echoes roar,
And JOY'S loud voice was heard from shore to shore—
Her graceful steps descending press'd the plain,
And *PEACE*, and *ART*, and *LABOUR*, joined her train.

(These lines were written by Erasmus Darwin (1731–1802) physician, botanist and theorist of evolution, grandfather of Charles and friend of Josiah Wedgwood. The theme was taken from an engraved medallion, modelled by Wedgwood in clay brought from Sydney Cove. Its allegorical figures represented 'Hope encouraging Art and Labour, under the influence of Peace, to pursue the employments necessary to give security and happiness to an infant settlement'.)

INTRODUCTION

'There are innumerable questions to which the imaginative mind can in this state receive no answer: why do you and I exist? Why was this world created? Since it was created, why was it not created sooner?'

(Dr Samuel Johnson)*

The arguments for and against creating a British colony in Australia were rehearsed for some years before the First Fleet of compulsory convict, military and naval emigrants left England. They continued after the Fleet arrived in New South Wales, and the controversies have raged intermittently ever since.

The archetypal, traditional reason for the settlement turned on the need to dispose of at least a proportion of Britain's supposedly growing population of convicts, especially after the loss of the American colonies which had offered a dumping ground for them before the American rebellion. These arguments have been set out many times.†

It took, nevertheless, a long time to formulate the theory. Firm documentation and scholarly exposition were both scarce. Confusion and secrecy were the keywords of government 'policy' in the 1780s. The Commander of the First Fleet and first Governor of New South Wales, Captain Arthur Phillip, RN, was a man of few words. He shared to the full the normal naval officer's concern to preserve official secrecy where naval strategy was involved. The Governor's records are patchy until 1800. Phillip's successor, Hunter, another naval officer, shared his predecessor's caution and may have taken the most secret records with him to England when he left for home in 1800, resolved to present the case for his conduct as Governor to HM Government and prove his numerous critics at fault. Many other records were 'censored', so that they 'fell short of accuracy, completeness and precision'. Many were omitted from the collections of records published for the history of New South Wales (1892–1901) and later for the history of the Australian

---

* Boswell *Life of Johnson*, L.F. Powell's revision of G.B. Hill's edition, vol. I (Oxford, 1934).
† See G.J. Abbott and N.B. Nairn (eds) *Economic Growth of Australia 1788–1821* (Melbourne, 1969), for a collection of views which on balance comes down in favour of the convict solution to the question of why the First Fleet set sail in 1787.

Commonwealth (1914 onwards).* Many other decisions and policies were probably never committed to paper at all.

In any event, the 'histories' of Australia before the twentieth century took time to catch up with the revolution in techniques which was the greatest change in the writing of history in the nineteenth century. The Reverend Julian Edmond Tenison-Woods (1832–1889) produced, in 1865, his *History of the Discovery and Exploration of Australia*.†

Woods was a priest, a convert to Roman Catholicism, a firm believer in visions and a man of uncertain temper. A varied and often stormy career saw him established as a respected figure in geological and other scientific circles, holding a no less prominent but more debatable position as editor of *The Irish Harp and Farmer's Herald*, described by the *Australian Dictionary of Biography* as a 'politically oriented journal which contributed much to divisive diocesan quarrels [in South Australia]'. Woods's accounts of early navigators and explorers follows pretty faithfully the diaries, journals etc. they left behind them. His 'history' nowhere rises above an almost childish level of romanticism. Thus, on the arrival of the First Fleet:

> In this January, 1788, a great sight broke upon the view of the Botany Bay tribe. Ships they had perhaps seen before, but so many sailing in at once, and such large ones, was more than they had ever seen...

He continues his account; its interest lies not in any originality of treatment but because it was the version of the beginnings of Australian history three quarters of a century earlier in its popular, authorized form.

> Not only were ships anchoring in the bay in number beyond precedent, but boats were descending, determined to possess the land, whilst the ships possessed the water. The first boat came nearer and nearer, and all the crew made such demonstrations of peace and good intentions, that they forgot their right to the land; forgot the legend about the small shot in their countrymen's legs, and fraternised with the intruders. The leader of the company, who stood before them in the full splendour of naval cocked-hat, and gold braid, was no less a person than Captain Phillip, or Governor Phillip, who was charged by the Home Government to take away the land from the blacks, and give it to the men he had with him; who were principally sent out from England because they would not let other people's property alone. It was thought that they could thus reform.

* See Victor Crittenden *A Bibliography of the First Fleet* (Canberra, London and Miami, 1981), pp. 4–5.
† London and Melbourne, 1865, 2 vols.

Thus the picture takes shape: a multitude of innocent, gullible natives forgetful of their predecessors' rash and futile bravery in face of Cook's counter-strategy; the contrivance of the white crew to disarm any suspicions that might have lingered in their memories; the full naval uniform, commanding a gang of thieves and pickpockets, who were heirs apparent to the aboriginals' land and a hoped-for life of law, order, penitence and reform.

Historians of Australia have in the main accepted the 'convict' explanation for the founding of British Australia. Had not Edmund Burke declared that the 100,000 convicted criminals awaiting disposal cried out for a solution? Was it not true that the revolution in North America had cut off an indispensable aid to the solution of the problem by deportation, and that this had to be replaced by some other dumping ground? Critics might reply that Burke's 'statistics' were Hibernian hyperbole: John Howard, prison reformer, suggested a figure of 4,500. Most subsequent writers (down to 1952 at least) seem to prefer the Burkeian estimate. And they not infrequently cite the increase in population as an undoubted cause of the increase of crime in those years. This is often taken for granted, though it is difficult to know how it could affect public opinion and government policy, since almost everybody, down to the end of the eighteenth century, especially in government circles, was firmly convinced that the great risk facing England was a *decline* in population.*

It was the resounding achievement of T.R. Malthus, a former Fellow of Jesus College, Cambridge, to put paid to this misapprehension. To add to the confusion, the reasons he advanced for his theory (supported as it was by the first census of population in 1802) were more gloomy and disturbing than the beliefs they challenged. The nightmare of an under-populated England was merely replaced by a nightmare of an over-populated England, liable to mass deaths from starvation and poverty, being Providence's only remedy for the basic problem facing society.

Other later Victorian historians followed in Tenison-Woods's footsteps, fortified by the widespread popular acceptance of the Malthusian portrait of an increasingly overcrowded Britain, preserved from total disaster only by the continual fraying of its demographic edges by disease, starvation and crime. George William Rusden's *History of Australia*† faithfully expounds the convict origins of Australia in resounding Macau-

* Talbot Griffiths *Population Problems in the Age of Malthus* (Cambridge, 1926).
† 3 vols, Melbourne, 1883–97.

layan prose. Other lesser authors follow suit. The story remains for the most part narrative. Not until well into the twentieth century, with Eris O'Brien and A.G.L.Shaw, do we reach 'critical' versions of the 'convict' explanation which go into statistical details and rely on primary sources, carefully analysed.*

Most recently, the enduring fascination of the 'convict' colony has been brilliantly illustrated by Robert Hughes's *The Fatal Shore*.† Hughes sees the 'system' of convict transportation, with all its weaknesses, brutality and social corruption, as not a bad alternative to other competing penal systems proposed by contemporary reformers (e.g. Jeremy Bentham or Lord Stanley). Moreover, unlike most earlier proponents of the convict explanation, he maintains this view in the light of the work of innovative historians who, from the 1950s onwards, have expounded alternative theories to explain the fitting-out and despatch of the First Fleet.‡ These include the British desire to establish a base for maritime trade; to obtain a supply of flax, hemp and shipbuilding timber to replace or reinforce the Baltic and North American supplies; entry to the China trade, the South American trade, the fur trade, and whaling and sealing.

However, Hughes does not believe that the transportation of convicts was absolutely essential to the settlement and development of Australia. If Australia had not been settled as a prison and built by convict labour, he writes, 'it would have been colonized by other means: that was foreordained from the moment of Cook's landing at Botany Bay in 1770'.§

But would it? Would it 'simply have taken longer?' Is this not another of those errors of the 'counter-factual' historian which assumes that you can remove a single element from history and leave the rest unchanged? Who would have colonized a later Australia? Britain? Or Holland? Or Germany? Or France? These were the questions that worried contemporary statesmen, British in particular. For what *title* had Cook bestowed on his country?¶

* Eris O'Brien *The Foundation of Australia 1786–1800* (London, 1937). A.G.L. Shaw *Convicts and the Colonies* (London, 1966).
† London, 1987.
‡ K. Dallas *Trading Posts or Penal Colonies?* Tasmanian Historical Research Association, Papers, vol. I (1951–2) (Hobart, 1969). G.N.Blainey *The Tyranny of Distance* (Melbourne, 1968).
§ R. Hughes *The Fatal Shore*, p. 588.
¶ See my essay on 'Convicts, commerce and sovereignty' in *Business Life and Public Policy: Essays in Honour of D.C. Coleman* (Cambridge, 1986). French jealousy of the English settlement at Port Jackson was the animating sentiment of a long despatch from François Péron to General Decaen, Governor of Mauritius, printed in translation in Ernest Scott *The Life of Captain Matthew Flinders, RN* (Sydney, 1914), Appendix B.

1

TRANSPORTATION AND THE EFFECTIVE OCCUPATION OF AUSTRALIA

'Next ... an account of the transportation system ... as making for rapid colonization and as having valuable reformatory effects ... converting felons into
good colonists, to educate their children and train them for useful avocations.'

(François Péron)*

'My first appearance at a public meeting was to resist the influx of English
criminals, in which I never relaxed my efforts until the struggle ended in
triumph.'

(Sir Henry Parkes)†

There was nothing new about the serious and widespread nature of
poverty or crime in 1787. When Gregory King, an ingenious and responsible pioneer of social statistics, calculated the population of England
in 1696, he divided its five and a half million people or so into 'those
who increased ... and those who decreased' the wealth of the nation.
He believed his calculations proved there were more of the latter than
the former, that is, there were more people below the bread-line than
above it. This gloomy picture is confirmed by modern historians, who
have suggested that in seventeenth-century England, at least one third
of the population was either unemployed or underemployed.

This segment of poverty and crime was permanent – rural as well
as urban, residential as well as mobile. As well as the vagrants and
vagabonds who tramped from village to village, there was a sedentary,
almost hereditary, tribe of petty thieves, pick-pockets, poachers, prostitutes, drop-outs; some harmless, some ready to mug, rape and murder.

---

* François Péron to General Decaen, Year 12 (1803–4); manuscript, in translation in
Ernest Scott *Life of Matthew Flinders* (Sydney, 1914).
† Sir Henry Parkes *Fifty Years in the Making of Australian History*, vol. II, (London,
1892), p. 383.

Nearly every city, town and village had its thieves' kitchen. These squalid corners of England housed 'the Poor'. They were the nests from which came the regular flow of crime and criminals, and the latter were joined by a smaller contingent of victims of occasional misfortune: men and women who had fallen by the wayside.

Public anxieties about crime, poverty and unemployment were not, as is sometimes suggested in the British and Australian history books, a specifically British phenomenon. All over Europe the same anxiety was apparent. So too were the attempts of authority to contain and mitigate the evils perceived. Nowhere did anything but failure, or at most precarious and short-lived success, result. This was a universal problem: attempted solutions were generally even less humane than the British policy of transportation.*

This state of affairs continued in the nineteenth century, which was above all an age that debated continually the problem of poverty. Solutions included the improvement of agriculture, of trade, industry and productivity, combined with the provision of schools for the young, workhouses for the unemployed and almshouses for the old and infirm. By themselves, none of these contrived remedies solved the problems. They were alleviated and finally extinguished – at least in their extreme forms – by 'industrial revolution' – revolutionary changes in the whole economic and social system.

In the 1780s these changes had begun, especially in cotton textile, coal and iron production, and to some extent in shipping and overseas trade. But their early effects were to dislocate rather than improve social relations in manufacturing. The replacement of home and workshop hand production by factories equipped with machines was in the end to boost wealth and employment: in the short run, it seemed merely to displace land-workers and craftsmen, especially in the textile industries. The riots in 1768 and even more, the Gordon riots in 1780, were highly disturbing, but the participants were more likely to be Irish navvies or coal heavers, drunk on cheap gin, than unemployed weavers. Increased overcrowding, as a result of population growth, may possibly have contributed to such upheavals, and the anxiety they aroused for the safety of people, property and the preservation of law and order. The important point is that such conclusions are the result of later knowledge. At the time, the poverty and crime of 'the Poor' (who were always 'with' the more affluent) were taken for granted. There was nothing new about

* See C. Lis and H. Soly *Poverty and Capitalism in Pre-Industrial Europe* (Brighton, 1979); also, Michael Weisser *Crime and Punishment in Early Modern Europe* (London, 1979).

either phenomenon. What was changing was the climate of thought. Whatever it was not, this *was* the age of the 'Enlightenment', and amongst the more disagreeable, but unavoidable, ingredients it contained was penological theory and especially the theory of the deterrent power of punishment for crime.

There was one indubitably new element in the situation regarding crime and criminals. Virginia and Maryland were no longer available as a dumping ground for unwanted felons: but the extent to which they had ever received any important number of them is doubtful. There is no reliable evidence as to how many were transported, stayed, or returned. Berkely, whose plans for Virginia were highly regarded and influential, thought that the whole idea of using it for transported criminals was wrong and unnecessary. One source which describes a hundred or two transported annually, suggests that many returned.

If Charles Dibdin, ballad composer and writer, may be trusted, Botany Bay itself was a joke in the underworld in 1788; Newgate prisoners petitioned their jailers for permits to go there. John Howard, the prison reformer, himself denounced those who favoured 'the expensive, dangerous and destructive scheme of transportation to Botany Bay'.

The First Fleet

The critics of transportation as a means of dealing with crime had powerful arguments on their side. The First Fleet was an outrageously expensive enterprise, if this was its sole or even major justification. Its voyage took eight months, and covered 15,000 miles. It consisted of two warships, six convict transports and three supply ships. They carried 560 male and 190 women and juvenile convicts, and were guarded by nearly one-third as many naval and marine officers and ranks – 280 in all. No overseers or prison staff accompanied them. Medical staff attended to their health. Captain Phillip ensured personally that these aspects of the voyage were dutifully, and as far as possible, humanely attended to. The number of deaths during passage was forty-eight – for its day a very low figure. The cost in food, stores, clothing, medicines, etc., was enormous. So too were the risks – from disease, accidents, shipwreck, drowning – to officers, guards and crew. The chaos on landing could have brought fatalities on an epic scale, but these were in fact avoided. It would have been understandable if they had occurred, given the unavoidable absence of first-hand knowledge of the circumstances of disembarkation amongst those in charge. On the whole, the muddle was less than the inexcusable scramble and confusion of embarkation in England.

The expedition survived, but there was one consequence which, from the Governor's point of view, was disastrous. He had repeatedly pleaded to be supplied with the prisoners' dossiers: they never came. He had thus no means by which, in that age of indiscriminate punishments and administrative confusion, he could distinguish between trivial and serious offenders; between the harmless and the murderous. It was to prove a grave obstacle to establishing anything resembling an orderly society, and its consequences were to be handed down from generation to generation.

Before order could be established ashore, the prisoners got loose and a wild night of orgies ensued. The thieves thieved, the drinkers drank, the prostitutes plied their trade. They had, after all, something to celebrate. Not only had they survived; they had enjoyed the most expensive outing ever financed from the British Treasury. It has been estimated that the outward passages cost upwards of £300,000. The military garrison cost another £100,000. Other items brought the grand total to half a million pounds. Taking subsequent maintenance costs and losses into account, this represented £1,000 per prisoner: and so it was to continue. Little wonder that awkward questions began to be asked about the value of the whole enterprise.

Major Ross, commander of the military garrison, Deputy Governor to Captain Phillip, and a grim, argumentative Scot, as mean as he was contentious, wrote his conclusions to the Home Department in July, after the landing: 'This country will never answer to settle in ... it will be cheaper to feed the convicts on turtles and venison at the London Tavern than be at the expense of sending them here....' For once the Governor himself might well have agreed with his Deputy (it did not often turn out thus): he was to plead with Whitehall for volunteer farmer settlers to be sent out, as often as he had pleaded for the convicts' dossiers. Whitehall remained deaf to his pleas.

Fortunately, or otherwise, it has become clear in recent years that the long-cherished assumption that the sole object of the enterprise known as the First Fleet was to rid England of at least part of its criminal population, was a misapprehension. As the latest bibliographer of the First Fleet has observed, there are at least two alternative theories (both have emerged since 1952) to explain why the Fleet was despatched: he calls them respectively, the Naval Supplies Theory, and the Trade Development Theory.*

* Victor Crittenden *A Bibliography of the First Fleet* (Canberra, 1981) Introduction, p. v.

As the editor of the bibliography remarks: 'The "Reasons Why" has occupied the thoughts of most of modern Australians.' And, it may be added, of some others. Not the least purpose of this book is to explore the case for another theory: it might be called 'The Indispensable Occupation Theory'.

The Naval Supplies Theory

It was natural that the arguments about the origins of Australia should crystallize round the decision to transport convicts to Botany Bay. The convict issue was the one that had the largest social impact on Australia for well over half a century. Even after the policy of transportation had been abandoned, it lived on in the imagination of Australians; both those descended from convict lineage and those of 'free' origins. Its horrors, real and exaggerated, became the subject of a certain shame or embarrassment to the conventional, respectable middle class, and of an equal, if perverse pride to the rebellious or *avant garde*. As the bushrangers turned into figures of romance, a mysterious attraction developed for their (often) convict origins. The name Botany Bay stuck, in spite of Phillip's wise decision that it offered no future as a harbour; he moved on to Jackson Cove and the 'haven for a thousand ships' he named after the current Minister for Home Affairs, Lord Sydney. Sydney consisted, for its first decades, principally of convicts. Why complicate history by introducing new reasons for the establishment of Australia, when a perfectly good one existed, apparently with more supporting evidence behind it than its rivals?

In the nineteenth and twentieth centuries, British, American and Continental historians continued to modify standard orthodoxies on the nature and development of British and French imperialism, to re-channel the flows of commercial interest, strategic objectives and political ambition. One recurrent, irresistible object of interest was seapower. How exactly was seapower related to the ebb and flow of national power and wealth? How did the belief in seapower and the demand for the weapons it wielded, themselves affect foreign policy?

One fact stood out, as soon as men paused to analyse the character of British sea power, and that was the growth of the Royal Navy and the widening scope of its operations which had created ever-growing needs for strategic materials, including different kinds of timber each with its highly specific use and function. The basic brackets on which a ship was hung were of oak, decks and sides of decks of elm, masts and yards of pine. Sails were of flax; ropes of hemp. Waterproofing demanded vast quantities of tar and pitch. Students of seventeenth-century logistics were well aware of England's dependence on the Baltic for the Navy's (and merchant navy's) masts, yards, planking, cordage and pitch. Those who read the *Diary* of Samuel Pepys during the period of the second Dutch War (1663–7) knew how precious, even then, was the supply line from the Baltic; how profound his relief when three ship-loads of timber and naval stores from North America arrived in 1665. The drafting of the whole of the Navigation Laws emphasized the conviction of government administrators that the hair-raising antics of the Baltic Powers, Russia and Sweden especially, made it essential for Britain to find and conserve any alternative supplies of strategic materials which could be obtained from British-controlled sources. North America was at that time the most obvious source.

In 1926, a remarkable study by an American, R.G. Albion, *Forests and Seapower*, underscored the continuing, and indeed increasing danger in the following century. Between the end of the Seven Years War (1763) and the end of the century, the French Navy, under the vigorous direction of Choiseul and others, reached new heights in its mastery of tactics in warfare, weight of firepower and ship design and building. The odds were about even between the world's two greatest navies. When the Baltic Powers formed the Armed Neutrality in 1782, their objective was to challenge the belligerents – especially Britain – in the exercise of their professed (and essential) 'right of search' of neutral ships for 'contraband' cargoes of war stores destined for France.

Such considerations had often claimed low priority in the minds of historians who were more preoccupied with convict history when examining the reasons for the First Fleet's departure in 1788. But they were very much in the minds of the group of Australian historians who inaugurated the lively debates of the 1950s on the role played by naval needs in triggering off the search for new supplies of timber and flax. The trees which Cook and Joseph Banks had seen growing by the side of river and sea in New Holland might replace the Baltic spars and planks, Ukrainian – even North American – masts, even main ship timbers of English oak. On Norfolk Island grew great pines, which looked like perfect material for masts.

Then there was flax. Banks had noticed this growing in Australia. Lord Sydney – not usually easy prey to excitement – was stirred to remark that a supply of what seemed to be such excellent material for making strong rope cable – 'stronger than one made from European hemp' – could be 'of great consequence to us as a naval power'. Not only could these supplies be put to naval use. The eighteenth century had seen the production of Irish and Scottish linen overtake in quality and quantity, the Continental linen bleached at Haarlem and formerly exported by the Dutch merchants of Amsterdam in vast quantities into England. 'Import substitution' and the control of raw materials useful to employing manufacturers was a commonplace of mercantilist, natio- nalist economic thinking since the sixteenth century in England. It was the basis of the Navigation Code on which Britain's economic policy had been based since the mid-seventeenth century.

The need for timber and flax were the main arguments used by histor- ians such as Professor Dallas of Hobart and Professor Blainey of Mel- bourne against the older theories. They were far from convincing all their colleagues, but their evidence, though not abundant, was not neglig- ible. Their case gains credibility when it is looked at in the light of the *European* mercantilist tradition. Here, the national objectives of 'pro- fit and power' had long carried more weight than the problems of crime and the cost of criminals, certainly more than their comfort.

Nor is there any doubt that for some time after the first landings in New Holland and Van Diemen's Land, English interests in strategic materials continued. The most critical years for the Royal Navy were 1788 to 1804. This was when the supply of masts (from Russia) and planking (from Prussia) fell to their lowest point, with the impact of the Baltic Armed Neutrality at its sharpest, and supplies from Canada still not fully organized. This was the time when *jarrah* from New South Wales (and later *kauri* from New Zealand), were at their premium. In peacetime high freight costs made such a trade impracticable commer- cially, but it was by no means a negligible blessing in war. For many years after the Napoleonic Wars also, the Navy continued to draw masts and timber from these remote sources.*

One of the keenest students of this type of economic potential was Lieutenant Philip Gidley King, later promoted (by the first Governor) Lieutenant Governor of Norfolk Island. At first sight, Norfolk Island seemed full of promise with its giant pines and soil that seemed to grow good flax. Alas! the pines were most disappointing. The timber early grew rotten under the bark – in no way reliable material for ships' masts. The flax proved difficult to work. Everywhere it was found to be custom- ary for the aboriginals to pull up the growing crop before it was ready to harvest; they used it for fishing lines.

King refused to be entirely discouraged. What Norfolk Island might fail to produce, Van Diemen's Land might. After the navigation of the

* Albion *Forests and Seapower* (Harvard, 1926), pp. 364, 400.

strait separating it from the mainland, a British colony was settled at Risdon Cove, just outside Hobart. It was commanded by the youthful naval Lieutenant Bowen, who reported in some excitement that he had seen 'with his own eyes' the flax plant growing at Risdon. In his instructions to Bowen, King (now Governor of New South Wales) underlined the section dealing with economic potential: 'you will inform me whether the general timber in that country is fit for the purpose of being sent to England for construction of the King's ships, particularising ... the different species, length of trunk and diameter, also whether it grows mostly crooked or strait, and notice the facility of getting it on board ships...'.

Bowen does not seem to have been any more successful at following up his first observation than at most other things. He was soon recalled. But not the least ironical aspect of King's search for supplies was that the trees of Van Diemen's Land, which were to prove the source of what has been called 'the world's best boat-building timber', were named after the great French navigator and explorer, Huon Kermadec. The richest supplies of the Huon pine were to be found along the banks of the Gordon River, in the north west of the island. They were logged by convicts from the settlement at Sarah Island on the nearby Macquarie Harbour. The settlement was to build an astonishing number of excellent ships: the largest was a famous barque, *William IV*. It sold for the sizeable sum of £1,375.

Related directly to timber and the development of ship building was the discovery that the oceans surrounding Tasmania (as Van Diemen's Land was ultimately called), supported a vast population of seals and whales. These were, in turn, the source of rich supplies of skins, meat and oil. In the three decades after the voyage of discovery by Bass and Flinders, these came to represent half of the exports sold by Australia to the outside world (see Chapter 3).

What the influence of Australian supplies of timber, flax, seals and whales on world history might have been had inventions not revolutionized its economic aspects, is anybody's guess. In practice, the future was to lie with steam-driven ships built of iron. The economics of mercantilism were already outmoded by 1800. Their influence on the men of the 1780s is more difficult to assess; but it would be wrong to dismiss it as unimportant.

The Protection and Expansion of Trade

When the Centenary of 1788 was celebrated, the English historian, E.C.K. Gonner could propose that the popular idea that the despatch of the First Fleet was solely or primarily to dispose of a superfluity of convicts and remove them to a penitentiary *al fresco* as far away as possible, was nonsense. There were, he suggested, more forceful, 'nobler' objectives than these. He referred especially to the arguments of James Matra (a midshipman with Cook) and the other exponents of expansionism (such as Admiral Young); these were directed to measures which would ensure the protection, safety and expansion of British trade and British rule. Only the outbreak of the Revolution in France, and the onset of another war caused these objectives to be overlooked.

Gonner's article was published in the *English Historical Review*, the classic organ of Victorian historical learning. However, in more recent times, his perceptions have been further expanded. Historians have detected a change in the attitudes of strategies of the European powers (Britain and France, especially) in regard to the extra-European world, and this has been described in the phrase 'Swing to the East'. The older preoccupation with America as the most important area, where each thought the rest should be contained or from which they should be forcibly expelled, faded. It was replaced by a much greater curiosity about the opportunities offering in India, Asia and beyond. Of the traditional colonizing powers, only England and France survived. (The Netherlands were by now alienated from their former British ally by the quarrel over neutral rights, and the rise of the pro-French party against the House of Orange. The Dutch fleet had been sunk at Camperdown in 1782.)

France saw chances to recoup her losses in the West Indies, Caribbean and Canada by compensations in India, comparable to what Britain had gained by the victories of Clive and Coote. Warren Hastings and Louis XVI tried to establish their respective powers in Cochin-China. England financed James Cook on three arduous world voyages with objectives which included astronomical observation and research and the quest for a practicable route which would link the Atlantic with the Pacific by sea. The first voyage included, almost incidentally, the discovery of the Eastern Coast of Australia and the registration of British claims to sovereignty over those parts of Australia. But, thereafter, in characteristic eighteenth-century fashion, New South Wales had been forgotten – at least by government.

France, meanwhile, continued to strengthen, enlarge and train her navy. Under the aegis of the French Admiralty, a great deal of surveying and exploration was done in the Pacific and Indian oceans. In all, France sent ten full scale hydrographic expeditions to the East between 1784 and 1789. In full cry after their patriotic, mercantilist motto – 'Ships,

Colonies and Commerce' – British statesmen, politicians, nobility, and the lobbies of particular trading interests pursued the various means open to them of obstructing and hampering the national enemy, France, and those now associated with her, such as the Netherlands. And since the pursuit of imperial ends included not only theories and plans, but their execution by defensive and offensive arms, they took due note of the strategic importance of the Dutch-owned colony at the Cape of Good Hope, essential for the victualling of ships engaged in long distance voyages to the East. The growing interest in trade with China had already attracted an attempt at a free port settlement (1772–4) which failed. It was followed in 1786 by other attempts on the Nicobar Islands and Penang. A penal colony was tried on the Andaman Islands in 1785, where the pioneers doubtless knew of the proposals by the distinguished French soldier, sailor and explorer, La Pérouse, for a penal settlement in New Zealand.

The Need for a Maritime Base

The scholars who are less than satisfied with traditional 'convict' reasons for the despatch of the First Fleet have mostly put high on their list of objectives the widely-felt need for a maritime British base somewhere between the Indian Ocean and the Pacific. Its major functions would be to provide staging ports for the China and Pacific trades (including a projected link with Vancouver) and possible sources of supplies of naval stores, new fisheries, ship repair and maintenance facilities.

All these aspirations were to materialize to a greater or lesser extent; and while it is all too easy to read history backwards, there is sufficient evidence of keen and practical interest in the period of gestation of the First Fleet to warrant the possibility that they were in the minds of those responsible for the Botany Bay plan. In 1788, England had no port between St Helena and India, nor between India and the Pacific. France had purloined Mauritius from the Dutch and thereby acquired a valuable staging port to India, the Dutch-held Indies and China. England, as in the seventeenth century, was rich in her Eastern trades, but her sea lanes were – as James Cook's voyage had emphasized – disturbingly extended and vulnerable. The First Fleet's plan of operations derived directly from Cook and his Dutch predecessors in the Eastern Seas. Their predecessors, the Portuguese, had now left the scene almost completely. The Dutch were, overseas as at home, in decline. The new rivals here, as elsewhere on land and on the high seas, were the French. New South Wales, perhaps the whole of Australia and New Zealand, Cook's heritage, along with a few more unconsidered trifles like New Caledonia, were the ultimate prize in the international contest; it would go to the contestant best equipped in navigational skill, experience in the other varied skills required of an explorer – ship design and armament, crew management, marine medicine and health at sea, and, if necessary, how to fight a ship. As the organizers of the Cook voyages had also grasped, the more knowledge there was of geography, topography, *flora* and *fauna*, etc., the better. Such skills and knowledge had crucial effects on how the expeditions for prolonged and far-distant voyages must be organized – what must be carried, what could be picked up *en route*, how the limited space on board could best be allocated. Exploration was the most hazardous and precarious of adventures; the gap between success and failure was a hairsbreadth.

Rivalry of the French

Of all the possible European rivals of Britain the French were now the most formidable. If the legend of de Gonville were true (he was said to have sailed from Honfleur as early as 1503), they would also have been amongst the earliest contenders for power in the South Seas. In the eighteenth century, some dozen bold navigators had sailed east from Mauritius: Bouvet de Losier (1739), Marion Dufresne (1772), Bougain-ville the elder (1764), Kerguelen-Tremarec (1772), and St Allouarn (1772). Some (and many of their crews) were Norman or Breton. Ile de France (Mauritius) was a crucial centre for French naval and privateer-ing operations against English trade routes with India. Beyond Mauritius was the hope of finding a deep water port to supplement St Louis, expand-ing into a colony to link Ile de France with the Pacific.

The popular background to such expeditions was provided by readings in the Utopian fiction of writers such as Charles de Brosses and Cyrano de Bergerac. But the pre-Revolution explorers were like men walking on the moon: they achieved little in the way of occupation and settlement. The exception was St Allouarn: he reached the west coast of Australia. On 30 March 1772, an ensign from his ship, the *Gros Ventre*, landed at Turtle Bay and took possession in the name of Louis XVI, King of France. A parchment recording this was buried at the foot of a tree, with two French coins. St Allouarn then went on to Timor and back to Mauritius, where both he and his ensign died soon after landing, apparently from the debilitating effects of their voyages.

They had no immediate successors. If it was the case, as Professor Marchant has written, that France could acquire territorial sovereignty by a simple declaration of prescriptive right, St Allouarn's claim would have been enough, in his view, to justify French claims to have 'acquired' the western parts of Australia. But modern doctrine would not accept that a simple declaration, unaccompanied by continuous and undisturbed sovereignty of the claimant for a long period was adequate basis for a title. By this time, the British view, derived from Hugo Grotius and from Dutch practice, and adhered to by a growing body of international opinion, was that when an uninhabited territory was discovered, only 'effective occupation' by the discovering power could create the right to sovereignty.

The remaining French expeditions to Australasia were either – like that of the Comte de la Pérouse – more or less contemporary with that of the First Fleet, or subsequent to it. They took place in a period of peace between Britain and France. None of them challenged Cook's claim of two decades earlier to New South Wales and Northern Australia on behalf of Britain. It will never be clear beyond doubt why this was: did they recognize Cook's claim? Did they believe it would be imprudent to challenge it? Or was it that they were in too weak a position to challenge it? Or, had the Governor of the First Fleet taken those necessary steps to reinforce Cook's claim without which Cook's declaration of British possession would have been, after the best part of two decades of neglect, shaky indeed? We shall return to the French expeditions later.

The Occupation: January 1788

Intriguing and important as the historians' debates on the theories and plans behind the despatch of the First Fleet are, they have diverted attention from what is perhaps the most important evidence regarding the nature of the British occupation of Australia. This lies in the character of the occupation and of its execution. And, in these regards, international law and its history have at least as much to tell us as social or economic history. Yet until very recently historians have insisted on treating the settlement of New South Wales as if it was a civil project, undertaken for (or even by) the convicts. The function of the Governor, officers and military guard, in this view, was solely to transport the convicts out of England and dump them as far away as possible. This is not only quite misleading as a matter of the historical facts of 1788: it also introduces historical distortions into the purpose of the British Government regarding Australia, to say nothing of its subsequent relations with the colony.

First, the expedition was a military, not a civil, expedition. It was carried out by the Royal Navy under naval command. The Royal Commission conferred on Arthur Phillip as Governor was (I quote) a mark of reward for his 'loyalty, courage and experience *in military affairs*' (my italics). His writ was to run over the whole eastern half of Australia (which itself raises the question: why occupy half of Australia if all that was needed was a disposal centre for surplus convicts? Wasn't there more in the First Fleet operation than that?)*

From his arrival in Botany Bay, Phillip's arrangements were carried out with meticulous attention to legal detail. This was characteristic of him: in spite of one slighting comment on his appointment, Their Lordships of the Admiralty were obviously fully informed of his record, not only in the Royal Navy but with the Portuguese Navy too. His belief in absolute accuracy and propriety was doubtless sharpened by the sighting, on arrival at Botany Bay on 24 January, of two unknown ships, first assumed to be Dutch. They turned out to be French – *La Boussole* and *l'Astrolabe* – under the command of La Pérouse. Friendly contact was established (and continued). The presence of two French warships nonetheless probably hastened Phillip in the business of taking formal possession of the area of Australia entrusted to his care by his Commission. On the same day that La Pérouse dropped anchor in Botany Bay, therefore, the Governor and a detachment of marines and convicts went ashore in Sydney Cove. Phillip had no opinion of Botany Bay – for once disagreeing with the judgement of Cook and Banks. He later recorded his reconnoitre in a famous despatch to Lord Sydney: 'We got into Port Jackson early in the afternoon (23 January) and had the satisfaction of finding the finest harbour in the world, in which a thousand sail of the line may ride in the most perfect security....' He was not exaggerating. (But again, one must ask why, if the sole purpose of his mission was to establish a convict prison, he should be thinking of the future in terms of the anchorage needs of naval battleships?) No wonder La Pérouse reported to the French Admiralty that the British Lieutenant in charge of Botany Bay, whom he interviewed 'appeared to make a great mystery of Commodore Phillip's plan, and we did not take the liberty of putting any questions to him on the subject...'. La Pérouse was a soldier and a gentleman.

Possession Taken for His Majesty

Thus, on 26 January the Governor's party cleared a piece of ground near a run of fresh water, a flagstaff was erected, and, as Lieutenant

---

* Indispensable to the student of the early settlement is *The Voyage of Governor Phillip to Botany Bay*. It is best studied in the admirable edition by J.J. Auchmuty, Royal Australian Historical Society (Sydney, 1972).

King reported: 'possession was taken for His Majesty'. A Union Jack was displayed, and 'the marines fired several vollies between which the Governor and the officers who accompanied him drank the healths of His Majesty and The Royal Family, and success to the new colony'.

That, for the moment, was enough. In the following week or more, the expedition was kept busy unloading in face of heavy thunderstorms and overpowering heat. Whilst doing this, they had to ward off belligerent natives, who pelted them with stones. They were additionally diverted by the abundance of fish, the brawls amongst the convicts, and the need at night to ward off the swarms of spiders, ants and every kind of vermin which crawled over officers and convicts alike as they tried desperately to get to sleep on the hard, cold ground. The Governor was, meanwhile, preparing for a full-dress ceremony to betoken, beyond all manner of doubt, full and (God willing) permanent British occupation of Australia. The details are as important to Australians and historians as they obviously were to the Governor. Those officers who kept diaries – many did, probably under instruction from Arthur Phillip – recorded the occasion. Surgeon Lieutenant Bowes (one of ten surgeons accompanying the Fleet, all kept exceedingly busy) gives the fullest account of the much more extended formalities of Thursday, 7 February:

> This morning at 11 o'clock all who could leave the ships were summoned on shore, to hear the Governor's Commission read and also the commission constituting the Court of Judicature. The marines were all under arms, and received the Governor with flying colours and a band of music. He was accompanied by the Judge Advocate, Lieutenant Governor, clergyman, Surveyor General, Surgeon General, etc. After taking off his hat and complimenting the marine officers, who lowered their colours and paid that respect to him as Governor which he was intitled to, the soldiers marched with music playing, drums and fifes and formed a circle round the whole of the convicts, men and women who were collected together. The convicts were all ordered to sit down on the ground; all gentlemen present were desired to come into the centre, where stood the Governor, Lieutenant Governor, Judge Advocate, Clergyman, Surgeon etc. etc. A camp table was fixt before them, and 2 red leather cases laid thereon, containing the Commissions etc. which were opened and unsealed in the sight of all present, and read by the Judge Advocate (Captain Collins).

Phillip had been ordered 'as soon as conveniently maybe, with all due solemnity, to cause our said Commission under our Great Seal of Great Britain constituting you our Governor and Commander-in-Chief as aforesaid to be read and published'. His authority was defined in his Commission, in the Act of Parliament establishing the colony, and in the Letters Patent constituting the Courts of Law. The Commission instructed him to keep and use the public seal, to administer oaths, and to appoint justices of the peace, coroners, constables, and other necessary officers. He was authorized to pardon offenders in criminal matters (short of murder) at his discretion. The Act empowered the Governor to convene a Court of Judicature to consist of the Judge Advocate and six officers of His Majesty's Forces. The majority of the court would decide the verdict, except in capital cases, when five members must concur before convicting. Witnesses would be examined on oath. The execution of the judgement of the court was made the responsibility of the Provost-Marshal.

The Letters Patent established the Civil Court, which would consist of the Judge Advocate and one of two people properly appointed for the purpose. This court would hear matters relating to land, houses, debts, contracts and trespasses. On a complaint in writing to the court, the Judge Advocate would issue a warrant to the Provost-Marshal, who would summon the defendant to appear. Either party might appeal against the decision of the court, generally to the Governor, or, for debts exceeding £300, to the Privy Council. All executions required the consent of the Governor.

Instructions referred to the Transports:

It is intended that several of the transport ships and victuallers which are to accompany you to New South Wales should be employed in bringing home cargoes of tea and other merchandize from China, for the use of the East India Company, provided they can arrive at Canton in due time, whereby a very considerable saving would arise to the public in the freight of these vessels: it is our Royal Wish and pleasure that upon your arrival in Botany Bay ... you do cause every possible exertion to be made for disembarking the officers and men ... together with the convicts, stores, provisions and etc. .... and you are to discharge all the said transports.

Phillip was instructed to commence cultivation, especially of the flax plant, as soon as possible. He was directed to send the *Sirius* and the *Supply* to neighbouring islands to barter for supplies and livestock, and to establish a settlement at Norfolk Island as soon as circumstances permitted.

The instructions concerning the natives were precise:

You are to endeavour by every possible means to open an intercourse with the natives, and to conciliate their affections, enjoining all our subjects to live in amity and kindness with them. And if any of our subjects shall wantonly destroy them, or give them any unnecessary interruption in the exercise of their several occupations, it is our will and pleasure that you do cause such offenders to be brought to punishment.

The Governor was authorized to emancipate convicts for good behaviour and industry and then to grant land to them. Power to grant land to the marines was withheld.

The isolation of the colony was ensured by the last part of the Instructions:

> And whereas it is our Royal intention that every sort of intercourse between the intended Settlement at Botany Bay ... and the settlements of our East India Company ... should be prevented by every possible means: It is our Royal Will and pleasure that you do not on any account allow craft of any sort to be built for use of private individuals, which might enable them to effect such intercourse.*

In the meticulous precision of the acts by which he took possession of New South Wales, Phillip was following in the paths of Cook and Banks. Cook had sailed under instructions to take possession of such territories as seemed to him to be worth taking in the Southern continent, either with the consent of the natives (where there were any) or by leaving 'proper marks and inscriptions' proving first discovery and possession (where there were none). This latter situation was described by the phrases *terra* (or *territorium*) *nullius* ('no man's land'). To Cook and Banks, all the evidence they found in Eastern Australia suggested that it was *terra nullius*. There were few natives: never more than thirty or forty at a time or in one group. Their houses were merely hollow shelters. They were not 'residences', for the aborigines simply wandered ceaselessly in search of food. They had no possessions or clothes. They performed no labour, and they were too primitive even to see any point in accepting gifts.

New South Wales was in

> the State of Nature where the 'industry of man' had no place and where men had not yet even begun to develop any forms of social institution. They spoke a language and they were familiar with the social unit called the family. In all other respects they were in the most rudimentary stage of human civilisation.

There was no evidence that any other European explorers had set foot in Eastern Australia. In the West, yes: the Dutch had preceded them. But in the East, Cook assumed, rightly, that his was the 'first discovery'. After taking possession of New South Wales Cook left; thus

* Copy from Dr John Cobley's account.

there remained a gap in Anglo-Australian history which lasted until January 1788 and Phillip's arrival at Botany Bay. A year and a half later, St Allouarn had surveyed the west corner of Australia, and as far north as Darwin. After St Allouarn, France, like Britain, rested on her oars. She had, nevertheless, made a claim to a stretch of the coast of West Australia: it was less impressively supported by evidence than the claims of Cook in the East, but it could not be neglected. In 1788, it still stood unchallenged, but the presence of, first, La Pérouse, and after him, the Chevalier Bruny d'Entrecasteaux (who tried, but failed, to find La Pérouse's expedition which disappeared after leaving Botany Bay) made it plain that France was in southern waters and determined on serious business. In 1792 d'Entrecasteaux in *Recherche* and *Espérance* (commanded by the Breton, Huon Kermadec) got as far as Espérance. In 1800 they were followed by Nicolas Baudin and Jacques Hamelin, in the *Géographe* and *Naturaliste*. With a brilliant team of scientists, explorers and artists headed by François Peron, they advanced into Van Diemen's Land enumerating, analysing and describing the geographical, botanical and zoological data of that rich and fascinating country.

Did these French expeditions present a deliberate or immediate threat to the Cook heritage? Probably not. The latest historian to enquire closely into their expeditions, Professor Marchant (of the University of West Australia), thinks that British historians have exaggerated the predatory intentions of these great French explorers. He may well be right. Certainly they would have been unwise to ignore that the English had, thanks to Cook and Banks, gained a head start on them in many aspects of navigatory, geographical, astronomical and botanical science; for some reason, the English were better also at the everyday business of holding a crew together in reasonable health and spirits than the French, whose voyages were often marked by quarrels (like those which soured relations between Baudin and Peron). These quarrels seriously lowered morale and made for disasters. La Pérouse, a great soldier whose humanity in warfare was well known in England, was exceptional in this respect – an excellent leader of men and a chivalrous opponent.*

It is worth remarking also that not all the English commanders shared Professor Marchant's generous views. Philip Gidley King (later Governor) was not personally hostile to the French. He nevertheless harboured deep suspicions of the purposes for which their government had sent them southwards. He thought it prudent to safeguard the newly discovered passage through Bass Strait (plumb on the route between Sydney

---

* Leslie Marchant *France Australe* (Perth, 1983).

and Britain) by proclaiming King Island British. And at Hobart, the Governor defined the purpose of the small garrison there as being:

> to prevent the French gaining a footing in the east side of these islands ... to secure another place for procuring timber, with any other natural productions that may be discovered and found useful: [to assess] the advantage that may be expected by raising grain, and to promote the seal fishery....

The officer in charge was also commanded 'to counteract any projects or plans' which the French – now in the neighbourhood – might be harbouring. He was to be particularly vigilant in thwarting any attempt to 'form an Establishment anywhere', and the French Commanding Officer was informed of 'His Majesty's right to the whole of Van Diemen's Land'. But, there was to be no 'Act of hostility if it can be avoided'. Equally, however, on no account was the British Commander to suffer 'His Majesty's flag to be insulted'. Anything of that kind was to be reported 'in the most early and substantial detail'.

At that point, the British defence contingent faced the most formidable potential challenge which the French were to mount after the disappearance of La Pérouse. This was the Baudin mission, and in equipment and scientific staff, it far surpassed Cook's first venture. In fact, conflict was avoided, and after 1815 the missions of de Freycinet (1817) and Dumont D'Urville (1826) both passed off peacefully in the relative calm that followed the Napoleonic storm. From 1819, France was to be more concerned with the possibilities of setting up convict colonies in Western Australia and New Zealand.

King's tense reactions to the Baudin expedition revealed, nevertheless, the real risks that sooner or later there might be a serious conflict between England and France in Australia.

Professor Marchant in a brisk but perhaps not wholly serious article* has queried 26 January as an appropriate date for the bicentenary memorial of the foundation of 'Australia'. As well (says he) quote 14 May 1607 (when Virginians remember the founding of Jamesburg) or 1621 (when descendants of the Pilgrim Fathers may celebrate the landing of their ancestors) as the birth of the American nation. They did not: nor does 26 January, when the First Fleet landed in New South Wales, mark the foundation of Australia. The public persons who pick 1788 'either did not learn their history well, or they have been badly advised by their consultants'.

Both may be true. There are, nevertheless, cogent reasons why 1788 and the First Fleet have a better claim than Professor Marchant allows.

* *Australian*, 27–8 July 1985.

Cook (he says) was rushed out to counter the French mission sent out after the humiliations which the peace of 1763 inflicted on France at the close of the Seven Years War. Cook achieved his object, and more. But a year and a half after Cook had named and annexed New South Wales, France despatched the Kerguelen–St Allouarn expedition (already described). This (he argues) 'resulted in France claiming Western Australia as part of the new French Empire then being created to compensate for the loss of Canada to Britain'.

He adds that the French claim hung on (what he describes as) the French belief in 'the principle of prescriptive rights' of a discoverer to new and uninhabited territory. 'They believed that an act of proclamation [such as St Allouarn made] was in itself sufficient to add a territory to empire. And they believed that was the international law.'*

The English might say (he continues) that 'France had a substantive territory in Western Australia, and was actively exploring in and about the territory it had claimed...'. His picture is accordingly one of an Australian continent divided between differing (but presumably equally valid?) English and French claims: the French holding theirs by 'prescriptive right', and the English by 'effective occupation'. That is, 'possession was to be regarded as nine-tenths of the law'.

But this argument is surely defective. Let us consult the international lawyers (whose views have been singularly neglected by historians in a controversy where 'law is the root and branch of the matter'). A prescriptive title to sovereignty arises 'where no sufficient claim can be shown by way of occupation, conquest or cession', writes one authority,† 'but the territory has remained under the continuous and undisturbed sovereignty of the claimant for so long a period that the portion has become part of the established international order'.

This could certainly not be claimed by the French visitors who landed at what later became known as Turtle Bay (which none of them had ever seen), and departed after only a very brief sojourn. It could not therefore, by the same token, be claimed by occupation; nor, since nothing was said of the inhabitants (even if there were any), could it be claimed by conquest. As a distinguished Australian international lawyer has written: no one, in modern history, has ever strictly referred to one practice or theory in acquiring backward territory. Discovery, cession of occupation – all have been appealed to, sometimes at one

* This is also the gist of his argument in his fascinating study of eighteenth-century French exploration, *France Australe*.
† M.F. Lindley *Acquisition and Government of Backward Territory in International Law* (London, 1926), p. 78.

and the same time but, to prove sovereignty, 'The realities of territorial expansion ... were such that only actual settlement and administration, coupled with at least the presumption to exclude others, by force if necessary, invited the sanction of law.' Hence came the notion of 'effective occupation', inherent but not explicit in Grotius, Pufendorf, Vattel and others.*

This was the true significance of the First Fleet of Arthur Phillip. On 1 January 1788, there was in law little to choose between James Cook's territorial claims on behalf of George III in Eastern Australia and those of St Allouarn in Western Australia. By 1 March 1788, all that was changed. A series of solemn Acts of state confirmed and extended Cook's claim. A sizeable area of territory had been settled by a colony, military and civil, of over a thousand people who were provided with an authorized government and ruled by an articulate body of laws, criminal, civil, military, and naval. Any charge that the sovereignty of the territory rested solely on 'discovery' or 'conquest' alone was disposed of. It was clear for all to see that there was in force a recognizable machinery of state capable of enforcing law and order. That, in turn, implied the existence of a 'community', not merely a garrison subject to military law, important though that was in real life, where not only hostile aborigines, but Dutch or French intruders might attack at any moment.

In this case occupation was not wholly immediate. The title of New South Wales could be regarded as constituted *tout d'un coup*. Phillip's claims beyond that could not be validated except by gradual consolidation. It was open to other states to appropriate those areas – if they could. Fortunately, after 1815, there was no rival capable of contemplating any such action. But the activities of the French exploration parties between 1788 and 1802, and statements of French ambitions and intentions thereafter made it abundantly clear what *might* have happened.

The sceptics who throw doubt on the alleged fears of the British in the 1780s make some plausible points which deserve attention. First, no outward friction disturbed Anglo-French relations in the Southern Seas before 1788. Even the encounter with La Pérouse did not involve the slightest anxiety, once contact had been established. Thereafter, relations could hardly have been more amicable, courteous or chivalrous. As La Pérouse himself wrote (doubtless by way of explanation to his masters at home): 'All Europeans are countrymen at such a distance from home....'

It would be crudest unhistorical sentimentality nevertheless to confuse civilized conduct with Anglophilia. La Pérouse was a professional soldier

* D.P. O'Connell *International Law*, vol. 2, 2nd edn (London, 1970), pp. 408–17.

of France, always chivalrous in war (as his actions in Canada had proved), but ready to fight and die without question. Of the other explorers, Louis de Bougainville had been a most efficient aide to Montcalm in Canada; Kerguelen, a daring naval commander in the Seven Years War; Dufresne had been in command of the exercise for getting Bonnie Prince Charlie out of Scotland; Hamelin was later to be given command of the naval force assembled on the French coast to invade Britain, and later he was to be Director-General of the French Admiralty.

The mutual courtesies which Professor Marchant has rightly observed were important. They were an element which did something to soften the barbarities of war in a still feudal age when war was a professional tournament. (Such courtesies have disappeared from the democratic age of indiscriminate bombing and maiming of civilians – to say nothing of modern nuclear warfare.) They did nothing in themselves, however, to identify or mitigate the causes or the course of hostilities. The issues of peace or war were decided elsewhere: by princes or governments representing, or purporting to represent, the interests of the state or the people. The professional gladiators merely identified themselves with these decisions – whatever they were. With respect to Professor Marchant, we must not confuse chivalry or expediency with pacifism. The Australian historian, Sir Ernest Scott, had a point when writing of the historical irony inherent in this particular imperial exercise:

> The Englishman will fight to the last gasp to keep what he really does not want very much, if only he supposes that his enemy wishes to take a bit of it. It was in this spirit of pugnacity that he stretched a large muscular hand over the whole map of Australia and defied his foes to touch it.

Scott comes close to the same basic analysis of the causes of war when he describes them as more often rooted in mutual fear rather than in simple unilateral aggression.

Terra Nullius?

No international lawyer has denied that Australia was properly regarded in 1788 as a *terra nullius*. It was (as Lord Watson declared in a Privy Council decision of 1889) 'a tract of territory practically unoccupied, without settled inhabitants or settled law' at the time it was peacefully annexed. In 1837, a Select Committee of the House of Commons on the aborigines observed that the British settlers were 'brought into contact with aboriginal tribes, forming probably the least-instructed portion of the human race in all the arts of social life...'; so barbarous was their state 'and so destructive are they even of the modest forms of civil polity, that their claims, whether as sovereigns or proprietors of the soil, have been utterly disregarded'.

On this, Lindley has remarked, as facts presented themselves at the time: 'there appeared to be no political society to be dealt with; and whatever rudiments of a regular government subsequent research may have revealed among the Australian tribes, occupation was the appropriate method of acquisition'.*

As the Australian historian Alan Frost has written, it may be regrettable that the British failed in 1770 or 1788 to negotiate with the aborigines; but 'that does not mean they can be treated as marauders, plunderers, pirates and butchers cast in the mould of Swift's colonists described in *Gulliver's Travels*'. Latter-day critics who take this view are merely demonstrating precisely the same anti-historical ignorance with which they charge those whom they accuse of destroying the aborigines' culture.†

The Governor's inaugural speech of 7 February 1788, was at pains to underline the utmost importance of intercourse and humane relations with the aborigines. Anyone offending against his injunctions in this respect was to be punished. He remained true to this policy and undertaking. But the problems of 'negotiating' with the natives were to prove insuperable (see Chapter 5).

It is virtually impossible to avoid the conclusion that if Britain had not intervened in January 1788 to remedy the defects of the title Cook had claimed to New South Wales, some other European power would have done so – and France was the certain contender. Perhaps a French Australia might have been a brilliant success; a divided, part-French, part-English, Australia would have suffered all, even perhaps more, of the problems later faced in Canada. These are speculations. Relevant facts are, first, that the aborigines of Botany Bay got short shrift and more forceful impatience even from La Pérouse than they did from the unbelievably patient Phillip. Second, it is transparently clear that Pitt and his ministers knew perfectly well what the situation of New South Wales was in law and in fact, in the state of contemporary opinion. Given that they were concerned for British overseas trade for naval supplies, for the permanent threat from France, and – up to a point – for the convict and prison problem, they deserve good marks for an ingenious

* M.E. Lindley *The Acquisition and Government of Backward Territory*, p. 40.
† Alan Frost, of La Trobe University, in 'New South Wales as *Terra Nullius*: the British denial of Aboriginal land rights' (Historical Studies, vol. 19, April 1980–October 1981, (History Dept., University of Melbourne, Melbourne)).

plan which provided, not a wholly satisfactory, but at least a partial remedy to all their problems.

The Convict Question

With regard to the convicts, whose fate tugs hardest at the modern liberal conscience, be it Australian or British, two points need to be made. First, contemporary opinion was divided sharply on the respective merits and otherwise of English prisons and the Australian alternative – remember too that within a decade or so the greater fear became that Australia offered too soft an option. Be that as it may, there can be no doubt about point two (of which little has been said in the debate between historians): if it were desirable to preserve and develop the Cook heritage, what alternative was there to the plan accepted by the Government and executed by Phillip? *Voluntary* settlement on any scale by Europeans in Australia was out of the question. Individual settlers who could afford to contemplate emigrating simply did not exist. There were no organizations capable of organizing or bearing a tithe of the cost of a continuous flow of men, stocks and money which the situation demanded. It was, in any case, to be a prime source of controversy in Australia until after the mid-nineteenth century, whether the transportation of convicts should be abolished or continued – and if continued, on what terms?

Nothing divided the inhabitants of Australia (and a considerable number of thinking English too) so bitterly. The solution, or mitigation, of the convict problem was, of course, present in the minds of those who planned the First Fleet; but this was far from being the only, let alone the most urgent consideration. Transportation commended itself, not for its inherent social merits, but because it played an indispensable role in a package deal which offered a good hope of killing several birds with one stone.

One final question: why, the critics quite reasonably ask, is there so little written evidence expounding these policies? First – though too simple an explanation to bear the whole weight of an answer – the Governors' personal files only began in 1800. What happened to the earlier files is not known. Possibly Hunter, Phillip's successor, took them to England; at any rate, they have not been found – yet. They may still turn up. But even if they do, it is unlikely that they will provide any single, coherent, logically argued policy to confirm the propositions suggested above. Much of the state's business at the end of the eighteenth century was still done orally, and in discussion. This was particularly true of diplomatic, naval and military affairs, where national security and international relations were involved. A plan for taking possession of New South Wales was in all probability, automatically regarded as best kept secret. Why tell the French? We have it on the assurance of no less an authority than Nelson that one of the considerable advantages that the nation enjoyed as a naval power in battle was its rigorous security system: but (he added) France enjoyed more. Silence, as Plotinus said, was a wonderful thing.

In any case, much knowledge was largely taken for granted. There was no call for a school text book on the subject of empire. Few ministers in an eighteenth century cabinet were ever fully aware of the forces at work, much less in control of what was done. Assumptions were concealed. Other assumptions were too well understood between colleagues, *sub rosa*, to need writing down. This was especially true in 1788.

2

THE FIRST GOVERNOR AND HIS PEOPLE

'Australia is his monument.'   (*Marjorie Barnard*)*

'Phillip is one of the greatest British sea captains ... firm and courageous, lonely yet sympathetic, he laid the foundations of a British Dominion in the Southern Seas where development still continues and he did it with inadequate tools, intermittent support and in lonely isolation.'

(*J.J. Auchmuty*)†

Botany Bay, as it continued to be called – in contradiction of the facts – was a nine-day wonder. Like their twentieth-century descendants, the hacks of Grub Street rapidly lost interest in this faraway place that nobody had heard of, and its newly installed convict inhabitants, of whom the less men knew the better they were pleased. 'Australians' themselves had more urgent things to do than sit and philosophize, though that was probably the occupation some of the convicts enjoyed most. The history of the first sixty or so years was to be given over to essentials – scratching meagre crops of corn from the soil, finding water (and procuring rum), searching for land for cattle and sheep, shearing the wool, sealing and whaling, mining, and multiplying.

This left little time for the contemplation of their own history. Once the first flurry of narratives and diaries, real, doctored or fabricated, gave out, even the literary reminders of Botany Bay were no more. Daniel Mann's *Present Picture of New South Wales* (1811, with plans and illustrations) deserves a special mention for its attention to the convicts and their problems. On these subjects the author (private secretary to the third Governor, King) was well qualified to write with authority; he

---

* M. Barnard Eldershaw *Phillip of Australia* (Sydney, 1962–72), p. 345.
† In Introduction to Phillip's *Voyage to Botany Bay* (Royal Australian Historical Society, Sydney, 1972).

was himself a convict sentenced and transported for forgery. In the same year there appeared another account of *The History of New South Wales, From its First Discovery to the Present Time* by G. Paterson (a second edition gives him as G. Patterson, MA and describes him as 'a Literary Gentleman'). It was published at Newcastle-upon-Tyne and its circulation can hardly have reached a numerous public. Between such publications and the appearance of the official (that is, government-sponsored, printed and published) *Historical Records of New South Wales (1892–1901)*, little serious attention was paid to the history of Australia by Australians. G.W. Rusden's *History of Australia* (1883) is exceptional for its extent (three volumes) and thoroughness, though not in its frequent lack of accuracy and critical sense.

The Undistinguished Gentleman

In this period, then, history became a charade. The Centenary itself passed with the stage still occupied by Tenison-Woods's Punch and Judy Show, with Phillip in his cocked-hat and full naval uniform in the leading role, supported by a chorus of marines and convicts – male pickpockets and female street-walkers. The trials, like the achievements, of the first Governor, were all forgotten. *The Australian*, often distinguished by its regard for accuracy and intelligent comment, recently published a review* of a new book on Phillip, with special regard to his service in the Portuguese Navy. Its title was: 'The Undistinguished Gentleman Who Founded Australia'. The article is largely devoted to explaining that before 1786 Phillip was more unemployed (on half-pay) than employed; that he was estranged from his wife and Germanic by birth. All of which was perfectly true, but beside the point and of little importance. (Many great sailors had to face being laid off in the unpredictable pacific interludes between eighteenth- and even nineteenth-century wars. It was still a recurrent theme of musical comedies in the London Theatre between 1920 and 1938.) The true purpose of Kenneth McIntyre's book, *The Rebello Transcripts*, is to show that, partly as a result of the experience he gained while serving Portugal in the colonial war against Spain in South America, 'Phillip learned the skills of leadership, resourcefulness and the ability to survive in virgin country.' This left him 'uniquely qualified for the task of establishing a British Colony in Australia'.

Getting, or not getting, naval employment and command in Phillip's day was less scandalously a matter of knowing the right people than

* *Australian*, 31 March, 1 April 1984.

it had been before Pepy's reforms in the late seventeenth century, but it was still partly a matter of luck; and family influence was still very prominent alongside other factors. Phillip did not score well at either game. Lord Howe, First Lord of the Admiralty, who could have had little first-hand knowledge of Phillip, doubted, in what may have been a casual aside, if he was right for the First Fleet command. Here Phillip's luck was out; but Sir George Rose, his neighbour on his Hampshire farm and a high man at the Treasury, thought very well of him. This did something to counterbalance the First Lord's doubts. Family? Phillip's father was a German language teacher, an immigrant nobody, said to be of Jewish origin, who married the widow of a naval officer related to the Earls of Pembroke. A whiff of influence? If so, one so slight that he was educated at the Greenwich Hospital for poor boys of naval parentage – an institution which was virtually an orphanage. His provenance was therefore a mixed one, and it proffered few strings waiting to be pulled. But, though his career was to be an uphill one, he never wavered in his commitment to justice and the application of just principles to the situations which faced him.

Arthur Phillip has often been described as a man of the Enlightenment in his quiet, patient belief in the validity of human reason, his refusal to allow emotions of anger, hatred, jealousy – perhaps even of love – to take over. Running through his whole career is the same thread; each situation he met had to be examined, pondered, discussed – and tackled. The inefficiency, carelessness and idleness of the masters and servants of the ministries which all had a finger in the pie called the First Fleet: Admiralty, Navy Office, Home Office, War Office, India Office, Treasury, Board of Trade, Foreign Office, Privy Council, Board of Longitude, etc., left Phillip with his hands full of fireworks. Such responsibility left its mark on his never robust constitution. The portrait by Francis Wheatley in the National Gallery is telling: a good likeness of the inner as well as the outer man. Here is the small figure, the shrivelled face, the thin, beaky nose, dark eyes, high cheek bones, full chin, a certain tense but quizzical character in his look. It was the face and image of decision, and it needed to be. It is not difficult to accept the judgement – at first blush a little surprising – of a friend who credited this small, quiet man with a loud voice.

Fortunately, since the growing publication of a wealth of documents bearing on early Australian history from the latter nineteenth century until the present, Phillip has been the subject of study by a number of capable and dedicated scholars. From a sizeable choice of biographies available two combine close study with sympathetic understanding. They are *Admiral Arthur Phillip* by the Sydney historian, George Mackaness* and *Phillip of Australia* by Marjorie Barnard Eldershaw.† The first is notable for its mastery of detail drawn from a great variety of sources. If I state a preference for the second it is because of its outstanding qualities of psychological penetration. Phillip emerges as a fascinating mixture of philosopher, man of action, and meticulous administrator.

The Meticulous Administrator

It is this last quality that was so prominent in his first appearance on the stage of the mid-1780s. From the moment of his appointment until the embarkation of the Fleet, nothing escaped his attention. Unfortunately, the execution of everything essential (in his view) to the satisfactory despatch of the Fleet and its successful transportation of its passengers and their settlement on arrival in New South Wales rested more with an ill-chosen, ill-organized, contentious and unwilling body of what passed for public servants in a dozen ministries and institutions, and a venal and corrupt body of private contractors. With all these and their political masters, Phillip pleaded daily that the supplies, services and information essential to a successful operation should be made available. The results were below even the standards of the late eighteenth century (and these were in many respects below the standards of 1700). This was not, in what today would be called the 'public sector', an age of progress and improvement.

The First Fleet departed in haste and confusion. One *desideratum* – it was to cause Phillip the idealist much anxiety and trouble – was any systematic provision of his prisoners' dossiers. Two transports, the *Friendship* and the *Lady Penrhyn*, had full details of their passengers. Many of those in other ships had none, or at best defective accounts. Phillip, whose philosophical and moral intellect was much devoted to the study, theory and practice of law – especially the relationship between crime and punishment – was much put out by this particular defect in the arrangements. But before the administrative and judicial consequences became clear he had more immediate problems to face.

As Commander of the Fleet, he was responsible for eleven ships; of these two, the HMS *Sirius* and HMS *Supply* were small warships, the *Sirius* being a re-build of a former merchant ship that had been burnt.

* Sydney, 1937.
† London and Sydney, 1938.

Neither warship was a good sailer: the British Government was even meaner about making ships available than it was about supplies. Six others were transports for the convicts and a handful of specialists (carpenters, blacksmiths, etc.). Three were store ships. In all, they carried (the figure, like everything about the First Fleet is an approximation) 1,486 people; of these rather more than half were convicts and their wives and children, the rest were naval or marine officers, ratings or rankers, wives and children. To shepherd such a large convoy, with such a bizarre collection of passengers, half way round the world – the journey was at least 13,000 miles and probably much more – was a supreme test of naval and administrative skill. There was no precedent for it. Even if Phillip had been given tools adequate to the job, his achievement would have been in the highest degree praiseworthy. Given the additional problems, inevitable and unavoidable, that he was required to face, the safe arrival, in good order, of convoy and cargo, at Botany Bay was little short of a miracle.

Even before he left he had complained bitterly to Nepean, the official responsible at the Home Office (their friendship was to survive even the ordeal of the First Fleet), that the ships were overcrowded to a degree dangerous to health, order and decency. Neither flour nor anti-scorbutics was provided. There was no fresh meat for use while in port, no proper clothing for the convicts, no hygienic disinfecting ('smoking') of the ships. Some of the women convicts were already – and were long to be – a prime source of trouble. The lowest sweepings of the streets of London, they were almost naked, filthy, unwashed, often mentally retarded or sick, many suffering from either the clap or even syphilis. Some were pregnant.

While some of Phillip's complaints were attended to, more were not. He wrote to Nepean that 'the garrison and convicts are being sent to the extremity of the globe as they would be sent to America – a six week passage'. (His own voyage was to take over eight months.) He was (he added frankly) concerned not only about his public duty but his public reputation if half the garrison and the convicts were to be lost on the voyage.

In spite of all the hazards, Phillip got there. This is his first and unique claim to credit, equal in the scales of Australian and world history – when all is taken into account – with that of Cook and Banks themselves.

His second claim rests on his aims and ideals, as they were expressed before sailing on his great adventure and, doubtless, after viewing some of his unwilling and unattractive passengers. His words must have delighted the imperialists such as Matra and Young: they are still worth repeating not only to his inextinguishable honour, but as clarification of the priorities of his tastes. About the convicts, he said: 'As I would not wish convicts to lay the foundations of an Empire, I think they should ever remain separated from the garrison and from the settlers that may come from Europe.'

And that, he added, should continue even after their period of punishment had expired; Phillip may have been humanitarian, but he was also realistic.

Justice

Phillip's abiding concern was the law. British law should be the basis of law in New South Wales, for, 'There can be no slavery in a free land, and consequently no slaves.' Phillip's perception of his voyage was not mere responsibility for a giant version of a seaborne Black Maria: it was a grand vision of Empire, based on free men and free land. Upon emancipation, the convicts were to be granted land for the keep of themselves and their families. The 'emancipists' are sometimes seen as the brain-children of Governor Macquarie, but this is not the case; they were the invention of Phillip.

His letters to the Home Office and other departments were – necessarily – filled with complaints of shortages and defects in the stores that had been supplied in the dockyards or were sent out later. There is no room in this brief survey to do more than repeat that Phillip was ill-served by his masters in London. One theme recurs time and again: he had been promised that sooner or later, he would be sent some individual, free settlers experienced – preferably – in farming, and backed up by some experienced skilled artisans – smiths, tool-makers, carpenters, bootmakers, etc. But none arrived. There was though a stream of new convict arrivals – in much worse condition than those he had himself shepherded from England. Whitehall had learned nothing. Phillip protested repeatedly: fifty good farmers would be worth more to him and his settlement than a thousand more convicts. But it was all to no purpose. Virtually no free settlers arrived during Phillip's governorship. This created, or made worse, the recurrent periods of food shortage – amounting to famine – in times of drought or bad weather.

Yet, throughout, the Governor's morale remained high, and his patience almost unlimited. In such conditions, his task was made the more unpalatable by his own conviction that in a real crisis, the settlement must necessarily revert to an egalitarian system of distributing what food and other supplies of necessities existed. This in turn evoked criticism from – above all – his own officers; more particularly the marine officers.

His Deputy Governor and Commandant of the Marine Corps, Major Ross, dourest of Scots, was mean, jealous, resentful and greedy. To his way of thinking, Phillip was scandalously lenient with the convicts and far too generous to the natives. After rehearsing his grievances, against the world at large and Arthur Phillip in particular for some time, he hit on a means of taking his revenge. Ingeniously he thrust at Phillip by bringing the machinery of the law to a standstill. He knew that few things could cause the Governor greater concern in a still unstable, small and temperamental society.

The-tragicomedy was in two Acts; the plot of both was written by Ross. In the first, he supported another officer friendly to himself (but not to the other marine officers) in refusing to take part in the proceedings of the Criminal Court. Knowing that if this non-co-operation spread to other officers, it would be impossible for the Courts to operate, Phillip intervened. He was in the end supported by the whole body of officers and the quarrel was, after a lapse of time, settled. It was followed by a more serious attempt by Ross to throw military discipline out of the window by intervening in a court martial, pronouncing it to be out of order. When the officer in charge refused to accept his ruling (as illegal), Ross put all five officers operating the court under arrest. The officers protested; Ross demanded a general court martial. Phillip refused: the officers of the entire marine detachment were only eighteen in all. Five had already been suspended in one way or another by Ross. Ten out of eighteen were thus out of action. Who was to be responsible for duty, discipline and defence against disorder or aggression?

Ross quarrelled successively with almost everybody. As Marjorie Barnard has remarked: 'How the wheels of justice kept turning at all through this turmoil is a miracle.' But Arthur Phillip was by now good at performing miracles. In the field of law he had an able assistant in Judge-Advocate Collins. Collins shared many of the Governor's views on crime and punishment. He also held him in high esteem.

In his 'harangue' to the seated convicts on the occasion of the official foundation of the colony (see p. 18) the Governor had concluded his speech with an uncharacteristic (for him) fanfare threatening that any more behaviour of the sort witnessed in the orgies after landing would be visited with the most deadly penalties. According to some witnesses he carried out his threat. Statistics (kept by Collins) tell a different story. In four years out of five, only male convicts were executed (five, four, one, one); in the fifth year (1789), omitted from his journal, the count seems to be six soldiers and one woman. This, by the standards of the time, was by no means harsh. By the standards of naval discipline, which were especially ferocious, the demands of the law in New South Wales were mild.

Phillip shared the assumption, widely accepted by the penologists of his day, that crime could best be met with punishments designed as effective deterrents. To this he added a general rule that crimes should be graded as more, or less, serious *according to the damage they inflicted on society*. And by 'society' he meant the thousand-odd people who comprised Sydney and its surrounding countryside in 1788 and after. There was, for example, no point in fining convicts who had no money with which to pay; nor in depriving the settlement of the most valuable services of a competent fisherman at a time of acute food shortage. He was given severe physical punishment, deprived of his hut, but he kept his job. Another convict, sentenced to death, was offered his pardon on condition he accepted the gruesome office of public executioner.

Banishment to a faraway penal settlement – Norfolk Island, or (later), Macquarie Harbour in Tasmania – was to become regarded as the severest sentence. Phillip's successor, Hunter, wrote of the convicts that 'they would sooner have lost their lives; because it [Norfolk Island] is a small spot and they have no chance of escaping'. In general, punishment was designed to fit the crime and simultaneously do something by way of supporting the colony. Even from Norfolk Island, a letter 'received from a gentleman resident' there and published in *The Sun* on 27 May 1793, notes that about 300 acres of ground (it was pretty good at Norfolk Island) was cleared and worked by some 170 settlers, part sailors and marines;

> the rest are the convicts who have served their time and are now become settlers. ... I believe they have from one acre to four each man; some of them have already taken one man off the store [that is, the public food supply] and in the course of time will ease Government very considerably.

In such conditions, punishment inflicted, even law itself, became conditional, that is, relative to the gravity of the crime; and in New South Wales the gravest was not necessarily to be murder or rape: it was most likely to be theft of scarce goods, and in particular, of food. In the recurrent periods of starvation, men like James Collington were driven to steal in order to eat. 'He appeared', wrote Collins, 'desirous of death, declaring that he knew he could not live without stealing.' 'Their universal plea [for mercy]' (Collins again), 'was hunger; but it was a plea that in the then situation of the colony, could not be so much attended to as it certainly would have been in country of greater plenty.' Theft did most harm to others, therefore theft was the worst crime, and most crimes were due to hunger. The chastity of the food store was (as Collins said) 'as the chastity of Caesar's wife. With us it would not even bear suspicion.' The preservation and protection of the small flock of animals was basic to the very existence of the settlement.

This compelling logic sometimes had bizarre results. In September 1789 a private soldier, one Wright, was accused in the Criminal Court of the rape of an eight-year-old girl. Murder, sodomy and rape were capital crimes, but Wright's sentence was commuted to exile on Norfolk Island. Explaining this reprieve (while on the same occasion hanging another man for petty theft), the Judge Advocate declared:

> This was an offence that did not seem to require an immediate example; the chastity of the female part of the settlement had never been so rigid as to drive men to so desperate an act; and it was believed that beside the wretch in question, there was not in the colony a man of any description who would have attempted it.

The function of justice in such circumstances becomes not to vindicate Divine Law but to protect society against repetition of socially disastrous acts. Watkin Tench, one of Phillip's most intelligent and observant officers, author of one of the world's best diaries, noted that in this period of Phillip's four years, 'few crimes of a deep dye, or a hardened nature, have been perpetrated. Murder and unnatural sins rank not hitherto in the catalogue of their enormities; and one suicide only has been committed.'

Phillip himself certainly accepted the lines of thinking expressed by Collins and Tench. They may well have learned their philosophy of crime and punishment from his own steadily unemotional view of human nature. It must, in any case, have required the Governor's approval to commute Wright's punishment. Phillip was liberal enough to prefer reducing the severity of a penalty rather than increasing it. In any case, his ideas on methods of improving the quality of society changed as he observed how society worked. It was not only deterrents that made an important contribution to improvement; so did incentives.

Being a humane, as well as an honest and realistic disciple of the Enlightenment, he took a humane view of the sexual problems of the convicts. Even during the voyage of the First Fleet, he discussed openly with his officers the 'irregularities' that punctuated life at sea amongst the convicts, male and female, and sailors. At one stage he concluded that the irregular should be regularized, that is, that the females should appoint regular times of 'visiting'. For good or ill, nothing seems to have come of this initiative. The result was the unlimited orgy which took place immediately after the original landing. From this the Governor seems prudently to have averted his eyes, regarding it as beyond human power to control.

Originally, as we have seen, it was his idea that the convicts should be separated at all times from the free settlers. He changed his mind on this point. His reasons for pleading for more free settlers from the Home Department ceased to be exclusively directed towards improvements in agriculture and food supply. They began to include the moral example which the free men could provide for imitation by the convicts, who could thus be brought back into civil society as equal and respectable citizens. In a remarkable despatch to the Home Secretary he wrote: 'The vicious and idle are not easily reformed while they are incorporated in one body. Precept has little effect, but example will do much ... we shall still want some good characters to whom those people might look up.'

His conviction that the best arrangement would be for convicts to be assigned to settlers finally percolated through to the Select Committee on Transportation (1812), which endorsed his ideas:

> It would be better for them to live *en famille* in rural conditions than in urban gangs frequenting the stews of Sydney.... In the service of settlers they are likely to acquire some knowledge of farming ... if from convicts they become well behaved and industrious servants, a further possibility is opened to them of becoming prosperous and respectable settlers.

The Phillip leaven seemed to be working: and in many cases work it did (see chapter 4). Unfortunately, the delegation of responsibility for the convicts to private settlers was to lead to grievous and insoluble abuses. They were to grow and persist until transportation was abolished during the mid-nineteenth century. Initially, single-handed, Phillip made the system work. That it was grossly extravagant is undeniable; the one thousand convicts of 1788 swelled to three thousand by 1792, when Phillip left Australia. The total cost for this trifling relief of England's prison problem was nearly a million pounds, not counting the loss of two warships with all their cargo – *Sirius* and *Guardian* – in bad weather and impossible landing conditions; nor the fearful mortality in several of the fleets which followed the First Fleet. These later operations enjoyed nothing like the care that Phillip had taken with the First Fleet. Collins described the scene when the *Neptune* and the *Scarborough* disembarked their passengers from the Second Fleet. The portable tent-hospitals 'were filled with people ... labouring under the complicated diseases of scurvy, dysentery and others in the last stages of either of those terrible disorders or yielding to the attacks of an infectious fever'.

A woman convict wrote home of the landing of the *Lady Juliana* from the same fleet, when even Phillip's patience broke:

> Oh! if you had but seen the shocking sight of the poor creatures ... it would make your heart bleed; they were almost dead; few could stand ... they died ten or twelve a day when they first landed ... they were confined and had bad victuals and stinking water. ... The Governor was very angry and scolded the captains a great deal, and, I heard, intended to write to London about it, for I heard him say it was murdering them.

The costs of transportation were intolerable. That they were improved, even in Phillip's time, by his sole effort, in a way made things worse. The horrors of the 'system' were moderated: the virtues apparent – at least to English administrators, politicians and penological theorists 15,000 miles away – seemed to grow. Settlers – big graziers especially – welcomed the provision of cheap labour. The vice inherent in the system was clearer to Australia's own population. The life for many was isolated, claustrophobic and unnatural. Even the Governors, and naval and marine officers, let alone the convicts, were separated from their wives and families. Basic human problems – sexual especially – were solved, *ambulando*, by casual alliances. Most men, including inherently respectable officers (like King) had illegitimate children. Illicit heterosexuality was almost universal; homosexuality less so, but apparently frequent. Even when supplies of food and necessities improved, agricultural knowledge and productivity grew, the population increased, the sense of isolation grew less, the origins of 'Botany Bay' remained stamped on the psychology of the settlement. Society was divided into convict and free. The malodorous social and political consequences were to take a long time to eliminate; the longer because, in the meantime, the penologists, in the grip of deterrent fever, persuaded politically influential circles that what Australia needed was a more severe regime of punishment.

Phillip the Explorer

At Sydney Phillip made what perhaps will always rank as his greatest discovery; rejecting without a day's hesitation the verdict of Cook and Banks he left Botany Bay to its own devices and went straight for Sydney. Grand as the harbour itself was, the surrounding country left much to be desired. His first task was to find some decent agricultural land: he had after all, successfully farmed two holdings in Hampshire and knew good soil when he saw it. With the burdens of Atlas on his shoulders he had no time to carry out more than fairly short-distance exploration:

even so, he quickly nosed out an area up river which he christened Rose Hill (in honour of his neighbour and Treasury friend, Sir George Rose). There he noticed a heavier clay soil, better suited to growing crops than the lighter sands on the coast. Soon Parramatta (the aboriginal name) was yielding the best harvest the settlement had seen. He got as far as the Hawkesbury and Nepean rivers; some of his staff urged the settlement of the Hawkesbury, but Phillip disagreed. It was too isolated and his people were too few to be scattered over great distances. Better to concentrate efforts nearer home – on planning the broad streets of Sydney itself, a Governor's House, accommodation for officers, troops, stores, even convicts. By the time he left New South Wales in 1792 over a thousand acres were planted with crops, and over 300 convicts had been freed from their sentences and granted land.

The Governor's Auxiliaries

No doubt the Governor was glad of the occasional chance to get away from the tensions and squabbles of Sydney Village – above all to leave behind the malevolence of his deputy, Ross, who summarized his attitude to the new settlement in a few terse phrases: 'I do not scruple to pronounce that in the whole world there is not a worse country than what we have seen....' For the most part the officers preferred the company and personality of their Governor. Collins, the Judge Advocate, had 'an inexpressible hatred' for Ross. Like the Governor, whose ideals – especially his concern for the natives – he shared, Collins was a retiring man whose considerable merits were never rewarded by the British Government. Lieutenant Watkin Tench of the Marines – described by Professor Fitzhardinge (to whose meticulous editing we owe the best edition of Tench's vivid *Diaries*) as 'the first to mould Australian experience into a work of conscious art', must have been good company.

Another marine Lieutenant William Bradley, was a good naturalist, observer of aboriginal life and the settlement's first pianist; he brought his fortepiano with him. Lieutenant Dawes, in spite of a classic disagreement with Phillip, was also a scientist, useful on exploration, difficult only through his refusal to bend even a fraction his 'unbending principles'.

The surgeons were as indispensable on land as at sea. John White, Surgeon General, was highly competent; it was largely thanks to his ministrations that the First Fleet arrived with so few casualties from scurvy or dysentery. Arndell, of a gentry family, was another useful enthusiast for botany who was later to turn to farming and act as champion of the small settlers.

By 1791 the settlement had made considerable strides. When he could shut the door on Ross, forget the problems of the convicts and a pain in his side that nagged at him by day and night, Phillip was an excellent host for a party. Mrs Parker, wife of the captain of the visiting warship HMS *Gorgon*, and a budding travel writer, could write:

> Our amusements here, although neither numerous nor expensive, were to me perfectly novel and agreeable: the fatherly attention of the good Governor upon all occasions, with the politeness of the officers, rendered our *sejour* perfectly happy and comfortable ... it [Government House] always proved a home for me: under this hospitable roof I have often ate part of a kangaroo with as much glee as if I had been a partaker of the greatest delicacy of this metropolis ... our parties generally consisted of Mr King, Mr Johnson [the Chaplain, and a querulous bore] and the ladies who reside at the Colony....'

On walks she admired the flowering shrubs that sprouted from the rocks, white flowers that reminded her of English hawthorn, smelling both sweet and fragrant, the luxuriant grass, indeed all 'the natural beauties raised by the hand of Providence without expense or toil ...'. Only the hospital, filled with 'mere skeletons of men – in every bed and on every side lay the dying and the dead' was a 'Horrid spectacle'. She reflected (rightly) that 'It would be repeated so long [as] the present method of transporting these miserable wretches is pursued.'

The Natives

The Governor's exploring parties have another aspect that reflects the gross errors that confound so much early Australian history, and the behaviour of those who made it. They arise out of the attempt on Phillip's life and, later, a separate attack by aborigines in which his game-keeper was killed. Both Miss Barnard and Professor Mackaness tell the story of the attempt on Phillip's life in very similar terms. Hearing that a whale had been stranded on the coast at Manly and was being cut up for a feast by the natives, Phillip decided to row across the bay and see if his two favourite aborigines, Colbee and Bennelon were there. Upon his arrival, all was good humour and high banter. After all this had gone on for some time, a native unknown to Phillip or his party was seen approaching, spear in hand. Phillip approached him; Lieutenant Tench takes up the story:

> The nearer the Governor approached, the greater became the terror and agitation of the Indian. To remove his fear Governor Phillip threw down a dirk, which he wore at his side. The other, alarmed at the rattle of the

dirk and probably misconstruing the action, immediately fixed his lance on his throwing stick. To retreat, His Excellency now thought, would be more dangerous than to advance. He therefore cried out to the man Wee-re, Wea-re (bad: you are doing wrong) displaying at the same time every token of amity and confidence. The words had, however, hardly gone forth when the Indian, stepping back with one foot, aimed his lance with such force and dexterity that striking the Governor's right shoulder, just above the collar bone, the point glancing downward came out at his back, having made a wound of many inches long.

The native attacker then disappeared. All was confusion. Phillip's companions ran up to help, a few spears were thrown and a musket was discharged. No further casualties, however, were inflicted. The Governor was placed in the rowing boat, apparently in mortal pain, but the five-mile row back to Sydney was accomplished in a couple of hours. There the barbed lance, still stuck through his shoulder, was removed by Balmain, the assistant surgeon (White being away). Ten days later Phillip was up and about again: being scorbutic his wounds were slow to heal. Six weeks after the event he was back in good health.

The important point to be remarked is that Phillip refused to make anything out of the incident. It was (he insisted) the result of a misunderstanding for which he took the blame. He refused to accept that the attacker had any intention of doing anything but defend himself against what he believed was Phillip's intention to attack or capture him. He refused to contemplate for a moment any idea of reprisals. Most of the Command believed the outcome of the affair to be good, with better understanding and more intermingling of the native and white communities. It was at this point that Phillip readily acceded to Bennelon's pressing request for a hut of his own in Sydney. It was built at the eastern point of the cove, known down to the present time as Bennelong Point, and now the site of the Sydney Opera House.

Again, Phillip had carried out in the letter and spirit the terms of his commission enjoining on him the importance of opening intercourse with the natives, conciliating their affections and encouraging amity and kindness towards them. We shall see later how his sense of duty, patience and magnanimity have been rewarded by some later writers.

This brings us to the second incident involving the aborigines and Phillip's attitude towards them. Again, it arose from aboriginal attack, but this time it was mortal. The victim was Phillip's gamekeeper, by name M'Entire. He was not an attractive figure and had by his brutal behaviour brought down on himself the hatred of the natives. He was ambushed on 10 December 1790, while out hunting near Botany Bay with a party of marines and convicts. The assassin's attack was of exactly the same type as that on the Governor: but this time M'Entire was very seriously wounded. A man of enormous physique and strength, he dragged himself to Sydney but bled profusely all the way. Though the lance had penetrated his lung he hung on to life for some time, but finally died of exhaustion.

Following M'Entire's death, Phillip ordered two expeditions, in rapid succession, to go out, find the assassin and bring him and his companions in for punishment. This has led some followers of early Australian history to conclude that Phillip finally lost his temper and patience with the natives and ordered a campaign of personal revenge on the tribe responsible. (They were the Bid-ee-ga, a particularly bloodthirsty tribe who had been responsible for most of the seventeen killings of white men on the coast.)

This is the interpretation adopted by Professor Noel Butlin in his book *Our Original Aggression* (1984). His principal objective is to re-calculate, by a number of ingenious statistical computations and inferences, the size of the original native population of Australia and its subsequent drastic reduction. Unfortunately he has added to his calculations some unfavourable reflections on the First Governor and the First Fleet (see chapter 5, pp. 77–9). To a collection of possible misdeeds of the former he has added a character-change in Phillip, stemming directly from the assassination of his game-keeper.

The punitive expeditions, the order (alleged) to bring to him 'ten black heads in exchange for one convict body', the decision to 'send packing' the mutinous Lieutenant Dawes, whose conscience forbade him to participate in the punitive expedition Phillip ordered – all this, Butlin has written, is proof of an 'unfortunate ... major turnaround some time between 1788 and 1790, in Phillip's own attitudes to the blacks'. This leads him to conclude that one cannot rule out 'the various possibilities of deliberate action at some level' by a Governor beside himself with rage against the aborigines.

Apart from the fact that the chronology of any such historical interpretation is wrong (the great smallpox epidemic, which Butlin believes may have been an act of deliberate genocide of some kind by the 'whites' under Phillip's command, took place in April–May 1789, *before* the native attacks on either the Governor or his gamekeeper which are now said to have disturbed the fairly good relations that previously existed between whites and blacks) – the recorded facts contradict the Butlin assumptions. When Phillip ordered out the first search party, his orders included the following:

the Governor strictly forbids, under penalty of severest punishment, any soldier ... ever to fire on any native except in his own defence ... the natives will be made severe examples of whenever any man is wounded by them: but this will be done in a manner which will satisfy them that it is punishment inflicted on them for their own bad conduct, and of which they cannot be sensible, if they are not treated with kindness, while they continue peaceable and quiet.

This was no more severe than the language he had used to the convicts after the founding ceremonial of 7 February 1788, and less severe than some of the punishments he had meted out to white sailors and marines. It cannot for a moment be construed as an anti-aboriginal campaign *per se*. Lieutenant Tench (who himself thought the Governor's original instructions to the search party under his command were too severe) found Phillip his usual reasonable self when he went to him and said as much. Could not the number of potential culprits be reduced from ten to six? The Governor at once agreed: indeed 'if as many as this were necessary, he would hang two and send the rest to Norfolk Island for a period, which will cause their countrymen to believe that we have despatched them secretly'.

Nor did he fly into a temper and 'send Dawes packing' for questioning his orders. Dawes did not in fact leave New South Wales until a year later. Phillip's strict sense of duty and humanity never deserted him. His duties included the punishment of deliberate violence: murder (by white or black) was by definition to be punished by death. He told Tench he doubted whether he had been wise to allow other murders by natives to go unpunished. He had done so because of the possibility that they were caused by provocation or misunderstanding, like the attack on himself. As for the causes of this latest attack on M'Entire (he went on): 'I am fully persuaded that they were unprovoked and the barbarity of their conduct admits of no extenuation.'

He had scrutinized all the evidence and interviewed the natives best known to him – all to no purpose:

So that we have only our own efforts to depend upon: and I am resolved to execute the prisoners who may be brought in, and in the most public and exemplary manner, in the presence of as many of their countrymen as can be collected, *after having explained the cause of such a punishment; and my fixed determination to repeat it, whenever any future breach of good conduct on their side shall render it necessary.**

These are not the words of insensate rage or thirst for vengeance.

* My italics.

There was no 'turnaround' in Phillip's attitude to the natives. He knew them better than any later academic can hope to – their unpredictability, their quick wits in some matters, their hopeless confusion in others, their engaging frankness mixed with deepest duplicity when it suited them, their charm and their ruthless violence. Some of his colleagues were gradually provoked out their wits by what they gradually discovered to be the utter impossibility of dealing with the aborigines, but not Phillip. Product of the *Aufklärung* as he was, he continued to be fascinated by the Australian scene – its flora and fauna, above all its childlike, cunning people and their kaleidoscopic spirits. So that when the day of his departure to England arrived, he took with him not only timber, plants, birds, animals, four kangaroos and several dingo dogs but also Bennelon and Yemmerrawannee, his two favourite aborigines. They went 'voluntarily and cheerfully'. King George III, to whom they were introduced at St James's, was much interested – more interested than Bennelon who put up with England for two years. After that he asked to go home, was returned to Sydney where he left off his clothes, made for the bush and disappeared.

Phillip's Last Years: the Fencibles and Retirement

Phillip left Port Jackson on HMS *Atlantic* on 11 December 1792. He arrived at London on 22 May 1793. He was still suffering from the chronic pain in his side, possibly hernia, which had bothered him for a couple of years. On 23 July he formally applied for permission to resign the governorship – with 'the greatest regret'. Later, he recovered sufficiently to resume naval service, commanding HMS *Alexandra*, HMS *Swiftsure* and finally HMS *Blenheim*, a seventy-four-gun warship of the line. In 1799 he was promoted Rear Admiral of the Blue, and thereafter, via the White and Red (and five more promotions), to Admiral of the Blue (1810).

By this time, however, his sea-going service had long ceased. From 1796 to 1805 he was principally occupied with the command of the wartime organization called the Sea Fencibles, first in his own area of Hampshire, later in the whole of England. He had arrived home at a time of deep and prolonged political and diplomatic crisis, both in home and foreign affairs. In the mid-1790s and the year 1805–6 the risk of invasion was real – and the fear of domestic insurrection hardly less disturbing. The 'Fencibles' (from 'defensibles', implying 'liable and fit for active war service') were regular troops, one-third horsed, the rest infantry, for defence duty, the Napoleonic period forerunners of the

Home Guard and, like them, a kind of 'Dad's Army'.

To command the Fencibles he was appointed, without doubt, on the strength of his matchless record as naval and military administrator in Australia. George Mackaness makes it clear he lived up to his reputation. No part of the English coastal defences escaped his closest attention. After 1806 he finally retired, to spend his last eight years peacefully at Bennett Street, Bath. Here he entertained as hospitably as ever, drinking tea or madeira with a circle of old naval friends and visitors, playing cards with his second wife: going shopping in Bath, chatting to his pet parrot from Rose Hill. He seems to have basked happily in this late sunshine of relaxation and marriage. (His second wife was a greater comfort to him than his first: the latter's portrait, by George James, in the Dixson Gallery, needs no prolonged scrutiny to suggest that those tightly pursed lips and pert, inquisitive gaze, can hardly have been easy to live with.) He died in Bath in 1814, at the age of seventy-six, and is buried alongside his second wife at St Nicholas's Church Bathampton, where an unobtrusive tablet marks his final resting place. Very recently the patient efforts of local vicars and First Fleeters over nearly a century have added a tiny chapel of remembrance.

Phillip was able to create a state in Australia because the ideal of a state was in his mind long before he saw Australia. He 'approximated' the raw materials he was given to his concept – a free state with no slaves; paternal – in its early stages necessarily – but predominantly democratic, in times of crisis egalitarian. The *imponderabilia* he gave New South Wales were – Marjorie Barnard is perfectly correct – 'self-respect and trust in a just and impartial Government'. These were handed on and survived long enough to be renewed and continued by Governor Macquarie. Many, probably most, modern historians would agree.

Marjorie Barnard's portrait of Phillip is an honest one; he appears, to coin the phrase, warts and all. He was neither perfect nor wholly successful. He had no diplomatic gift for dealing with people. If he had emotions he rarely showed them. He was not cold but he was impersonal. He made few friends, at Sydney at least. The principles which gave strength and balance to his practical acts of administration derived from his supreme belief in the logic of reason, and this was not conducive to easy friendships. Sometimes it was a cause of his positive unpopularity, for convicts could not understand his regard for mere natives, and his officers felt humiliated when they compared his treatment of the convicts with his treatment of themselves. His very leniency won him the affection of nobody, even those who benefited by his fairness.

He was not, Marjorie Barnard thinks, an unhappy man. He was exceedingly brave, but his bravery was the bravery of a man who is not naturally without fear. It was the bravery of a shy, nervous, sensitive spirit who succeeded in rationalizing fear out of his life by facing it with all the 'reason' he could muster. His ceaseless attention to work and duty was similarly explained by the way he manipulated 'reason' to filter away the need for love, religious belief, social interests. There remained the loneliness, the sense of duty, the silent extinction of self.

In the end, as Marjorie Barnard has said, we can only guess what kind of man Phillip was. Perhaps his achievements have been best summarized by Sir Ernest Scott:

> There was not one among all the subjects of King George III whose place was more assured than his ... who amongst them all did a piece of work to compare with Phillip's. And who amongst them all overcame such difficulties with such imperfect material and reaped so small a material reward.*

It is no overstatement. Phillip was not just the First Governor; he was also the greatest.†

---

* Ernest Scott *A Short History of Australia* (Oxford, 1950), p. 48.
† This view is shared by Professor Auchmuty in his meticulous edition of Phillip's *Voyage*, Introduction, pp. xii–xiii (Royal Australian Historical Society, 1972).

3

THE YEARS OF STRUGGLE 1788–1860

'Almost everybody in this land calls Great Britain *home* and speaks with desire respecting returning thither.'

(James Backhouse)*

The history of Australia's economic expansion and development has been thoroughly, if unevenly, attended to. A number of themes of great importance have been treated, after appearing as this or that historian's *leitmotiv* of Australian progress or lack of progress. The place of labour, of labour organization, wage regulation, the trade unions' role, have been a major area of study. Equally enthusiastically, another school has emphasized the role of economic freedom as the creative context of Australian growth and prosperity. The opposing view, that Australia has been caught fast in the grip of economic imperialism, first of Britain, later of the United States has also been very influential. These, and other theories, all continue to recruit support today, even though the interpretation of such themes as 'imperialism' has to be modified – some would say twisted – to accommodate contemporary circumstances.

This chapter is concerned with the period from about 1788 to 1860. Here the major themes must surely be the geographical expansion of Phillip's original settlement; the growth of population and its character; the development of Australian 'farming', meaning – primarily – pastoralism; and the emergence of dominant exporting trades and industries which in turn helped to pay for Australia's vital needs of goods that could not, in these early stages, be provided or manufactured in Australia itself.

In some of the best modern writing in economic history, the source and spring of Australian economic growth – a truly remarkable phenomenon – is seen to lie in the early development of export industries. The early emergence of fine wool as an export has been featured by generations of writers. Only recently has it been more clear that exports

* *Extracts from the letters of James Backhouse 1838–1841*, vol. I, Part 4, p. 7.

– in disguise – continued to be of primary importance in the second half of the nineteenth century as they had been down to 1850. Our period therefore set a pattern which was to last for another half century. For Professor W.A. Sinclair, 'The source of economic growth . . . in terms of rising output per head, continued to be land-intensive exports.'*

The development of mining, especially of alluvial gold, then copper, brought up the average rate of immigration of settlers hitherto unattracted by the modest prospect of rural agrarian life in a country thousands of miles from the nearest white settlements. Its exports therefore stimulated the growth of cities, building, transport and the further general exploitation of natural sources and secondary industries. Tangible, eye-catching 'growth' was postponed until well into the later nineteenth century. That postponement was in no way a consequence of British 'imperialism' in the nineteenth century, nor of American (or even Russian or Japanese) 'imperialism' in the twentieth.

To revert to the earlier period, sophisticated economic theory has little place in the interpretation of its economic history. The settlement created by the First Fleet was about the size of a large village, a drop of humanity in a vast bucket of largely empty space, whose potentialities were as unknown as its problems and slower to reveal themselves. At the end of Phillip's term of office he wrote to Dundas (Sydney's successor in Whitehall). He was cheerful, rightly, that he had 1,000 acres under crops and 4,844 bushels of corn – even allowing for 1,500 bushels of maize having been stolen.

These figures illustrate the immense effort that had gone into Phillip's enterprise. It is not easy for us today to appreciate what a formidable task it was to clear and cultivate 1,000 acres with a force of labourers that cannot have reached an average size of 500. And this, accomplished as it was against an unfamiliar climate, widespread and frequent sickness and mortality, ignorance, idleness and bloody-mindedness, inadequate supervision and primitive and badly-made implements supplied by fraudulent contractors, constituted a very great achievement on the part of Phillip.

By 1860 the picture was transformed. The white population had grown, by convict transportation, by the immigration of free settlers, and by natural increase, to nearly 1.2 million people. More of them still lived

* W.A. Sinclair *The Process of Economic Development in Australia* (Melbourne and London, 1976), p. 171.

in rural areas than in cities, but the cities that are still Australia's great capitals were growing. The oldest was Sydney – until the mid-century the largest – but the gold rush of 1850–60 in Victoria brought hordes of treasure seekers swarming into Melbourne. Its mushroom growth ensured that it caught up with and soon overtook Sydney: in 1861 Melbourne had over 125,000 inhabitants, whereas Sydney had about 100,000.

The rural population had reared and sheared a sheep population of twenty-one million, and bred and herded four million cattle; raised fifteen million bushels of wheat, oats, barley and maize; reared half a million horses and over a quarter of a million pigs. Perhaps most important of all, the colony was exporting at least two of its products on a very large scale: the value of wool was very high – five million pounds; but wool had already been overtaken in value by alluvial gold. Its value now stood at just under ten million pounds.

The footings of this expansion were the geographical flow of settlement, fanning out into the west, north and south from the original settlement at Port Jackson. The first movement, as we have seen, was Phillip's development of farming on the better lands round Parramatta (Rose Hill). Gradually there followed the occupation of the whole area of the Cumberland Plain. The navigation of the Bass Strait and the settlement round Hobart and Port Dalrymple was followed by agrarian development, aided by the transportation of huge consignments of convict labour. By the second decade of the nineteenth century, explorers were probing westwards in attempts to ease the growing pressure of sheep and cattle on pastures hemmed in by the Blue Mountains. They were crossed by the patient and intrepid trio – Blaxland, Lawson and W.C. Wentworth – in 1813. But not until 1820 did the reigning Governor, Macquarie, allow more than a mere caterpillar of stock to cross into the new territory. His decision to relax was triggered off by a series of droughts and cattle plagues on the now crowded Cumberland Plain.

The later years of the eighteenth century and the first decade and more of the nineteenth century were a time of fluctuating economic fortunes. A basic source of uncertainty for everybody, but most of all for the Governor – who under the customary form of commission laid down in 1788 ruled like a tribal chieftain – was the numbers of convicts transported per annum. Would the number this year be larger or smaller than last? Nobody knew: not even Whitehall knew until the unlucky dip took place. During the time of the European wars, under Phillip's three successors, numbers were small. Under Macquarie they were large; more than twice as many a year as under Phillip. And it was the size of the convict immigration which guided the Governor in deciding how much labour to assign to stock raising and how much to cereal farming. Beyond using his wits or tossing a coin there was little prophetic guidance, little help he could seek.

Thus it was not until about 1820 that the economic trends seem to point upwards. Britain had come out of the French Wars triumphantly. Her old rivals in trade, the Dutch, were in eclipse. Her traditional political enemy, France, after threatening Britain at home as well as abroad, had been despatched. Phillip's 'Fencibles' could go home, the army could disappear and the Navy be put in mothballs. Now there was time and money for better things.

The three decades between 1820 and 1850 were the rich core of this half-century of expansion. Sheep and wool were its enduring claim to imperishable Australian fame in the second half of the century, thereafter to be joined by mining. But between 1800 and 1830 sealing and whaling were at their height as the leading Australian export-orientated industries. Sealing fell away sharply after 1830: whaling went on longer, until after 1850, but that decade saw its end as part of a major but transient sector of the economy.

Sealing

Captain Cook noted in his diary for 1773 that at Dusky Sound, New Zealand, seals were to be found 'in great numbers ... on the small rocks and isles near the sea coast'. Hunter, sailing in with the First Fleet, saw 'many animals' which he took to be a sort of sea-otter, 'playing alongside' the ships. In 1806, Joseph Banks was in hopes that the 'almost innumerable' seals of Van Diemen's Land would form the base of an industry for the new colony. The beaches were 'encumbered' with them and visitors to their haunts could kill them more easily than the victuallers' servants 'who kill hogs in a pound with mallets'.

The first grounds to be exploited were the coasts of Bass Strait. The earliest sealers came from Sydney or London. In 1798 the brig *Nautilus*, skipper Captain Charles Bishop of Sydney, collected nine thousand skins at Tasmania; Bishop grew the first peas and potatoes produced there. The Sydney sealers were followed by others based in Massachusetts, New York, Nantucket, Canada and Tasmania. It was a Nantucket sealer, the *Favourite*, which landed the world's largest haul of seal skins – 87,000 – at Canton, in January 1807.

After some ten years, the focus of sealing moved from the Bass Strait to the south coast of Tasmania and the Southern Islands. Sealing was a rough business. The 'half-castes' of the Straits, a breed of maritime bushrangers who took one or more aboriginal 'wives', fought the seal gangs from Sydney. They in turn fought the sealers from Boston. It was a world of peril and profit, as violent and cosmopolitan as the Newfoundland cod-banks. Its last scenes of glory were at Macquarie Island, deserted by 1830 except for occasional visitors buying and selling the popular, now extinct Macquarie Island parrots.

Whaling

The first British whaler, the *Emilia* of London, entered the Pacific via Cape Horn in the year the First Fleet anchored in Botany Bay. Three years later British whalers following the same route were loaded with convicts and stores for Sydney. It was an Enderby whaler, *Britannia*, that killed whales off the coast between New South Wales and Tasmania. But this enterprise was illegal, infringing as it did the monopoly of trade in the area claimed by the East India Company. The whaling lobby got to work: by 1801 Australian waters were open to them.

By 1804 nine London whalers were said to be operating on the New South Wales coast: their registration might be British; their skippers were all from Nantucket, refugees from the British blockade of American trade in the revolutionary war. By 1841 Tasmania had thirty-five whaling stations, manned by a thousand fishermen. There were others in Victoria, South Australia and Western Australia. Bay whalers from Sydney and Hobart were active in New Zealand where they married Maori wives, fought in the Maori wars and acted as interpreters to other white settlers.

Down to the 1850s Sydney and Hobart were the centres of the deep-sea whaling companies. They had ousted the old 'bay whalers' which took the whales close in to the coast. Deep-sea whaling was more costly in capital and labour. In 1848 Hobart had thirty-seven deep-sea whalers, manned by crews totalling over 1,000. By 1859 they were down to twenty-seven, with crews totalling 680. Like sealing, whaling was a cosmopolitan business, with Portuguese, Americans, British and French all joining in, 'enriched with oleaginous spoils'.

The Australian whaling industry was small beer by 1860, its cargoes down to values derisory by comparison with the great days of the 1850s. The reasons for the decline – unlike the demise of sealing – are not clear. Sealing went because the fur-seal was hunted to extinction. The value of the oil produced by the other members of the seal family was not worth pursuing for itself alone. The rise of costs and risks against the relative fall in the value of oil was probably at the bottom of the trouble. Only the gigantic sperm whale produced the precious ambergris used in perfumery and even then rarely. Ambergris is 'a morbid product resulting from digestive disorders ... taken only from sickly whales ...'.* Hunting the humpback whale was revived in the twentieth century. Modern techniques of killing the whale and extracting its products – meat meal, dried solubles valuable in nutrition, and whale oil – actually made profits in the 1950s for whaling stations on the coasts of Western Australia, Queensland and New South Wales. They fell victims not to economic decline but to increasingly humanitarian public opinion. Whaling was, first, controlled; then more recently, abolished.

The days of the pre-eminence of fisheries in the economy of New South Wales, Van Diemen's Land and what was to be Victoria were numbered. As in English history, they have received too little attention from economic historians. In 1830 the value of fish and products derived from fish as exports was still nearly double the value of wool exports. During the 1850s their value continued to rise, but the value of wool exports rose much faster. Thus, sealing and whaling were only an interlude – though a significant one – in Australia's economic history; again, repeating earlier English history, where the first sign of an 'industrial' trend, clearly visible in statistics, came with the rise of the shipping industry in the seventeenth century. A prominent role was played by the shipping within the triangle formed by the English West Country ports, the Newfoundland cod banks and the Mediterranean markets for dried fish.†

Ships and Shipping

The importance of ships and shipping was a staple argument used by 'mercantilist' writers and polemicists. It had some force. Of the governors of New South Wales, Phillip believed in it. Philip Gidley King, Phillip's protégé, and in many respects his disciple, outdid his master in his basically 'mercantilist' faith that profit came from power and vice versa. Both were rooted in ships and naval strength: and for King, France was the most dangerous rival. King recognized the importance of places of strategic and economic importance – Norfolk Island, Van Diemen's Land, the area later known as Port Phillip and the Bass Strait – rather

---

* *The Australian Encyclopaedia* vol. IX (1958), p. 272.
† Charles Wilson *England's Apprenticeship* (Harlow, 1984), p. 170.

better than some of the other Governors. King has often been criticized for his pernickety interference with administration which would (his critics argue) have been better left alone. He was, it is true, a worrier. Amongst his worries were the seal and whale fisheries. As a conventional mercantilist he saw them as essential, basic activities. So from his time onwards we see a growing interest not only in the fisheries but in the transport of goods, people and the multiplication of communications between Sydney, Hobart, Port Phillip and the ports of the south-east coast in between.

The importance of this cannot be adequately measured simply in export or import statistics. It needs to be borne in mind that not only the volume of shipping, exports, imports, Australian shipbuilding and ancillary industries, but the skills of navigation and ship-handling and management were a vital consequence in a new set of triangular trades between the mainland and Van Diemen's Land. Australia's future was to lie with agriculture, pastoral activities, and mining; but vital to all these were earnings from overseas trade which enabled Australia to borrow the capital without which economic enterprise would never have begun to move, let alone continue in movement and growth. Fishing was one of the first; the other, steadily overtaking all else in importance, was the growth and export of wool. Both demanded ships, shipbuilders and the skill of deep-sea sailors.

Wool

The story of the Australian wool industry, its (alleged) origins in the fanatic zeal of John Macarthur, and its meteoric rise in three decades to be the prime industry of the young colony, has been told many times and is still being refined and modified in detail. Here it is only necessary to make a few basic comments. Its origin lay in the seventy sheep brought with the First Fleet by Phillip from the Cape. They were added to and more highly bred for wool by Macarthur. Macarthur was undoubtedly an excellent sheep breeder; he was also a man of uncertain and contradictory temper. Uncontrollably quarrelsome, he fell out violently with three Governors in succession. He was at the centre of the rebellion against Governor Bligh and as a result spent eight years in enforced exile in England. Here (until 1807) he pursued his research into sheep, wool, its manufacture and markets in England, while his wife managed his affairs at home. Elizabeth Macarthur was a remarkable woman; while she fulfilled the Victorian ideals of womanhood – she was beautiful, dutiful and faithful – she was also highly intelligent and an excellent business-woman. She continued the breeding of sheep for fine wool instead of coarse wool-and-mutton combined, which was the early practice.

Whether the Macarthur flock at Camden Park was the sole source of the quality of merino wool is not certain. Without doubt, the Macarthurs gave the same kind of boost to pastoral management in Australia as Coke of Holkham gave to arable farming in Norfolk. In England and Holland since the sixteenth century the fine qualities of the Spanish merino had long been recognized by cloth manufacturers. (At the height of the seventeenth-century economic warfare between the two countries, there was a much debated plan for England to pre-empt the entire yield of merino wool in order to ruin the Dutch cloth industry at Leiden and elsewhere by cutting off its major supply of fine wool.)

By the 1820s not only was Australian merino recognized by Yorkshire manufacturers as the finest in the world; its production was spreading rapidly as the plains beyond the recently conquered range of the Blue Mountains were opened up for pasture and arable farming. By its quality, price, and in association with a rapid development of the Yorkshire cloth industry, wool growing became the major industry of Australia, replacing meat and corn production in the rapid pace of its development. The settlement of the Port Phillip area to the south, across the Liverpool ranges and in Van Diemen's Land offered seemingly unlimited opportunities for more pastoralism. The mode of production was two-fold: by settlers who bought their land, and by 'squatters' who leased it, usually on extremely favourable terms.

Settlement

This was not quite what the authorities had wanted. From the first, Phillip had had his own vision of Australia as a colony of small free settlers. That vision never materialized. There followed an expanding flow of convicts which encouraged the growth of very large estates by well-to-do or speculative ranchers and 'squatters', whose imaginations and pockets boggled at nothing in their ambition to operate on the largest possible scale.

Reformers (like Edward Gibbon Wakefield) who theorized about actual and ideal models of colonization were worried by what they saw as the risk of emancipated convicts and fly-by-night immigrants picking up land cheaply, selling it off at a profit, and decamping with the proceeds. Wakefield's views (published in *A Letter From Sydney* (1831) – a place he never visited) were in part adopted by the British Government. His major principle was to keep the price of land high enough to restrict anybody, except those with a serious intention of settling in to farm their purchase, from buying it: the proceeds were to be devoted to subsidizing the travel costs of suitable and desirable immigrants. It was the dream of a yeoman colony cherished by Phillip and scores of British idealists, and it was to haunt British and Australian politics for at least another century.

In Australia it never materialized as the full basis of official policy. A minimum price of one pound an acre *was* set on land but observed as often in the breach as in the letter. A *part* of the proceeds of land sales was put into the subsidy fund for immigrants' passages from Britain to the colony. The powers of government were too weak, the momentum of demographic and pastoral expansion too strong, to allow Wakefield's ideas to work. Government looked on helplessly as New South Wales grew in the 1830s. The stream of convicts continued, and a sizeable proportion of them were 'assigned' to settlers and squatters as shepherds and labourers. More sheep were shepherded per shepherd.

Australian expansion of wool production was most vividly reflected in imports into Britain, and especially in their successful competition with Britain's earlier major supplier – Germany. Between 1830 and 1840, the value of Australia's wool exports increased seventeen-fold; from *c*.35,000 pounds to *c*.566,000. Between 1830 and 1850, while German wool imports into Britain (by weight) fell by over a half, Australian imports rose seventeen-fold.

Expansion on this scale was only possible with the application of capital. This was to come in stages. The first British capital made available in Australia had come in the shape of 'the store' – money made available to the military for the convicts and themselves and supplied from public funds. During the early decades of the nineteenth century it came from first, private pockets, and then in the 1820s and 1830s from bank loans. The Bank of New South Wales (1817) – still in existence today under the newfangled name *Westpac* – was followed by four more large banks by the 1830s. All these opened branches spread widely throughout the areas of settlement, old and new. Some Australian deposits were lent to pastoralists and farmers, but a large part of the loans represented British investment made via British Banks: for example, the Bank of Australasia and the Union Bank.

The growth of pastoral production, and the spread of settlement (north into what is now Queensland, south and west into what was to be Victoria, South Australia and Western Australia) were made possible by

British capital. This too lay behind the growth of the port and city of Sydney and the later cities, such as Melbourne, Brisbane, Adelaide and Perth. It was British capital which made possible the boom of the 1830s, the mining booms of the 1850s and 1890s, the construction of railways and public utilities.

The flow of British capital into Australia increased sharply in the second half of the 1830s as the boom gathered force. It declined equally sharply with the collapse of business in Britain between 1840 and 1845. In the mid-1820s Australians became aware for the first time that while international economic relations had their advantages, they brought corresponding disadvantages. The buoyant exports and capital imports of the 1830s enabled them to import sophisticated manufactures from Britain and Europe; some were essential to the building of cities, factories and highways, others went to pay for the embellishments of more comfortable, even luxurious living. The Reverend J.D. Lang (to whom we shall return later) thundered to his Presbyterian followers and readers that the depression of the 1830s resulted from the drought which the Lord used to demonstrate his displeasure with the greed of the speculators and usurers. Others thought, more pragmatically, that bankers, paper money and foreign capital were to blame. When the cycle of depression repeated itself in the 1840s, astute observers noted that Australia was, by her exports and imports, connected closely with Britain. They also noted that Britain herself was experiencing another depression at this time, and that the demand for wool in Yorkshire had fallen sharply.

Such fluctuations were henceforth to become a recurrent feature of an economy increasingly linked with external trade and world economic trends. The next phase of economic development was to witness not only radical changes in what we may call the 'technology of pastoralism' but a sudden revelation of untold mineral riches so far hidden from the human eye. And on these more ample material foundations was to be built a new and, gradually, characteristically Australian culture.

4

TRIALS OF 'THE TYRANTS'

'The law, Sir? I am the law.'   (Governor Bligh, 1806)

'It is a pleasure to acknowledge the high type of men appointed governors.'
(Sir Henry Parkes, Premier NSW)*

It has often been remarked that from Phillip to Macquarie the Governors
of New South Wales wielded absolute power. Some historians have described them as 'tyrants'. The first statement is correct in the sense that
the early Governors were answerable only to their home government.
That state of affairs came to an end with Macquarie – 'the last of the
tyrants'. After Macquarie the Governor was, by statute, to be advised
by a small council; and, as precept broadened down to precedent, its
size and ultimately its power, became a check on the personal power
of the Governor. As to the charge of tyranny, it is, of course, false.
Neither Phillip, Hunter, King and Macquarie, nor those who followed
them with their gubernatorial powers reduced – Brisbane, Darling,
Bourke, Gipps, Fitzroy – were by nature tyrannical. Only Bligh might
lay claim to the title, and his period of office ended in ignominy and
in gaol.

More important are the political vicissitudes which all these Governors
in turn suffered. All were naval or military officers of high rank achieved
through distinguished service. All (except Bligh) were experienced in
the administration of colonial territories. All were men of talent and
intelligence. Yet most of them ended their days in Australia broken men.
Phillip, a rare blend of philosopher and commander, survived to continue
in military duties, but only after retirement necessitated by serious illness,
possibly the consequence of stress. Hunter, a tough old sea-dog who
had survived at least three shipwrecks, was, like his predecessor, an
honest and able administrator determined on clean government; he got
as little support from Whitehall as Phillip, and was recalled in 1800

* Sir Henry Parkes *Fifty Years in the Making of Australian History* (London, 1892).

with belated and grudging recognition that he had not committed any crime.

King

Philip Gidley King, Phillip's true protegé, was, like Hunter, a tough and able naval officer, an enthusiast for Australia – he was an accomplished artist who left some fascinating sketches of aboriginal life behind him – keen to see its agricultural and economic life flourish and diversify. By 1806 he was weary, disillusioned and suffering from chest trouble which could have been heart disease, cancer, or tuberculosis. He collapsed completely on going aboard his returning ship and died soon after reaching England.

Bligh

King's successor was William Bligh (already famous as 'Bligh of *The Bounty*'. His appointment was an inspiration of Sir Joseph Banks, and it was not the only occasion when that great man of science showed regrettably poor judgement in other matters. Bligh, though unbelievably brave and an excellent sailor, was coarse, greedy, and incorrigibly quarrelsome. In New South Wales he demonstrated his abilities by quarrelling with everybody, including all the marine officers, and especially John Macarthur, whom he put in gaol. The Lieutenant-Governor promptly released Macarthur and put Bligh (who had hidden under a bed in his residence) in gaol instead. Joy and chaos reigned jointly in Sydney; for a year New South Wales managed without a Governor. Bligh was promoted Rear-Admiral for his pains but, wisely, was never again entrusted with political office.

Macquarie

Lachlan Macquarie, a colonel of the 73rd Highland Regiment, was a man of quite different ideas. A Highlander of clear if dour intellect, diligent and orderly, Macquarie was to win impressive claims on Australia's gratitude. Many have judged him its greatest Governor. He extended the settlement, helped to design what are still some of Australia's finest Georgian public buildings, and gave unequalled impetus to the emancipation of those convicts whose sentences had expired, so that they could be integrated into its free population. His reward was to be hounded out of the colony where he had done so much to create a land of hope out of a morass of inglory. Less fortunate than Bligh, he received no promotion, military or civil. He returned to England a broken man, sunk in disappointment and bitter resentment.

Brisbane

Sir Thomas Brisbane, another Scot and professional soldier with experience of warfare both in Europe and the colonies, entered on his duties as Governor with a determination – if it can be so described – not to repeat his predecessor's error of excessive attention to his business. Brisbane's character was best described in a lapidary note by another fellow-Scot, the Reverend J.D.Lang (see chapter 8). He was, wrote Lang, 'a man of the best intentions, but disinclined to business and deficient in energy'. These agreeable qualifications did not rescue him from either the hostility of the liberated emancipists nor the attentions of wily financial adventurers who swarmed round him like a honey pot. The truth was that Brisbane's heart was not in the arts of terrestrial administration but in the science of the stars. He preferred his observatory (which he built at Paramatta) to his office at Sydney, where he was content to leave the business to the so-called 'heads of departments'. It was not long before his masters in Whitehall called him home. He retired, not unwillingly, to Scotland where he continued to scrutinize the heavens to some effect. He was showered with academic and scientific honours and pronounced to be 'the founder of Scottish science'.

Darling

With the arrival of Sir Ralph Darling in 1825 the wheel of Australian fortunes turned once more almost a full circle. Within a week of landing he declared: 'I shall begin and reorganise the whole.' The wife of a leading settler shrewdly noted in her diary: 'General Darling, if I mistake not, will be Governor in Chief and ... all will find themselves subjected to the power of Major General Darling.'*

Darling was a Dubliner of humble origins: his grandfather kept a pub, his father was an army sergeant. Darling himself had risen swiftly on his own merits. He was brave and diligent, as good on the battlefield as on staff duties. He swiftly applied himself to the main task of stopping up the considerable holes in Brisbane's loosely decentralized system of government. But New South Wales was no more pleased with his reforms than with the system crying out for reform. Darling acted firmly, brought

* B.H. Fletcher *A Governor Maligned* (Oxford, 1985).

the bushrangers under better control, ensured fairer treatment of the natives, judiciously tried to conciliate the Irish Catholics and to hold the balance between farming and pastoralism. In this latter sphere he was unlucky. In the late 1820s, as the Reverend J.D. Lang mordantly declared: 'the heavens became as brass and the earth as iron' with a monstrous drought.

Tensions rose once again. Amongst the Governor's bitterest enemies were W.C. Wentworth (the rising political star in the firmament across which was strung the magic words 'Self-Government') and Chief Justice Forbes. It was not long before the Colonial Office, its feet once again cold with apprehension at another Australian row, weakly recalled him. Wentworth saw him off with a great party at his mansion, Vaucluse House. A brawling, blaspheming, belching mob full of free gin showed that Wentworth knew as well as Jack Wilkes how to organize mob rule.

Back in London, Darling was no safer. In the House of Commons he was hounded by an Irish-Radical group led by Hume and the O'Connells. It pressured a desultory House into appointing a Select Committe to investigate the former Governor's conduct. Fortunately for Darling, he had the unswerving support of an old friend: Sir Henry Hardinge (later to be Governor-General of India) was as skilful at political as he was at military tactics. Darling emerged from his trials bloodied but unbowed. He lived to a ripe old age and died in the bosom of his devoted family, half-blind, deaf and crippled by gout. All this did credit to his powers of survival, but also added another political disaster to the already lengthy list.

Bourke

The successor of this 'much maligned Governor' was another soldier, also Irish, but of totally different origins and quality. Sir Richard Bourke – his knighthood was a sore blow to Darling's pride – came from an old landed Anglo-Irish family. Where Darling was straightforward and abrasive, Bourke was urbane and conciliatory. This (so the Colonial Office assumed) was very necessary in the wake of Darling's upset of the antipodean apple cart.

Bourke had achieved a considerable degree of success as acting Governor of the Cape. Against the doubts and fears of white settlers, English and Dutch, he had set to work conscientiously to conciliate (and convert) the Kaffirs. With his liberal aspirations, he seemed to those dismayed by Darling's tactics of confrontation to offer a welcome chance of relief.

And so, up to a point, he did.

Bourke liked to govern with whatever consensus he could muster. He certainly took his Legislative Council into his confidence with much greater frequency than Darling had ever done. Yet his liberalism roused as much opposition as support. His proposals for a system of general education funded by the state upset large numbers of Protestants, Anglican and Dissenters. The 'exclusionists' suspected him of 'soothing' the convicts too much, and they found themselves in the sympathetic company of the Colonial Office in thinking Bourke was in altogether too much of a hurry to press on with elective government.

He can at least be partly credited with the rise in the numbers of free settlers during his governorship through his so-called 'Bounty' system of supported immigration (which did not supplant but complemented the existing schemes organized by HM Government). And, in the new areas round Port Phillip, he insisted on bringing expansion by big 'squatters' under greater control.

In short, this was a civilized Governor, popular, cultivated and conscientious; genuinely liberal and public-spirited. Yet even he had in the end to admit failure, resigning over a disagreement with his Colonial Treasurer who was known as an 'exclusivist'. If Bourke had a fault, it was that his enthusiasm for his own principles often tended to outrun his political discretion. Even Bourke could not win in this contentious society.

Gipps

Sir George Gipps (1837–47) inherited a legislative Council which became even more anti-emancipist (exclusionist) after the reforms of 1842 brought in a majority of big graziers. Gipps consistently propounded the doctrine that state lands were only held in trust on behalf of the Crown. Any such notion was an anathema to the big squatters. They were determined to hang on to the lands they had occupied, often illegally. They roared their disapproval. Led by Wentworth and his journalists, they bitterly opposed Gipps's proposed terms for licensing their stations.

Gipps, like Darling, was no tactician. He was guilty of too much straightforward honesty of purpose; to this he added occasional bungles in timing and explaining his proposals for public finance, education and aboriginal policy. Early in his term of office he had thwarted a 'job' by the formidably unforgiving W.C. Wentworth. Wentworth had planned to acquire twenty million acres of land in the South Island of

New Zealand at a price of 1,000 acres for a farthing: it was in Gipps's words 'a job on a larger scale than Robert Walpole had ever contemplated'. Wentworth never forgot or forgave.

An influential section of the press followed Wentworth. Gipps was in head-on conflict with the squatters, the business community, the small settlers – and, of course, the omnipresent Reverend J.D. Lang. When he vacated the governorship, the *Sydney Morning Herald* observed that 'eight years mature observation had convinced them that Sir George Gipps had been the worst Governor New South Wales ever had'. Later opinion was very much more favourable. Abrasive he certainly could be, but he was a totally dedicated and capable Governor, uniquely in command of his responsibilities, generous and a man of judgement.

Gipps was killed by his job and his enemies. He died, utterly exhausted in body and spirit, on his return to England in 1847.

Fitzroy

Sir Charles Fitzroy (1846–54) was in every respect in total contrast to Gipps. Although nobly born from both sides of his family, Charles inherited no silver spoon in his mouth. But being impecunious taught him that honey may catch more flies than vinegar. Earl Grey might tell Lord John Russell that Fitzroy was 'a most incapable Governor of so important a Colony', but it was Fitzroy who emerged triumphant from one crisis after another. It was Grey's policies which brought New South Wales nearer to revolt against the parent country than any other politician in its history.

Charles Fitzroy was a man of the world who seems to have inherited a gift for getting things done by being almost universally liked. There was an attractively casual air to his political stance. Time after time he pulled political rabbits out of his proverbially aristocratic hat. Was there to be a gold rush in 1851? The Governor was, incredibly, ready with a policy for licensing every digger for thirty shillings a month and ensuring law and order rather than chaos. He tended to favour the big pastoralists. The natives occupied less of his time than they had of some of his predecessors. He was also a man of his day; he was for *laissez-faire*, *laissez-passer*. If occasionally this went off the rails (literally, in the famous miscalculation over the best gauge for the railways), if his tariff policy misfired, or postal arrangements met with troubles, nobody seemed to mind much.

He had a gift for soothing the colonists' passions – all, that is, save the Reverend J.D. Lang, who could not refrain from moving an amendment to the colony's farewell address deploring Sir Charles's term as Governor as 'a uniform conspiracy against the rights of the people ... deleterious and baneful', adding more than a hint that the moral atmosphere of the Governor's residence was not what it should have been. (This may well have been true. Sir Charles as a widower loved the company of pretty women.)

His success was remarkable. It showed that even Australians were prepared to love, if not a lord, at least the scion of a noble house. Not so those in the corridors of power at Whitehall and Westminster. Charles Fitzroy got no support from Grey, or indeed from any other of Her Majesty's Ministers. His modest request that his term of office be extended, in 1854, was met with resounding silence.

After the mid-century both economic and social life as well as government in Australia were to undergo radical change. Between 1788 and the 1850s, there is a recurrent pattern of personal disaster among the Governors. In one way or another, they were all broken on the wheel of duty. Yet, with the exception of Bligh (who, whatever other tasks he might have been fitted for, was incapable of governing a colony), they were all men with a strong sense of duty; and all, except perhaps Brisbane, were men of high courage and powers of decision. What went wrong?

Circumstances, as well as men, made the Governor's problems almost insuperable. Change, and the rate of change – economic, social, political – was no more susceptible to measurement or prediction than it is today. It involved at least five categories of people: the serving officers, the convicts, the agrarian class, the urban class, the aborigines; and of course those in Whitehall and Westminster who would today be called the decision-makers. The interests, functions and behaviour of each of these classes interacted with those of the rest. The Governor's task was to preserve law and order with one hand while with the other attempting to mould some sort of balanced society out of as odd a collection of humanity as had ever been assembled thirteen thousand miles from their native shores.

The Governors, as we have seen, were all chosen from the military or naval professions. All were battle-hardened. All, to a degree, were autocratic by training. Yet (Bligh apart) their deeds as well as their words prove them to have been not ill-chosen. From Arthur Phillip onwards, they all had considerable and varied achievements to their credit. Not only they but the lesser figures – Lieutenant Governors of Tasmania, like Sir George Arthur and Sir John Wilmot, were of the same mould. No Governor has been more frequently or more ignorantly libelled than

Arthur. The best biography of him shows him as the model of a devout evangelical Christian, holding enlightened views on the duties of the whites to the aboriginals, and on the importance of combining education, training and incentives to virtue in the convict system at Port Arthur.*

Unluckiest of all was Arthur's successor, Sir John Franklin. Franklin was a kinsman and shipmate of the great Flinders, and, like Flinders (and Bass) a Lincolnshire yellowbelly. His integrity, and his intentions for improving Tasmania, were beyond doubt; but he too was defeated by the bitter, internecine feuds of the islanders. Worsted, and in total disillusion, he went back to Arctic exploration, disappeared and was never seen again. The epitaph in Westminster Abbey to this relation of Flinders and the Tennysons was written by Alfred, Poet Laureate, husband of Franklin's niece (see Preface, p. x).

> Not here! The white North has Thy bones;
> and thou,
> Heroic sailor-soul,
> Art passing in thine happier voyage now
> Toward no earthly pole.

The Governors were responsible to their political masters at Westminster and in turn to their ministries in Whitehall. They were a long way away, ships and posts were unbearably slow. Knowledge of conditions in this, as in other, distant colonies was patchy, unreliable and biased by rumour, myth and legend. Ministers rarely showed up well. The office responsible for colonial affairs was a sub-department of the Home Office. From Sydney to Gladstone, ministers, with the possible exception of Bathurst, showed little willingness to pay serious attention to the needs of Australia as a growing, developing society. At the beginning, Botany Bay represented a combination of two functions: a strategic-commercial strong point to be defended against the risk of French aggression in the Eastern Seas, and a means of satisfying that part of English public opinion which sought a haven for some of the criminal elements which seemed – as always – to be on the increase.

But transportation, once begun, tended to continue. The first settlers could not be left to starve, even after the threat from France disappeared. Indeed, successive ministers and their underlings began to be rather satisfied with the 'system' even as many Australians were becoming more certain that it ought to be abolished. There was little response to such feelings among what were called the 'Public Officers', later known as

* A.G.L. Shaw *Sir George Arthur Bart. 1784–1854* (Melbourne and London, 1984).

the Civil Servants. The public administration was a curate's egg. From 1780 there were signs of 'reform', but reformers were more concerned to reduce public expenditure and encourage honesty than to make the service more efficient. Offices were still bought and sold, part and parcel of the prevailing system politely called 'influence'. It was possible to find able men in Whitehall; but no steps were taken before the mid-nineteenth century to ensure that efficiency was a prime quality of persons appointed to the service. Whitehall did not, then or later, lead public opinion. In a slow, instinctive fashion, it followed it. In any case, the twelve public officers who comprised the total staff engaged on colonial affairs in 1787 could hardly have been expected to exercise a powerful influence even if their numbers had been multiplied ten-fold.

Thus, when London decided that Governor Macquarie was spending too much money and making too many enemies, Lord Bathurst did not send out a public officer or Commissioner in charge of his enquiry. He sent J.T. Biggs, a London barrister with no knowledge of Australia or its problems whatever. His instructions, between the lines, implied his main duty: to get rid of Macquarie. And that, employing a mixture of cold venom, total ruthlessness and a humiliating superiority of tactical skill, is what Biggs did. Time and again, ministers made up their minds about Australia first and looked at the facts later. Gladstone (then a Tory) recalled Governor Wilmot from Tasmania to answer charges against him that were totally without foundation; they were invented in the Colonial Office which never understood that the convict system Wilmot was required to operate never had paid, and never could pay, its way. Too late, Gladstone apologized: Wilmot was dead of exhaustion and indignation.

Transportation and Penal Reform

Earl Grey, who foreshadowed ideas of a self-governing federation of the (then five) Australian colonies with remarkably prophetic foresight in 1850, was in other respects a narrow aristocratic Whig of the old eighteenth-century school, and singularly blind. After the Reform Bill (in which he had played so notable a role) a Select Committee of the House had recommended, after a full enquiry, that transportation of convicts to Australia should be abolished. This recommendation was accepted, save for Norfolk Island and isolated penitentiaries in Van Diemen's Land.

Once again, the 'mind of Whitehall' demonstrated its inability to understand what was happening in Australia. Following the 'abolition' of transportation, there happened to be, once more, an apparent surge of crime in England and shortage of gaols. Once more the pressure grew for a revival of transportation. Van Diemen's Land was still a hole in the bucket. After 1840 a stream of convicts was poured into her penal settlements. They became so dominant that they ran their own newspaper, threatening to kick the free settlers out of the colony as 'puritan moralists'.

While Van Diemen's Land was saturated with convicts, HM Government ingeniously (as they believed) found another solution to their problem. A system of 'reformatory' treatment passed convicts through carefully devised 'moral cleansings' in England at Millbank and a new prison at Pentonville. Here they spent a year or two under special disciplines. They were then granted 'conditional pardons'. After that, a proportion of favoured convicts were selected for transportation to the colonies to serve the remainder of their sentences as free men. The first batch chosen by the Prison Commissioners were given permission by the Government to go to the recently formed settlement at Port Phillip: in fact to Melbourne, already a thriving town.

There were vigorous protests from Melbourne, from Hobart too. The action of the British Government, though carried through without the slightest consultation with the Australians, and abhorrent to most of the citizens of the areas affected, got some support from the big land-owners: they had felt the pinch of the labour shortage that resulted from the abrupt ending of transportation. The 'Pentonvillian' system (as it was called) offered them at least a reprieve, and they brought heavy pressure on government for its continuation. Gladstone (himself a partner in a Port Phillip sheep station) and Earl Grey were both in its favour. But not the people of Melbourne.

On 8 August 1849, the *Randolph* entered Port Phillip with convicts on board. Here, and later at Sydney, the citizens made it clear that they would oppose the renewal of transportation, if necessary with the use of force. Newspapers recently launched in both cities – the Melbourne *Argus* and the *Sydney Morning Herald* – denounced the system as 'an abominable system of misrule and total depravity'. Fitzroy, in New South Wales, with characteristic sleight-of-hand, diplomatically passed on the convict ships to Queensland. He knew, better than Gladstone or Grey, the temper of his colonial majority on the transportation issue.

That Grey never saw the folly of his ways uncovers some of the sources of the Governors' dilemma. The Boston Tea Party might as well never have happened. To Grey, and many others, the colonies were simply a basket into which the parent country could dump its unwanted criminals. By 1868 there had been, in all, 160,663 transported. But the robust reaction of Melbourne and Sydney marked a real turning point. In 1855 – two years after Grey wrote his book *Colonial Policy*, still defending transportation – the 'system' came to an end everywhere. The voice of colonial independence had been heard for the first time raised in anger.

Land and Labour

The attempted revival of 'convictism' had also highlighted the long-standing feud between the free settlers and the big pastoralists. The problem of the values, occupation and titles to land never ceased to vex Australia and those who tried to govern it. The land immediately surrounding Port Jackson was poor for tillage and stock alike. In 1803 Joseph Banks had thrown cold water on Macarthur's experiments with sheep breeding. Sheep, he said, would never thrive in New South Wales; the climate, soil and pasture were unsuitable for them. As in a number of his judgements, he was hopelessly wrong; but at the time, before the crossing of the mountain ranges that hemmed in the early settlement, his view seemed rational enough.

After 1820 matters were different. Wide, seemingly unlimited expanses of good land were available. Thousands of acres were granted to persons of standing and persons of none. Heiresses received a thousand or more acres as marriage portions. Convicts received official slips of paper entitling them to settle 'wherever they pleased'. Millions of acres were disposed of by free grant or at trivial quit rents. The Australian Agricultural Company received half a million acres free.

A 'squatter' originally was somebody who occupied land to which he had no title. Many were criminals, bushrangers and ticket-of-leave men. But many were simply adventurers. Being unfavoured by authority with free land, they set off into the great empty plains beyond the mountains to stake out their claims to vacant areas. Governor Gipps wrote with philosophical resignation of their enterprise: 'As well attempt to confine an Arab within a circle traced in sand, as to confine the graziers or wool growers of New South Wales within bounds....'

Later on in Australian history it became common retrospective wisdom that all this prodigality had been a great and terrible mistake: especially to English liberals and socialists, nostalgic for a vanished peasantry. But in the great days of expansion this was not the problem as men saw it. Then, as Ernest Scott has written,* 'The problem was to get

---

* *A Short History of Australia* (Oxford, 1958), p. 185.

men for the land. Only later did it become a problem to get land for the men.'

Big graziers and squatters wanted land and labour – cheap labour. They therefore supported transportation of convicts and subsidized immigration for settlers. The free settlers thought otherwise. So did the native-born young Australian 'cornstalks', the 'currency lads and lasses'. They were the small farmers who grew wheat and farmed the good lands along the Hawkesbury River using their own family labour. Or they worked as travelling shearers or drovers, independent men, often unmarried, earning much higher wages than the ex-convicts who worked as shepherds or hut-keepers on sheep or cattle stations. Here was a rural society divided on questions of *price*: the price of land and the price of labour. And was it to be the labour of free men or of slaves – assigned convicts?

The remaining problems of the relations between immigrant European whites and aboriginal blacks will be discussed elsewhere. Successive Ministries in Britain after 1788 committed themselves to their care and protection. Yet everywhere, especially in Van Diemen's Land, tension existed, frequently flaring up in violence, murder and massacre. This is not the place to apportion blame. It was the custom in earlier days to put it on the blacks; today the positions are reversed.

Relations were by no means everywhere or always unsatisfactory. Phillip had set a splendid example; Bennelon and his tribe remained his friends. In the 1820s Pamphlet, a white explorer, was one of four who were wrecked on Moreton Island and treated with great kindness by the local chief of the aboriginals. In other places there were different cases. Peel's colonists at Swan River, the founders of Western Australia, were attacked by the local aboriginals who feared the loss of their hunting grounds. The settlers fought back and shot their attackers. There were similar episodes in early Victoria and much worse in Van Diemen's Land. Here relations were at their worst. Both the efforts of the Governor, Arthur, to segregate the aboriginals by military force, and the attempt of George Robinson, a Methodist bricklayer and philanthropist, to conciliate them by persuasion, failed equally dismally. In 1835 he corralled the pathetic remnants of the *homo tasmanianus* – 203 of them – on to Flinders Island, in Bass Strait between Van Diemen's Land and the Australian mainland. Here they simply pined away. The last one died in 1860.

The problems of governing Australia were complex – each colliding with the others to create a never ending succession of crises. If there was a basic cause for this instability it was continued transportation. This at least was the considered verdict of two men who saw the convict problem at first hand. Captain John Maconachie, who volunteered for service in charge of the penal settlement on Norfolk Island, invented for its inmates a system of marks for good conduct. Sentences became flexible instead of fixed. Maconachie had the strong support of the Governor, Gipps, but the Colonial Office were against him. They were swayed by that body of 'liberal' opinion in England which held that conditions for convicts in Australia had improved too much: they should be made worse, not better. Maconachie was sacked. He had, in any case, made his views clear to the Select Committee on Transportation. They were a remarkably detached and perceptive analysis of Australia's malaise:

> The fretfulness of temper which so peculiarly characterises the intercourse of society in our penal colonies [is due to] the convict system. Degraded servants make suspicious masters. Masters soon begin to suspect their equals and superiors, as well as their inferiors [leading to] impatience and irritability under government regulations and judicial decisions, however well-founded [class relations are distorted] ... every difference of opinion constitutes a ground of quarrel and disunion becomes expensively prevalent [the result is] a regime of virtually unchallengeable authority, enough to exasperate even the mildest spirits. ...

A similar, even more sweeping, interpretation of social ills came from Captain Cheyne, the Director General of Roads:

> The habit which the free settlers contract, of treating convicts with contempt, has become extended to everybody else. Hence a whole variety of evils ranging from sexual immorality to the licentious state of the press. ... [there had grown up] a prejudice of caste [which encourages the free to take on notions of their] superior distinction and consideration ... while forgetting their relative duties.

Charles Darwin, on shore leave from the *Beagle* in the 1830s, similarly remarked that there was 'much jealousy' between the 'rich emancipist ex-convicts' and the free settlers: but he differed from Cheyne in thinking that it was the ex-convicts who hated and despised the free settlers as 'interlopers'. Whichever way you looked at it, the continued practice of transportation was a source of social antagonism, a canker in the commonwealth.

Thus did thinking men philosophize, like Greek Aristotelians, over the ills of the Australian body politic. They were not far off the mark; for this was, like ancient Athens, still a city state. In fact, the local administrators saw more clearly than the great Etonian and Oxonian Whigs at Westminster (who should have learned from their ancient history) that it was time to purge the body politic of its sickness.

Sir Leon Radzinowicz's monumental *History of English Criminal Law** is the most authoritative warning of the pitfalls of making easy generalizations about the state of law, opinions and morality in eighteenth-century England. The social evidence is in fact complex and very difficult to interpret. For example, capital punishment applied, in theory, to a multitude of crimes, from high treason downwards. Yet serious charges were as often dismissed as accepted. In practice, Judges and Court magistrates steadily ameliorated the full rigour of the law. It is impossible to say whether crime was actually increasing: no reliable statistics exist. If it seemed to be increasing, or even if it *were* increasing, it may have been, paradoxically, because society was living a more urbanized life at higher standards of wealth: opportunities for easy pickpocketing and other thefts were more plentiful. The apparent risk of transportation perceived by some English witnesses was that it provided too soft a way out for real criminals.

There were enough convicts of respectable family origin and education to cast serious doubts on any simple 'class' interpretation of the criminal law. It is difficult to quarrel with Radzinowicz's conclusion: there was still much that was brutal and degrading in the law, as in the society which created it and was ruled by it: but the inclination of the eighteenth century, growing more and more marked with the nineteenth, was for its unjust theoretical rigours to be abated by more lenient practice. Punishment and practice were real and pretty evenly applied for crime, regardless of the origins or status of the criminal.

As to the benefits or otherwise of the transportation system for Australia, the problem and answer may be represented by a line or curve on a graph moving downwards. Without the convict system it is difficult to see how Australia could ever have made a start, costly in human life, human dignity, and money though it was. After a decade or two it became a regular and accepted feature of Australian (and English) policy. The pastoralists throve on the cheap labour it supplied. But even as their approval grew and distant politicians in Westminster and civil servants in Whitehall applauded complacently, a (probable) majority of vocal Australians rebelled against the convict system and its social consequences for them. Support for it fell sharply until its final and total abolition throughout the whole of Australia by 1868.

Yet, as Professor A.G.L. Shaw has pointed out in a cool assessment

* (Pilgrim Trust, 1948, vol. i)

of its results, the system had countervailing benefits. In the absence of an adequate supply of voluntary labour, even poor quality convict labour was better than none. And it was to a large extent convict labour which explains the miracle of Australia's development as a spreading, growing agricultural producer of wool, corn and meat.

Finally, though numbers of convicts broke loose to terrorize the countryside, burgle, murder and rape its inhabitants, many others reformed: their children were even more ready to reform. Many were to be contributors to the cultural, artistic and musical life of Australia as well as to its economic prosperity, its political and social progress.

5

THE DARK PEOPLE

'A thousand times have I wished that those European philosophers whose speculations exalt a state of nature above a state of civilization could survey the phantom which their heated imaginations have raised ... [and] learn that a savage roaming for prey amidst his native deserts is a creature deformed by all those passions which afflict and degrade our nature, unsoftened by the influence of religion, philosophy and legal restriction.'

(Captain Tench)*

'... a people for whom I cannot but feel some share of affection ...'

(Captain Tench)†

The Aborigines

When Cook (and Phillip) landed in Eastern Australia, its only inhabitants were native aboriginals – 'blacks', 'blackfellows', 'dark people' as they were variously described by the white settlers. They were not in fact black; they were dark chocolate, and they were a separate race from the Negriforms, though tribes of similar appearance and characteristics may be found here and there in South India, Malaya and eastwards to New Guinea. This may well be the route by which they reached Australia, landing on what became the Cape York Peninsula. When? It is impossible to say. As Professor A.P. Elkin wrote in 1938: 'We do not know whether the aborigines have been in Australia one [thousand] or many thousands of years.'

The earliest contact with Europe may have occurred in the late Middle Ages or Early Modern period. It may have been French or Portuguese: neither presumption is beyond doubt. Authenticated evidence of discovery comes from the early seventeenth century: it was made by the Dutch and has been fully described by chroniclers and historians many times.

---

* From *Sydney's First Four Years: Being the Diaries of Captain Watkin Tench*, L.F. Fitzhardinge (ed.) (Sydney, Melbourne and London, 1961), p. 291.
† Ibid.

It persists in the numerous Dutch names which decorate the map, especially of the large island which used to be known as Van Diemen's Land and is now Tasmania, both names being those of Dutch East India Company figures. Of aboriginal evidence of white discovery there is none. Unlike the Polynesians, the Australian aborigines have no historical traditions or even sense of history or time.

The Aboriginal Way of Life

They are hunters and food-gatherers. They are not cultivators, nor do they breed animals. Their food is the kangaroo, wallaby or emu, nuts, fruit and, in coastal areas, fish, shellfish and turtle. Within certain territorial boundaries more or less fixed by immemorial custom, they are nomads. Their social unit is the horde or group, made up of individuals related by definable systems of kinship. The hordes make up the tribes; but the tribe is merely a linguistic group, without political unity or organization. There are occasional ceremonial gatherings but – as the white settlers soon found – it was never possible to discover any political entity with which they could negotiate. Figures came and went. They had names. Their personalities became familiar to Arthur Phillip and his officers. Some, like Bennelon, were generally friendly. Now and then, someone of this kind would act as interpreter or go-between when there was trouble. But generally they were as difficult to identify and trace as the secret religious rituals which formed such a prominent feature of their communal life. 'Magic' was everywhere. 'Sorcery' was a common occasion of inter-tribal warfare. Predatory raiding for land and property, so common in other outwardly similar environments, was rare. The only property that occasioned warfare was women, whose abduction was a daily occurrence.

The 'condition' of the aboriginal has been a matter of debate since 1788. Early opinion was not usually favourable, though Phillip, Watkin Tench and others found some lively and entertaining qualities to redeem the generally low order of intelligence and development more commonly the subject of remark. Barron Field, best known as the first white inhabitant of Australia to compile a book of verse, was a judge, though he was better as a writer of prose than as a judge or poet. His opinion of the aborigines was clear, if damning. They possessed:

> quick conceptions and a ready process of imitation ... but no reflection, judgement or foresight. Thousands of years of inbreeding, untouched by contact with any external civilization, had created a people without anything but immediate wants ... the only savages in the world who cannot feel

or know that they are naked ... at home only by themselves, in their own world of the bush ... the dark people had their past, a cloud that the wind took.*

Today, Barron Field's views of the aborigines are unlikely to find much favour with fashionable opinion. It has become fairly widely accepted that the aboriginals' lack of possessions of any kind (including clothes or tools) may have been an advantage rather than a burden to a nomadic people; that their innocence of technological knowledge of agriculture or trade may have been offset by their 'magic' and uncanny knowledge of bush lore, tracking ability and the like. Thus is constructed an argument that these primitive Stone-Age peoples really represented a culture naturally moulded to their environment.

Aboriginal Decline

The question follows: why then did their numbers dwindle, generally gradually but sometimes, as in Tasmania, frighteningly swiftly? The official (government) estimate of aboriginal numbers suggested throughout the nineteenth century was c.150,000. A British anthropologist who emigrated to Australia, Professor Radcliffe-Brown, believed this figure was too low; in 1930, he re-examined the whole problem and doubled the number to 300,000. A hundred per cent increase may seem statistically dramatic. It is not dramatic enough for Professor Noel Butlin of the Australian National University, whose book, *Our Original Aggression. Aboriginal Populations of Southeastern Australia 1788–1850* (1983), takes Radcliffe-Brown severely to task for proposing so low a figure.

Arthur Phillip is said to have hazarded a guess that there were probably a million aboriginals living in Australia in his day. Present estimates of aboriginal numbers put them at little more than 50,000 of pure blood, and perhaps three times this figure of mixed blood. Finally, more than one authority has expressed the view that this sharp drop in the native population does not necessarily mean that the race is inevitably doomed to extinction; enlightened policy may still arrest or reverse the decline of the last two centuries. There is no question that for one reason or another the aboriginal population has steadily declined. The reasons why remain controversial.

A major difficulty in reconciling such hopes with reality is another change in historical opinion. We have noted that opinion as to the rela-

* Marjorie Barnard *Macquarie's World* (Sydney, 1941).

tionship of aboriginals with their environment as it existed before white settlement has become more favourable; parallel with this, opinion as to the aboriginals' ability to exist in or in proximity to an alien culture has become correspondingly pessimistic. The early white immigrants, not least Phillip, believed that a just and rational relationship could burgeon, provided the white invaders attended faithfully to their paternal duties to the blacks and the blacks behaved in accordance with the elementary rules necessary to law and order. As time passed, these hopes faded. Although Phillip, and his successors as Governor, continued to abide by the terms of their mandate of good faith, problems of law and order increased. Phillip could still take Bennelon to England to demonstrate, in good *Aufklärung* fashion, the nobility of his savages. But the end was the black wars in Tasmania.

The resulting state of opinion has become one of turmoil and a range of controversies varying from differences of degree to – increasingly – violent and irreconcilable conflict. A (mangled) paragraph taken from a letter sent by Lord John Russell in London to the then Governor in Sydney, Sir George Gipps, on 21 December 1838, illustrates vividly how statements of the best intentions can lead into a chaos of misunderstanding: the letter followed a British government enquiry into the action of the New South Wales police who fired on an innocent native while pursuing other natives who were guilty of crimes against the white settlers:

> You cannot overrate the solicitude of HM Government on the subject of the Aborigines of New Holland. It is impossible to contemplate the condition or the prospects of that unfortunate race without the deepest commiseration. (I am well aware of the many difficulties which oppose themselves to the effectual protection of these people, and especially of those which must originate from exasperation of the settlers on account of aggressions on their property, which are not the less irritating because they are nothing else than the natural results of the pernicious examples held out to the Aborigines, and of the many wrongs of which they have been the victim.) Still, it is impossible that the Government should forget that the original aggression was ours.

In commenting on this letter, Professor Butlin's omission of the passage in parentheses is important and may lead to misunderstanding. In using the words 'original aggression', the Minister was referring solely to the action of the police, not, as might mistakenly be inferred, to 1788. He concluded by assuring Gipps, whose conduct *vis-à-vis* the natives was always impeccable, that he would receive every support from London in his efforts to secure justice for the aborigines and 'every social advantage' which it was the colonists' duty to impart to them.

It is common amongst 'radical' historians of today to dismiss such declarations of intent as Victorian eyewash. But such opinions are relatively new. Sir Ernest Scott's *Short History of Australia* is probably as balanced a study of its kind as ever appeared. Scott was an outspoken champion of the British–Australian link. He stood up for Dalley and his decision of 1885 to back Britain in Egypt; he approved Australian participation in the South African War (1899), in the suppression of the Boxer Rebellion, and in the 1914 war. For Scott, Britain, its qualities and its cultural heritage belonged to Australia; so too its mistakes and its weaknesses.

Scott ranked the record of relations with the aboriginals amongst the latter. The aboriginals (he wrote) were not an organized, warlike people like the Maoris or the Bantu. They thieved and murdered admittedly, but they did not commit military aggression. They were as low in the history of human development as it was possible to go. If for no other reason, the fact that they had no conception of private property inevitably led to conflict with the whites. The limitation on their hunting grounds added further fuel to the fire. Disease and drink were also factors. But: 'The worst features of the fading out of the native race arose from sheer brutality and treacherous murder by white settlers and their convict servants.'*

Scott's comment is reasonable and just. It largely exonerates the British Government and the Governors: as we have seen, their record of intentions was high in regard to the aborigines. But they were a long way from the scene of the crime. Their knowledge of conditions was limited; resources for maintaining law and order far away in the bush even more limited. No one knew this better than those much maligned officers, Governors Macquarie, Gipps, Darling, Arthur.

Smallpox: a Deliberate Infection?

As to the settlers, we shall come to them and their problems a little later. Let us first revert to Professor Butlin, his proposed analysis of the reasons for the decline of the aboriginal population and especially the suggested guilt of the first Governor, Phillip, and/or his officers, for the outbreak of smallpox in 1789. Its effects were dire.†

* Scott, *Short History of Australia*, p. 190.
† For the full exchange of opinions between Professor Butlin and myself, see *Quadrant*, March, June and July 1985.

There is no doubt that the surgeons accompanying the First Fleet brought with them materials for inoculating persons suspected of developing smallpox during the voyage. This was common form and common sense. There was general consternation, nevertheless, when a very serious outbreak of smallpox occurred amongst the *aborigines* in 1789. That no case occurred among the *white* population brought some comfort, but added to the mystery of the origins of the outbreak.

From the superb (and very careful) diary kept by Lieutenant Watkin Tench, we know that the possibility that it might have originated from the surgeons' supplies of *variola* (smallpox scab) was canvassed, but was dismissed, in Tench's phrase, as 'a supposition so wild as to be unworthy of consideration'.*

But not too wild for Professor Butlin. Among the 'evidence' he uses in his search for an explanation of the outbreak (to which he assigns the primary role for the start of the reduction in the aboriginal population), Professor Butlin includes the First Fleet surgeons' *variola*. While he concedes that Phillip could hardly have been so wicked – one might add stupid – as knowingly to arrange deliberate infection himself, he believes that '*it cannot* be beyond reasonable bounds that Phillip was pressured into action'. Later, this becomes a 'likely' possibility as 'a deliberate exterminating act'. The effect was to begin a series of smallpox epidemics which reduced (he believes) the aboriginal population of the south-east corner of Australia from around a quarter of a million in 1788 to around 10–15,000 by about 1850. This could have been (he suggests) a case of deliberate genocide.

I have explained (*Quadrant*, July 1985) why I find myself unable to agree with Professor Butlin's proposal to pin responsibility, directly or indirectly, on Phillip, or even on his staff. Let me repeat and clarify my reasons for purposes of simplicity. First, any deliberate infection of the natives would have been utterly pointless. Phillip, from the start, took the terms of his commission and especially his duty to the natives in deadly earnest. Second, there is not the slightest evidence of any conspiracy between Phillip and Tench, or any other officer, to victimize the natives. Though sorely tried, Phillip kept his patience and carried out his duty to maintain law and order without rancour, rage or sadism. Third, the 'evidence' of responsibility in 1789 in the Port Jackson area is shaky enough; it is even shakier for other supposed outbreaks – in what was later Victoria, for example.

---

* *Sydney's First Four Years: Being the Diaries of Captain Watkin Tench*, L.F. Fitzhardinge (ed.), p. 146.

Professor Butlin's evident distrust of Phillip and Tench and his approval of the only officer to oppose the Governor virtually to the point
of 'mutiny' (sic) – Dawes – only add to my feeling that Professor Butlin
has here forgotten his own urgings to historians to be 'dispassionate'
in their views and arguments on the causes of Australian history. Our
Original Aggression begins to look like yet another chapter in the campaign to trace the blots on Australian history solely to the white Australians.

The proposal to treat the First Fleet surgeons' variola as the likely
source of the 1789 epidemic, whether as the result of accident or design,
is flawed in one vital respect. Variola remains effective as a virus carrier
only in cold or cool conditions. The variola in question would have
been some three years old at the time of the 1789 epidemic. It would
have passed en voyage through tropical temperatures ranging from 82
degrees upwards. Phillip's Voyage speaks of his Fleet as 'exposed to
violent heat' while in equatorial zones in June 1787; of the 'great heat
attended by heavy rains' in July at Cape Verde; of gales, heavy seas
and leaking ships throughout the voyage. It is hardly possible that a
substance demanding cool, dry conditions for its preservation could have
remained active in such conditions for such a period of time.

There are also alternatives to the Butlin interpretation of the 1789–
1850 demographic decline which link it with quite other, non-white,
origins. Dr Judy Campbell has analysed in minute detail the possibility
that smallpox infection may have come across from Macassar (Celebes)
with the fishermen who came in search of trepang (sea slugs), a delicacy
much favoured by the Chinese.* This was part of a vast area of Asia
where smallpox was endemic. It is distinctly possible that smallpox in
Australia came, as did tuberculosis, syphilis and other venereal disease,
from Asia, which in turn may have received them from America.

The problem of assigning responsibility for the 1789 outbreak of smallpox bristles with probabilities – and improbabilities. Among the less
probable is infection by Europeans. This may have come later, naturally
transmitted by the convicts or the sealers, whalers or sailors. The evidence
for direct transmission by whites in 1789 is utterly unconvincing, indeed
non-existent. Modern knowledge of medical microbiology has reduced
its credibility to virtually nil.†

If there is no certainty – and there cannot be by the very nature of
things – that the decline of the aboriginals can be blamed on external

* See Historical Studies vol. 20, no. 81, October 1983.
† Review of Medical Microbiology, 17, December 1985 by Jawetz, Melnick and Adelberg
(Los Altos, California, 1970).

factors, why did they fade away in such numbers? Why were they lacking in those still mysterious but undoubted springs of collective revival that helped, for example, Europeans to restore their numbers by increased numbers of births in the wake of epidemics and other demographic disasters such as wars, tempests and floods?

Watkin Tench's editor, Professor Fitzhardinge, has written of him that 'his real interest was in man and what man would make of the country'. He was not to be dismissed as the mere purveyor of a sort of journalistic charm of writing. His whole career was one of alert, intelligent response to challenge and opportunity. It would be stupid to ignore what he thought and wrote about the aborigines. They were (he wrote): 'a people for whom I cannot but feel some share of affection'. They might be lazy and untruthful, but they were not simply stupid. On the contrary: 'All savages hate toil and place happiness in inaction ... hence they resist knowledge and the adoption of manners and customs differing from their own....' They were intrepid in war but not implacable; superstitious but not debauched. One feature he noted may be a significant pointer to their fate: occasionally the barbarous ferocity one tribe showed to another was loosed on their womenfolk. The women were:

> in all respects treated with savage barbarity; condemned not only to carry children but all other burdens; they meet in return for submission only with blows, kicks, and every other mark of brutality. When an Indian (aboriginal) is provoked by a woman, he either spears her, or knocks her down on the spot: on this occasion he always strikes her on the head, using indiscriminately a hatchet, a club or any other weapon which may chance to be in his hands.

Tench's general description is borne out by the detailed description of the punishments meted out by those favoured aboriginal ambassadors, Bennelon and Colbee, to their wives. Bennelon, a particularly intelligent, shrewd and resourceful fellow, would pursue his wife for days at a time when she displeased him, apparently intent on murdering her. He was thwarted only by the Governor and his officers. 'Pre-contact Australia' as Professor Butlin calls it, was no Utopia, particularly for the females.

We need not rely on Tench alone for such evidence of the violence that was traditional in much native life. Paul Wilson's *Black Death, White Hands* arose from the revelations made in the trial of a young aboriginal from Weipa charged with the murder of his female friend. The question was put: could his actions be explained, if not justified, by the historical events surrounding his life? There were communities in Queensland, it appeared, where the incidence of homicide was amongst the highest in the world ... 'at least equivalent to ... the poorest and most violent ghettos of New York'. Violence, rape, murder, suicide and mutilation were everyday happenings; but the most marked feature of the evidence is that it was women who were most often the victims, women who were most often beaten, raped and killed.

The 'progressive' solution for such troubles is to dissociate aborigines from 'white justice'. In the words of the author of *Black Death, White Hands*:

> To eliminate our paternalism, increase Aboriginal decision-making powers and provide black people with their own land. Only then can we begin to erase from our collective conscience the guilt of all those black deaths that have, directly and indirectly, flowed from our white hands.

Other writers, historians included, follow a similar line. Henry Reynolds's *The Other Side of the Frontier* (1981) describes the 'response' of the blacks to white immigration: they were not a primitive, unchanging mass, they were 'pioneers, struggling to adjust to a new world of experience'. There is some archaeological and antiquarian support for this; it is unfortunate that the accompanying rhetoric does little to justify the picture of primitive values Mr Reynolds holds up for us to see. Few thinking people today doubt that the blacks were often brutally treated by white settlers, but prejudice has not been erased: the balance of prejudice has simply shifted away from the blacks to the whites. This may represent change. It does not represent progress.

Mr Keith Willey's account of the destruction of the tribes of the Sydney region in the first six or so decades of settlement, in *When the Sky Fell Down*, is strikingly well written. It is sad that he too thinks it unnecessary to waste any time on understanding the conditions in which the settlement of 1788 took place. His account, like so much current writing on early settlement, is marked by almost total ignorance of its European background. Like Mr Reynolds, Mr Roger Millar (in *Waterloo Creek: A Colonial Cover-Up*, 1981) and the academic collective which organized the mass onslaught on Professor Blainey in 1985 are engaged in rewriting history. There is no harm in this. It has been recognized for as long as 'scientific' historiography has existed that each generation rewrites its own history; and this is all to the good – so long as the process is directed toward eliminating ancient prejudices, false interpretations, and errors of fact, and toward bringing new and more accurate facts to light. This unfortunately does not seem to be the object of many of the current reformers.

Mr Willey has convinced himself that the first Governor's *instructions* were nothing more than threadbare hypocrisy. Rumpole-like, he parses with pseudo-judicial solemnity the sentence in which those instructions lay down the terms of native protection. 'If any of our subjects shall wantonly destroy them ...'. 'Hold', cries Mr Willey. ' "Wantonly" is a let-out, an escape to allow whites to argue that when they killed blacks, they did it not "wantonly" but justly and judiciously. Just as' (to continue) ' "or give them *unnecessary* interruption"; "unnecessary" is inserted to allow the white subjects to argue that their interference with blacks was strictly necessary and therefore lawful.'

Such nit-picking is revealing. Anyone with elementary experience of drafting a law knows that verbs and nouns of a general character and meaning must be defined if they are to be accepted and enforced as just and reasonable. In this case, the laws were drafted to support and justify the Governor's officers as well as to protect the natives against the indiscriminate violence of white convicts or other malefactors. Mr Willey shows no signs of having reflected on the nature of contemporary law, opinion or standards of behaviour or misbehaviour, humanity or inhumanity, in contemporary society. I recommend him to read Leon Radzinowicz's *History of English Criminal Law* (vol. 1), which describes such matters with a lucidity which will not be lost on even the most determined progressive. Phillip himself knew from experience that to be effective the law had to be clearly defined. Defendants had as much right as plaintiffs to know what the law meant. They, after all, were innocent until *proven* guilty.

Nor need he seek even so far. Nearer home there is C.D. Rowley's *Destruction of Aboriginal Society* (Canberra, 1970). Rowley is not only a scholar with a fine sense of the nuances of history and social relationships, but an administrator with wide experience of native rights and problems in Papua New Guinea and other colonial territories, developed and undeveloped. His is an altogether more balanced and sensitive account of race relations in Australian history. He does not, like some would-be 'reformers', see all settlers or native policies as the embodiment of brutal retribution and prejudice aforethought. He allows that the problems of integrating the legal systems and customs of whites and natives were formidable: not all settlers were profit-maximizing tyrants. He can understand the exasperation of the pastoralist faced, on one side, by urban philanthropists to whom aboriginals were 'great pets', and on the other, by blacks who had acquired guns, a taste for other people's beef and an unquenchable thirst for liquor. He can follow the tragic logic. The blacks take to spearing an occasional steer belonging to a settler for their own use. They are remonstrated with, but continue to kill. The squatter at length takes up arms; the blacks spear him or his stockmen when they find them with their backs turned. War begins, and continues for months or years.*

Rowley recognizes that settlers of humane and liberal inclinations had no alternative but to accept this tragic decline into violence. It happened to the Duracks, Irish settlers and pastoralists who came to operate on an enormous scale, made deservedly famous to a wide audience by (Dame) Mary Durack's classic account of her ancestors' adventures and vicissitudes in *Kings in Grass Castles*. Her grandfather (she wrote) held it as an ideal to absorb the aboriginal into the white man's economy. He successfully trained many natives as stockmen, riders and farmhands with this object. Others in their parts of Queensland did the same.

> ... had they been encouraged and subsidized to bring in and train many more natives, the situation might be very different today, for it was the behaviour of the outside, or bush blacks who, in failing to co-operate with the new regime, in killing cattle, horses, and sheep, and committing a number of unprovoked murders that led to the settlers having to call in the protection of the police. . . .†

This in turn led to the 'extermination' of the aboriginals. And this, Rowley claims, proves that even white settlers as well-intentioned as the Duracks unconsciously reveal the fatal consequences of the native police.

Whether this is fair or reasonable comment must remain a matter of opinion. To an outsider, the pendulum seems to have swung too far. Opinion – and Australian opinion can be very mobile once it starts moving – has shifted rapidly from all-out white sympathy to all-out black sympathy. Rowley does not, however, join with those who condemn wholesale British Colonial policy, Colonial Secretaries of State and Colonial Governors in the critical years 1830 to 1850. Men such as Lord John Russell and Gipps (he writes) discussed the issues of justice for the aboriginals on 'a level of penetration and understanding of the administrative issues involved not to be heard again on the Australian continent for a long time'. This is high praise from a fundamentally critical observer. Did the discussions lead to a solution? Apparently not, even where (as in Western Australia) Colonial Office control was maintained for another two decades.

* C.D. Rowley *The Destruction of Aboriginal Society* (Canberra, 1970), p. 154.
† Durack *Kings in Grass Castles*, p. 290.

Was it then the case that the aboriginal decline was caused by exasperation and fear, the mutual violence of aboriginals and native police, white neglect of native evidence, the failure to agree terms by which blacks who wanted to be independent could live under their customary rules in the bush? Or was it that aboriginals were vulnerable to their own violence – in tribal warfare and domestic relations – as well as to lethal diseases? If the latter, who then brought the diseases? The whites (as Professor Butlin proposes), or other neighbouring peoples from, for example, the Celebes (as Miss Campbell believes)? It was not, we must remember, only smallpox that was concerned; it was certainly the most spectacularly lethal, so far as our fragile evidence goes. But various types of venereal disease must have added to the fragility of the female aboriginal, diminishing the chances of improving birth rates.

It is significant that the Australian aboriginal population does not seem to have shown any of the resilience which Western populations showed in achieving quite startling rates of demographic recovery from epidemics and the disastrous mortality they entailed. Why was this? We simply do not know; we must therefore scrutinize the cries of politicized compassion carefully, even though we attract the inevitable charges of prejudice. The historian must always ask himself what are the *reasons* behind his motivation to adopt this or that theory. We have, after all, the authority of that great debunker of conservative humbug, the late Professor E.H. Carr, to demand to know who wrote the history we are expected to believe, and why. Only if we do so have we the right to probe the motivations of others.

The Land-Rights Controversy

Let us, for example, take the case of Dr Marc Gumbert, whose attack on the conventional ideas of aboriginal anthropology is the *fons et origo* of his book on native land rights, *Neither Justice nor Reason*.* In place of the closed and permanent 'horde' proposed by the older anthropologists, Gumbert has laid it down that the old 'model' must be abandoned in favour of a new one which envisages 'society in a continual state of re-formation'. Each individual aboriginal 'was equipped not with a single absolute title to a defined patch of.land but each had a veritable portfolio of shared and variable rights to a wide variety of lands'.†

All this has the blessing of a jury at the Sorbonne which included not only the Head of the Department of Anthropology at Sydney, but,

* Queensland, 1985.
† *University of Sydney News*, 24 January, 1984.

perhaps a little surprisingly, the former Labour Prime Minister of Australia, Mr Gough Whitlam. Now it is not difficult to agree with Dr Gumbert's pronouncement that 'the unique Aboriginal society is not, and never was, a pallid imitation of the European'. Dr Gumbert merely seems to have propagated a myth that Europeans invented the idea of the 'horde' because it represented 'a close parallel with the European concept of the sovereign state, and meshed with the colonial practice of indirect rule'.

This seems to be a quite inaccurate inference. Nothing resembling indirect rule was possible between the Australian 'state' (in any form at any stage) and the 'horde'; and certainly not over aboriginal land rights, which seems to be Dr Gumbert's main preoccupation. From 1788 onwards, Britain regarded the parts of Australia it gradually occupied and settled as a *res* or *terra nullius* – nobody's land. By 1800 this line of thought would have been accepted universally. Even the Supreme Court of the United States put its *imprimatur* on it in 1823 in a case heard between the State of Virginia and an Indian tribe. The court took it as final that while the European nations had respected the rights of the natives 'as occupants', they universally asserted 'ultimate dominion' to be in themselves. In consequence they claimed and exercised 'a power to grant the soil while yet in the possession of the natives'.

From Grotius and Vattel (the fathers of modern and international law) down to our own day, 'effective occupation' of a *terra nullius*, to be recognized as valid, demanded not only 'discovery' (which Britain could rightly claim) but an 'intent and will' to act as sovereign (likewise) and the 'adequate exercise or display of sovereignty'. Of this latter there had been no doubt since Arthur Phillip's original declaration and ceremony of 7 February 1788. That had included the specific provision for the Governor's powers to grant land to the convicts where desirable. That the policy was not deliberately directed against the aboriginals is demonstrated by Phillip's specific exclusion from the privilege of land grants of all the marines.

A similar resolution in support of the Crown's reservation of land rights to itself was visible in 1835 when Governors Darling and Bourke found themselves faced by a settler of considerable courage and enterprise, especially in the acquisition of land. John Batman, of Launceston, in Van Diemen's Land, had originally proposed to Darling that he should be allowed to take over the failed Westernport settlement (Victoria); it had been set up to deter the French from selecting a site there and was no longer necessary for such defensive strategies. Darling refused. It was not (he wrote) within his power to comply with Batman's request.

Undeterred, Batman stuck doggedly to his plan to acquire a private land settlement on the mainland north of the Bass Strait. In 1835, with the backing of a syndicate of fifteen Launceston men, he landed at Port Phillip and recorded his impressions of what he saw in his journal: 'I never saw anything equal to the land; I never was so astonished in my life.'

He followed up his reconnaissance by including a 'treaty' with some friendly aboriginals whom he encountered. Encouraged by gifts of knives, scissors, blankets and the like, eight of the 'chiefs' who showed willing 'signed' long rigmaroles prepared by Batman's lawyer on impressive rolls of parchment. These claimed to be their 'grants' to him of territories roughly the size of a fair-sized English county with livery of seisin and other suitable legal mumbo-jumbo. Totally ignorant though they were of the letter of the law, the aboriginals entered into the spirit of the occasion with gusto. Mystical signs marked what Batman claimed were their names – Jaga-jaga, Cooloolook, Mommarmarler. (Batman looked after the signatures himself: they were inscribed by a Western pen guided by an experienced Western hand.)

The legal importance of this festive occasion did not lie in the aboriginal 'grants', nor in Batman's claims based on them. It lay in Governor Bourke's response: this ran as follows:

> Whereas it hath been represented to me that divers of His Majesty's subjects have taken possession of lands of the Crown (such persons are notified they will be regarded as trespassers and will be dealt with) as other invaders upon the vacant lands of the Crown ... God Save the King.

Bourke defeated Batman. But he did not and could not halt the expansion of settlement by settlers whose common motto was 'all I see I claim', unsupported by feudally-embellished parchment treaties. Possession was ten-tenths of the law. All Bourke could do was to send his special magistrate, Captain William Lonsdale of the 4th (King's Own) Regiment to exercise what government authority could be exercised in the interest of the natives and of law and order in general. He was to conciliate the natives, protect them where necessary and 'improve by all practical means their moral and social condition'.

In 1836, some 177 settlers were already resident on or near the site of what was to be Melbourne. They were grazing 26,000 sheep or more. Some 800 blacks were also present. They had no conception of private property in land or stock and were innocent of any notions of law or order. They stole and devoured any sheep they could spear. The settlers, unsatisfied by Captain Lonsdale's intervention, had recourse to self-help.

Batman was unlucky. His end – years of paralysing sickness, litigation, and crippling debt – had some of the dimensions of real tragedy. Even his reputation as founder of Melbourne is impossible to substantiate, and he died in poverty and estranged from his wife.

There were no more 'land-grants' by native 'chiefs' after Batman. His enterprise had served only to show the tenacity with which the Government monitored its claim to complete sovereignty and – in so far as it came into question – the grant of the soil.

Dr Gumbert's new model is only the most recent 'academic' development in the evolving controversy over land-rights. Will his model of 'high flexible land entitlement, in which cross-cutting alliances of people have a multiplicity of rights over wide-ranging lands' strengthen the moral or political case for extending still further plans for giving land-rights to the aboriginals? It is difficult to see how it can. Indeed, it is difficult to see how it can avoid weakening the case for such land-rights. For at the root of the argument for treating newly-discovered Australia as a *terra nullius* lay the practical problem of how to create a system of government, how to preserve law and order in a real world while at the same time protecting the natives *as occupants*. When Radcliffe-Brown's reputation was at its height, and the 'horde' still seen as giving some kind of cohesion to aboriginal society, there remained possible figments of credibility in ideas of ancient, customary land-rights. With its patrilineal grouping, a 'horde' owning and exploiting the resources of a specific parcel of land might plausibly be imagined as some sort of political unit. Dr Gumbert's 'multiplicity of rights' is much nearer the chaos which faced Phillip and his successors whenever they tried to meet face-to-face with the aboriginals to discuss day-to-day relationships of blacks and whites – rights to fish, gather fruits and plants (like flax), stealing, cattle killing, murder, etc. 'Negotiation' was a contradiction in terms. The more often the attempts at it were aborted, the more justified became the basic assumption of 1788: that Australia was a *terra nullius*.

Alan Frost* has written in just defence of the early settlers:

> However much we may now regret the British failure to negotiate with the Aboriginals, to consider Cook and Banks, Pitt and his colleagues, and Phillip and his officers as marauders ... is not only to do them scant justice but also to make the same error in assessing late eighteenth-century British culture as the representatives of the culture made in assessing the Aboriginal one – that is, of judging according to inappropriate criteria....

* Alan Frost, in 'New South Wales as Terra Nullius', *Historical Studies*, vol. 19, 1980–1, University of Melbourne.

In fact, Cook, Banks, Pitt, Dundas, Nepean and – above all – Phillip were ahead of their time in their recognition of the need for tolerance and understanding of the problems of race relations in New South Wales.

On the spot the Governors, their officers and public servants were thwarted above all by the insoluble problem of communicating with the aboriginals. Alert, skilled in every bush craft, endowed with extraordinary intuition as they were, the aborigines remained remote, virtually inaccessible. Their moods and movements were both erratic, evanescent. The horde might appear for a meeting or discussion; before talk could begin it had dispersed. No reasons could be divined. Mercurial as globules of quicksilver, their motives, hopes, fears and beliefs were beyond human analysis. Dr Frost has suggested that it was the failure of even the best-disposed of the white immigrants to 'accommodate the fact of the Aborigines', rather than 'evil intent or callous disregard' that shows up the limitations of even the most flexible of Europeans.*

It may well be that the newcomers were limited in their understanding. In 1788 it rested on observations that had lasted for months rather than years. But even this moderate and reasonable judgement misses a vital point. The task in 1788 was to set up some workable *modus vivendi* for maintaining law and order. The repeated failures of attempts to establish any form of dialogue between the whites and the aborigines wore down the patience of the most patient whites just as it aroused the fears and predatory instincts of the natives. Nomadic hunters and gatherers by nature, they were unattached to the land and therefore had no laws or understanding of 'ownership'. If the Gumbert thesis is nowadays to be more convincing than that of Radcliffe-Brown, the dilemma of 1788 becomes even more stark. It is worth pondering the words of the late Professor D.P. O'Connell, probably Australia's most distinguished international lawyer. When decisions were made in 1788 as to the alternative modes of occupation and acquisition of Australian territory, men were not concerned to divide such territories into 'civilized' or 'uncivilized'. What counted was whether they were 'organized' or 'unorganized'. In New Zealand, the North Island was regarded as having been acquired by 'cession'. No comparable evidence of 'political' understanding or responsibility was forthcoming in New South Wales. 'Since' (wrote O'Connell) 'the Australian Aboriginals were held incapable of intelligent transactions with respect to land, Australia was treated as *terra nullius*.'†

* Ibid.
† D.P. O'Connell, *International Law,* vol. i (London, 1965), p. 470.

The Aboriginal Problem Today

This appreciation of the problem of 1788 (and later) combines the perception that the men of the day considered both the philosophy and practice of law and government. There was no way of getting the aborigines out of the Stone Age into the world of the late eighteenth century. Whether it is possible to bridge the gap between their world in the twentieth century and the rest of the world in that century remains to be seen. The optimist will believe the long secular decline that has decimated their numbers can be halted. Others will be sceptical; for opposing reasons. One school of opinion will pay most attention to the change in the aboriginal way of life itself. How can it survive in a world where it is no longer necessary? Others will ask whether – if it can be maintained at all – it will be maintained as a kind of liberal, well-meant but inherently disastrous form of *apartheid*? Yet, whatever happens, no one can suppose that even the greatest island is sufficiently great and remote to afford them an existence of dreams in the Never-Never Land, isolated from the rest of the world. Nor is this a future that they themselves would be likely to welcome.

The problems of Australia's official interpretation of its discovery and settlement have been further confused by recent Senate proposals (1983) for a compact or *Makawata* with the aboriginal peoples. This, in turn, seems to be envisaged as resting on the principle that Australia was not 'settled' in 1788 but 'conquered'. Any such fundamental shift in international legal status could have far-reaching effects on the entire concept of Australian sovereignty. Meanwhile the tragic decline of the Australian aborigines goes on.

6

PASTURES, PROGRESS AND GOLD
1850–1900

'... an immense injection of energy, of democratic spirit, of youth and confidence, at which the whole country leapt forward with new life.'

(H.M. Green)*

From the middle of the nineteenth century, Australian life took on new aspects as it turned in new economic directions. The first six decades of the new nation's history had seen some noble individual achievements. Administrators, explorers, settlers – convicts too – had overcome the most daunting obstacles and terrifying hazards with unbelievable fortitude and tenacity. But not all their good deeds succeeded in casting much light into the depressing murkiness of the naughty world they perforce inhabited. Noel Butlin does not exaggerate when he characterizes the predominantly convict and ex-convict society of 1830 as 'sordid'.†

Butlin goes on to epitomize in a classic paragraph the transformation of that society out of all recognition by the combined forces of pastoral expansion and gold. By 1860 it probably attained the pinnacle of *per capita* growth in terms of 'real product'. 'Subsequent development to 1890 represented a prodigious and effective effort to achieve control of a new continent, converting a primeval wilderness into a capital-intensive and highly productive economy....' The rates of *per capita* growth (Butlin has calculated) moved up until they were 'close to those of the western world'.

1891 saw the climax of this grand phase of expansion. The labour troubles of the previous year petered out reluctantly and bitterly as the major unions involved (sheep shearers and shipping workers especially)

* *History of Australian Literature* (Sydney, Melbourne and London, 1961), vol. i, p. 146 (on Australia 1850–90).
† *Essays in Honour of (and of) W.C. Forster*, p. 284.

ran out of funds and gave in rather than run head-on into total bankruptcy. After that the workforce went on growing until the First World War but output lagged behind. It was an interlude of 'drastic retardation'* in the economy and society at large. The political system itself was revolutionized by the entry of aggressive Labour parties into the wages and employment aspects of politics.

The Gold Rushes

The years of glory began as they meant to go on. Between 1851 and 1900 there were to be 'strikes' of gold in all the Australian States; but the two great gold 'rushes' were in Victoria in the 1850s and in Western Australia from 1882 to 1900. These not only initiated the transformation of the whole Australian economy but set a large proportion of the Australian population in motion (to the gold fields) and acted like a magnet in the world outside, drawing in prospectors and speculators not only from Britain but from other parts of Europe and the United States. The Australian population trebled in the first decade after the rush of 1851. By 1939 Australia would have added some £715 million to the world stock of gold. (This figure was calculated in 1944 but it is well to remember Professor Geoffrey Blainey's timely warning in his own study of *The Rush That Never Ended*: 'Sharp inflation harms the historian particularly because it breaks one of his most useful measuring rods, money.')

There had been sporadic reports of the discovery of gold long before 1851. The Polish explorer, Count Paul Strzelecki, crossing the mountains of the South-east into the area he christened Gippsland, after the then Governor of New South Wales, found particles of gold amongst decomposed rock. Geologists pointed to the resemblance between these geological formations and those of gold-bearing areas in the Urals. A Sydney geologist, W.B. Clarke, found specks of gold in the Bathurst area; there were other such finds, small, widely disparate, too unexciting to spark off a gold rush, but disturbing enough to put authority into a stew. The hopes of finding gold threatened the prospects of the peaceable development of Australia. 'Put it away, Mr Clarke, or we shall all have our throats cut', said Governor Gipps. Strzelecki deferentially left out all references to his own discoveries when he wrote his account of his journeys. When a piece of gold was found at Berrima in 1848, the Government in Sydney refrained from ordering a geological survey, lest it should end by 'agitating the public mind'.

---

* Ibid.

Reports of discoveries multiplied in the late 1840s; but it remains one of the unanswerable 'ifs' of history whether there would have been an Australian gold rush in 1851 if it had not been for the sensational gold rush which had already caused the vast upheaval in California in 1848. What seems certain is that Clarke deserved the distinction, ultimately granted to him by government, of having first found and identified gold in the Blue Mountains. Clarke, an Anglican parson, had come to Australia almost by accident, for his health, which was frail. He was one of a group of Cambridge *savants*, all important in the evolution of modern science out of classics, religion, mathematics and literature. Sedgwick, a Woodwardian professor, was their leader. (Sir) Humphry Davy, Edward Daniel Clarke and W.B. Clarke were all members of Jesus College (Davy and E.D. Clarke Fellows). W.B. Clarke was to become a scientific pioneer of great distinction, FRS, founder of the Australian Royal Society, authority on coal in New South Wales as well as gold in Victoria, and finally winner of the £3,000 reward offered by New South Wales to the first discoverer of gold. He was a small, bearded patriarch, a warm friend and a fearsome adversary. 'Considering you are a clergyman' (remarked a geologist colleague), 'you are very bellicose.' Clarke sought out his scientific targets with uncanny imagination and hit them with deadly accuracy.

Clarke had prophesied in the 1840s that the country would be found to be rich in gold. But Gipps need not have worried: such academic observations had little impact on a generally apathetic Australian public. The burgeoning Australian (and English) press did nothing to help. John Fairfax, editor and proprietor of the *Sydney Morning Herald*, did his best to extinguish with dousings of the coldest water any enthusiasm speculative shipowners might raise in prospective passengers for California. Here the gold rush was well under way by 1848–9. Fairfax and other journalists portrayed the whole enterprise as a series of swindles, the gold fields filled with Mormons, fanatics, humbugs, rogues, thugs and tarts. But Tasmanians, already known for an unorthodox flair for the *dolce vita*, were not to be taken in. Hobart began to tingle with excitement at the thought of limitless wealth, bottomless gold mines. The incubatory fever infected New South Wales. Men were impressed by the promise of wealth and plenty; women by the reported shortages of female company in San Francisco.

There was something of an exodus from Australia. It included all sorts and conditions of men (and women). These included the remarkable Edward Hammond Hargraves – orphan, sailor, hotelier, adventurer and publicist. Hargraves was a big, ebullient man full of big, ebullient ideas.

In California he learned how to pan gold and make and use a 'cradle'. This he taught to several companions. Hargraves had no intention of becoming a digger himself: that he left to others. With them he returned to Australia and steadily rode round on his great horse, until one day, he jubilantly declared to his colleagues he had found gold. 'This', he cried – according to his autobiography, 'is a memorable day in the history of New South Wales. I shall be a baronet. You shall be knighted, and my old horse will be stuffed, put in a glass-case and sent to the British Museum.'

In fact, Hargraves had found no gold; but his old mates did, early in the winter rains of 1851 as the rock surfaces were washed down and exposed. As suddenly as it had begun, the rush to California ground to a halt; it was replaced by a rush to Bathurst. Traffic from Australia to America was replaced by traffic in the opposite direction. Three hundred diggers were attracted to the field now claimed by Hargraves as his own discovery and named *Ophir*. By mid-June the Bishop of Sydney reported that he found 3,000 people at Ophir. A few weeks later numbers rose to 10,000. Aborigines struggled in and made uncommonly high wages as trackers, labourers and builders. 'Black fellow rich now' they cried as they hurled their boomerangs for the entertainment of the ignorant, looked after horses while their owners went a-digging, and smoked cigars too large for the diggers yet to afford.*

Hargraves enjoyed his predicted glory, but it was short-lived. He won his prize of £10,000 for discovering gold. Prizes and trophies were showered on him. He became a Commissioner of Crown Lands and a Justice of the Peace. At great cost he visited England and was received by Queen Victoria. On his return, disaster awaited him. His former partners commenced law suits against him. They were successful. His prosperity in South and Western Australia failed. He was to die a poor man. But he had succeeded in one respect: he may not have found gold, but he had publicized it so effectively that thousands of others were drawn into the search for it.

Major fields were found at Ballarat and Bendigo, at many places in between, and to the west of a line drawn from one to the other. Alluvial, surface gold, easy to find and dig, came first and as quickly went, scrambled for by thousands of diggers attracted from other sites and occupations by the dazzling prospect of quick riches. The immigration from overseas – usually from Britain – created an entirely new Australian workforce and doubled the population in the 1850s.

* Jay Monaghan *Australians and the Gold Rush* (California, 1966), p. 178.

Gold production shot up to a peak in 1856, lifted by a change in the source of gold from individual, hand digging to richer seams deeper below the surface. After the peak, production declined slowly; the people originally attracted by the gold rush remained, to be absorbed into other industries – house building, manufacturing and pastoral farming. Geoffrey Blainey has noted that 'all Australia's large inland cities of the 19th century were mining cities, and gold made Melbourne for half a century the largest coastal city in the land'.*

The region of this first gold rush is still filled with monuments and relics of an age of epic energies, riches that were enormous but often as quickly dissipated as won. Much that is still to be seen is more historic than beautiful: the ruins of the vanished Bank of Victoria which at its peak housed seventy-two tons of gold, Bendigo's vast baroque Shamrock hotel, the rotunda of the Mountaineer Brass Band of Walhalla, once a busy mining centre, now a few old cottages, a cemetery, and nostalgic memories. There are extraordinary Chinese ceremonial towers at Beechworth where hundreds of immigrant Chinese miners were ritually buried at their deaths. Rutherglen's Star Hotel still commemorates the Scottish participation in the renewed gold rush of 1860 in which its creator, John Wallace, took part. At Bendigo the vast clock-tower still rises above a curving slate roof reminiscent of a Belgian railway station. Not far away is the classical grandeur of the Capitol Theatre; the Alexandra Fountain recalls the visit in 1881 of the Royal Princes who named it for their mother, the future Queen. In the 1860s Castlemaine was still the second city of the South, digging what were believed to be infinite reserves of gold and prophesying a future population of a quarter of a million. That vision faded, but Castlemaine's buildings – the impressive classic market entrance, for example – are superbly preserved. History lives on at Castlemaine. If the former gold fields of Victoria seem of lesser architectural quality than the towns of Tasmania, it is largely because they are nearer to us in time and experience.

In the countryside, progress and change were less dramatic but hardly less important. The caprice of natural water supplies had from the start been among the pastoralists' major hazards. Now they were supplemented by supplies made available by planned systems of water conservation. Thus improved, pastures were fenced with high wire fences. In this way the number of sheep raised on a given area of land was markedly increased, and the cost of shepherds' labour further reduced. There were more lambs and heavier fleeces. The animals were healthier and graziers

* G. Blainey *The Rush that Never Ended* (Melbourne, 1963).

able to concentrate on breeding from the best stock. Fencing was wide-spread in Victoria by the 1860s.*

By the 1870s New South Wales had followed suit on an even larger scale. The sheep resumed its role in the Australian export trade as industry and trade boomed in Britain, Australia's major market. In New South Wales alone the number of sheep pastured rose from just over 6 million in 1860 to over 56 million in 1890. But wool was never again to occupy the leading role it had assumed in the first half of the century. The first gold rush had combined with industrial changes in the outside world – Britain especially – and with the growth of international trade, to foster the growth of local manufacturing industries, railways, and building, to diversify what had earlier been a dangerously monolithic economy.

From 1882 to 1900 Australia was galvanized once more by news of a gold find in the Kimberley district of Western Australia, so far exclusively dedicated to cattle and sheep stations and mostly populated by English settlers. Through the 1880s the finds in Kimberley, Pilbara and Yilgaru fields built up to an important, but not sensational, level. That came, quite suddenly, in 1892 with a find by two remarkable prospectors – Arthur Bayley, a Queenslander, and William Ford, from the Ararat mine in Victoria. Thus was born the famous 'Golden Mile'. The city of Kalgoorlie grew like a mushroom. It was quickly flooded by miners who flocked west from all over Australia. By 1900 Western Australia had added over £22 million to the world's stock of gold.

Nor were new discoveries limited to gold. In 1883 a small syndicate of miners and shepherds unearthed a mountain of silver at Broken Hill in the far west of New South Wales. Their discovery turned them into millionaires and yielded additions to the world's stock of silver, lead and zinc to the tune of over £175 million. Further deposits of copper, already well developed in South Australia, were found in New South Wales, Queensland and Tasmania. Gold, silver, lead and zinc discoveries in the 1880s led to the age of the 'resource economy'. Australia was still 'the speculator's El Dorado.'†

However, none of these could compare in any dimension with the discoveries in Western Australia. There the digger gave way to large companies, backed by large volumes of capital and the technological skills necessary to exploit the deeper reefs which emerged along the Golden Mile. The new technology was in large part borrowed from the

* See chapter 13, p. 234, for details of the Fairbairn Stations.
† E.O.G. Shann, *Economic History of Australia* (Cambridge, 1930), pp. 303–4.

mining developers of the South African Rand. As a result, gold mining became less an adventure, more a complete industry propped by science, technology and capital.

The population – 25,000 in 1890 – grew more than four-fold by 1900, most of it associated in one way or another with gold mining. Before 1897, the 60,000 or so hopefuls heading for Coolgardie travelled on foot or rode horses or camels. After that they were able to travel by rail from Perth. Rail building in the 1860s had already successfully linked up Melbourne with the Victorian gold field. Now Perth and Adelaide were linked to their industrial and agrarian hinterlands.

Two questions now need to be posed: what was the effect of the gold rushes of the nineteenth century in Australia? How was the money provided to execute the vast economic and constructional operations stimulated and made necessary by the mining discoveries? The effects of gold have been summarized in a classic statement by the late Sir John Clapham, historian of industrial Britain and, in particular, of the Bank of England:

> It is said that the precious metals cannot of themselves produce prosperity, but they certainly promote activity. They fire the imagination; and economic progress needs the fired imagination, not merely the grasping hand and the patient, bowed back. Man labours, contrives and invents to get gold. When he has got it, the price rise that follows stimulates all kinds of enterprise.

This seems to me to square, broadly, with the verdict of a leading modern economic historian of Australia.*

General recovery of production, trade and general economic activity, not only in Western Australia but in the South and East, was stimulated by the gold discoveries. The Victorian gold industry revived as prices and costs fell and gold mining became more profitable. As Clapham added (with his usual Yorkshire caution), there was plenty of waste in mining, and even more in the far-flung enterprises to which mining gave rise in the 'multiplication' process. In spite of this, the stimulus afforded by gold (and silver) was real, and the growth of wealth real as well as apparent.

Now to the second question: how were the means of mining and industrial development provided? First, the problem of finding the wherewithal for economic development was not peculiar to Australia. To some degree, every area or state undergoing this process needs more

* W.A. Sinclair, *The Process of Economic Development in Australia* (Melbourne, 1980), pp. 153–4.

'capital' than it possesses; it therefore borrows from some other area better endowed. Late medieval Northern Europe borrowed from Italy; sixteenth- and seventeenth-century Spain borrowed from the Netherlands; seventeenth- and eighteenth-century Britain borrowed from the Dutch; the nineteenth-century world – Europe, North and South America, Canada, Australia, New Zealand, South Africa, India, Egypt – borrowed, on a larger scale than ever before, from Britain.

Australian (and other) economic historians of left-wing or 'liberal' persuasion have argued, under the influence of Marx and Lenin, that such borrowing was essentially a form of 'imperialist' tyranny. Brian Fitzpatrick produced the classic, and most eloquent, version of this kind. His picture of Australian subordination to British economic imperial domination emerges in a highly simplified version of history. British domination kept Australia, as it kept other colonies, in tow to London capital dictation. Instead of developing as a commercial and manufacturing nation, Australia remained (it is argued) an agrarian, pastoral land producing raw materials – wool, meat, butter, cheese, and of course gold and minerals – for the benefit of the British. A long succession of governments – municipal, state and federal – continued to pay tribute in the shape of 'usurious' rates of interest for the privileges of remaining in a state of humiliating subordination to the imperialist forces of Whitehall, Westminster and their masters in the City of London, the Stock Exchange and the Bank of England. And so on, and on.*

The Fitzpatrick thesis has more recently been elaborated by Professor Wheelwright.† Wheelwright foreshadows prophetically the outlines of a 'true' history of his adopted country. 'Such a history might', he suggests, 'show the following: how capital came to Australia dripping with blood and dirt, in the form of, first, the expropriation of the original owners of the land and their virtual extermination; and second, the Australian version of slavery, known as the convict system ...' Passing over some curious problems of chronology and fact raised by this lively introduction, let us pass on. The new history will show how the national bourgeoisie came into existence, how Australian nationalism developed, and how much this depended on the Australian working class. It is illustrated how this nationalism never broke with British imperialism but became side-tracked into militaristic jingoism in support of it, how much of Australian economic development was due to two world wars, when

* See e.g. Brian Fitzpatrick *The Highest Bidder: A Citizen's Guide to Problems of Investment in Australia: A Polemic* (Melbourne, 1965).
† E.L.Wheelwright *Radical Political Economy* (Sydney, 1974); E.L.Wheelwright and K. Buckley *Essays in the Political Economy of Australian Capitalism* (Sydney, 1975).

the imperialist links were weakened, and why there was an opposite effect in the Great Depression. And it is also shown how, after the Second World War, Australian capitalism slipped out of the orbit of British imperialism into the American variety; and, finally, to what extent the Australian bourgeoisie became a partner of world imperialism, having foreclosed any possibility of self-sustaining Australian capitalism, and is now becoming aware of this, only when it is too late.

We shall return to this, and even more recent, if possibly more confused, interpretations of Australia's history, later. For the moment it is enough to say that the foregoing passages contain all the major distortions of Australian history paraded by xenophobes of Left, Right and Centre; they beg every vital question in Australian history and ignore the fact that the Australian people enjoy, in the decade of their bicentenary, one of the highest standards of living in the world, and can claim a larger share of sovereign independence, democratic government and personal freedom than most. But first, it is necessary to insert an historical condition without which it is impossible to understand Australia's development, but which is almost invariably omitted from the history books.

This is most clearly and eloquently stated by Marjorie Barnard. She would not (I suspect) think of herself as an economic historian, but she talks better sense about the subject than many of those who specialize in it. 'Australia', she has written, 'is an epitome of all social history.' Because it was a great island cut off from the outside world, the people living in scattered settlements and homesteads equally isolated from one another, there was enacted, over more than a century and a half, 'under practically test conditions, an evolution such as in the old world worked itself out either in pre-historic terms or certainly before the age of scientific observation'.*

'The settlement began at scratch . . .', and any of its activities – agriculture, pastoralism, trade, education – turn out, when examined, to have passed through all the stages of evolution '*at an accelerated pace, because Australia had the more advanced old world to draw on for experience and supplies*'.†

The Land

Pastoral industry developed out of its original condition 'of biblical simplicity of nomad shepherds to the scientific management and highly

* Marjorie Barnard, *History of Australia*, p. 13.
† Ibid., my italics.

mechanized conditions of today'. The same was true of arable farming, which developed new machinery such as Ridley's stripper (1846) which reaped ten–twelve acres a day with one man and two horses: it greatly lowered costs of producing, amongst other crops, new grain of high-milling, high-yielding quality, more strongly resistant to rust and disease, developed by William Farrer. Farrer was a Cambridge mathematician who emigrated for health reasons to be a farmer in New South Wales. His most popular wheat ('Federation' of 1902) changed the whole appearance of large areas of landscape: for 'Federation' was not yellow, like the old straws, but a dull bronze. Sheep and cattle breeding proceeded briskly as farmers turned their eyes towards the meat as well as the wool market, and the cattle men competed to produce the best strains of Hereford cattle. Mining in its early stages worked the alluvial topsoil mineral deposits by hand. Later, first in Victoria, later in Western Australia and everywhere else, the miners penetrated to deeper-sunk reefs. This called for mechanical equipment; and this in turn called for capital, and capital called for management, for partnerships and companies – private or, later, public.*

As Miss Barnard has said, 'civilization' could not be imported. It had to evolve. But the physical, basic foundations of civilization could be, and were, imported. Again, to quote Clapham, economic activity is not the 'most important' human activity, but it is the 'most fundamental'. Without tools, inventions and investments, man is left without the means for better things ... 'chances to practise high arts, organize great states, design splendid temples and think at leisure about the meaning of the world'.† This was felt more acutely by Australians just because they were having to cram the essential tasks, which others had had thousands of years to achieve, into a century and a half; hence, in a large measure, the vast import of British capital, especially from 1870 to 1904. Its nature, operation and results form a major controversy among historians, Australian historians especially.‡

British Investment

From 1788, Australian settlement had been largely financed by Britain. The First Fleet, and its supplies, were at the cost of British public funds.

* See e.g. Geoffrey Blainey *The Rise of Broken Hill* (Melbourne, 1968).
† Clapham *Concise Economic History of Britain* (Cambridge, 1949), Introduction.
‡ For scientific analysis at the highest level of refinement, readers may refer to N.G. Butlin *Investment in Australian Economic Development* (Cambridge, 1964) and A.R. Hall *The London Capital Market and Australia 1870–1914* (Canberra, 1963).

These continued to finance emigration, both convict and free, and supplies for 'the store' necessary to supplement the shaky, precarious product of the settlement itself. Private settlers soon (but at a slow rate) added private imported funds of cash to the 'national' stock. Borrowed funds, the property of a few large companies such as the Australian Agricultural Company and the Van Diemen's Land Company, and bank loans, were gradually added from the 1820s onwards. But it was from 1870 onwards that very large-scale investment by Britain reached Australia, after half a century of experience gained (sometimes painfully) in the Americas and Europe. When George Paish, a celebrated expert in public finance, read a paper to the Royal Statistical Society in 1909* he concluded that while the vast sums invested overseas (including Australia) involved considerable risk, the economic results were, by and large, good. Britain obtained on balance more good, reliable investments than bad; the recipients were enabled to develop their economic potential in ways and to an extent which would otherwise have been quite impossible. To obtain (by 1910) an annual income of £140 million, Britain had invested some £2,700 million at an average rate of return of 5.2 per cent. How had this capital been spread?

Geographically, about half went to the countries of the British Empire, half to 'foreign' states. As to the purposes of investment, more than half of the grand total by 1910 had gone into railway construction – either by companies or – as in Australia – by governments. The rest had gone into a wide and miscellaneous range of companies – banks, breweries, distilleries, lighting and power companies, gas companies, mining companies (gold, copper, silver, lead, tin, diamonds), chemicals, plantations for producing rubber, tea, coffee, cable companies, tramways etc.

The largest group of borrowers by value were overseas governments – national, state and municipal. Such, in brief, was Paish's account of British overseas investment. He concluded by comparing the brisk continuation of the process in the time he was speaking (1909) with the later eighties, when Britain had experienced her previous record boom in overseas lending – especially to Australia. It was rolling on even as he spoke. Australia alone received over £12 million from 1908 to 1909. He had no doubt that investment in Australia had benefited Australia as well as increasing wealth and income in Britain. 'By building railways for the world, and especially for the young countries, we have enabled the world to increase its production at a rate never previously witnessed,

* Reprinted in *British Overseas Investments 1907–1948*, Mira Wilkins (ed.) (New York, 1977).

and to produce those things which this country is specially desirous of purchasing – foodstuffs and raw materials.' In short the Australian borrower, public or private, was provided with credit to buy the goods he needed, and to increase Australian production to pay interest on the capital borrowed, and also to buy increased quantities of British exports.

In the decade of the bicentenary, many – in fact, almost all – of the inventions, developments, ideas, policies and moral concepts of Victorian, indeed pre-Second World War, society are under attack. This applies to *laissez-faire* capitalism, British imperialism, railways as a form of economic development and the export of capital by Britain and (see Wheelwright, Fitzpatrick, Dunn et al.) the import of capital by Australia, together with many other things, institutions and people.

Let us now see how a sober, down-to-earth, recent Australian appraisal sees such things. We cannot do better than draw on Professor W.A. Sinclair's account in his *Process of Economic Development in Australia* (1976).

Australian Investment

By 1870, Australian investment opportunities were popular with British investors, and growing ever more popular. During 1871–75, the rate of capital inflow was 21.2 per cent up on the previous period. In 1876–80, it was 77 per cent up. In the 1880s, especially 1884 to 1890, capital movement was enormously vigorous. With capital available and gold to be mined, Australia was a new country to be reckoned with: a land of boundless prospects and plenty of prospectors.

From 1850, Australian banks – in Victoria and Tasmania, the Colonial Bank, The National Joint Stock and the National – were added to the number of English banks in operation. The Bank of New South Wales dates from much earlier; but at that time it came nearer overseas capital operations by opening an agency for recruiting British funds. All these banking developments helped the farmers and graziers by enabling them to offer land as collateral for mortgages. Pastoral land finance companies acted as go-betweens in the country. Building societies helped similarly in the towns and recruited the small savers' support for expanding the great cities like Sydney and Melbourne.

Under popular pressure, State governments in all the States, including Tasmania, played an increasing role in economic life and policy. Public investment (at some 40 per cent of capital formation) represented an element in the economy probably unique in the history of those developing areas of the nineteenth-century world that stemmed from Britain. This was partly the result of the deep roots 'government' had struck from 1788 in Australian soil. At that time, government 'intervention' was indispensable; by 1860 it was continued into the age of expansion and industrialization partly because the lower houses (if not the higher) in the developing parliamentary system were responsive (via representatives elected on universal manhood suffrage). If railways, mining and pastoralism needed capital, let government make whatever arrangements were necessary for it to be there. If manufacturing industry seemed to need protection, let government consider providing it. In Victoria it did, by means of the 1871 tariff, powerfully advocated by the Melbourne paper, *The Age* and its editor, David Syme. If large-scale pastoralists seemed to be proliferating too freely and doing too well, let government control them: land 'selection' followed. It may have facilitated the increase in wheat farming by smaller farmers. The growing population benefited from more abundant wheat supplies in an area stretching from the north west of Victoria to the south east of South Australia. It was good wheatland.

All these developments – fencing the sheep and cattle stations, building railways, developing arable farming, developing (especially in Victoria) manufacturing industries – mopped up capital, local and imported. It mopped up, too, the labour that was going spare when the mining boom subsided and diggers were looking for work. In Queensland, things were different. Queensland grew sugar and raised cattle.

Growth of Cities

In each State, at least one city burgeoned as the capital. Melbourne, half the size of Sydney in 1850, mushroomed with gold and by 1880 was bigger (at over a quarter of a million inhabitants). But Adelaide and Sydney both grew impressively; Perth and Hobart grew, but more slowly. House, office, factory, quayside and harbour building, like fencing and railway construction, took up idle labour. Pastoralists benefited from price inflation induced by gold and from the growing demand for wool in post-Great Exhibition England. With their profits on exports they were among the front shoppers for imports – mainly British. Nobody else could compete on price or convenience. Britain in a boom carried an Australian boom on her back; later, time would show that Britain in slump carried Australia down with her.

The older generation of Australian historians (Fitzpatrick excepted) rarely doubted that Australia made great strides in economic, social and political organization during the second half of the nineteenth century. The present generation has not reversed this particular aspect of Victorian history, nor, in general, the notion that the import of capital was beneficial in its effects. Indeed, they have rather underscored the extent, breadth and depth of the growth and improvements of the period. Economic and social development as seen, for example, by N.G. Butlin includes emphasis on urban growth and house building. They were not merely the fringe outgrowth of demographic increase, nor merely the provision of necessities, but of amenities of life for a population with rising standards of living. The results were also enduring.

Not everything was satisfactory in the phenomenal growth of cities like Sydney or Melbourne. Behind the elegant architectural creations of a remarkable crop of designers of genius (headed by the incomparable Francis Greenway but containing, especially in Van Diemen's Land, architects of almost equal gifts) lurked different and less agreeable sights and scenes. From the start Sydney had had it slums, brothels and red-light quarters where crime and violence festered. When Henry Parkes fled from Birmingham – itself not the apogee of urban civilization in the 1830s – and landed in Sydney, he found to his horror he had jumped from the frying pan into the fire. Its slums, misery and degradation were indescribable. Sewage disposal was conspicuous by its absence. Typhoid fever was responsible for a very high mortality. Factories poured their rich contribution of effluent into the rivers and bays regardless of the consequences. Melbourne was no better in such respects than Sydney. Elsewhere, cities were not yet big enough to suffer the worst features of overcrowding and slum conditions.

Pollution or not, the growth of Sydney and Melbourne alone was proof that many Australians – say, a quarter of the population – either found it necessary to live in cities or preferred to do so. The building of cities, with or without planning, must mean some sacrifice of natural amenities. Equally it meant the creation and addition of 'artificial' amenities – entertainment, amusement, social recreation, sport, games – all means of passing the time, providing rest, recreation or spiritual as well as physical renewal; all thing which social, civilized man has striven to provide throughout the ages. Australians, like Greeks, Romans and their successors to city life ever since the passing of the Ancient World, often preferred the social and cultural opportunities of life in a large city to the natural attractions and deprivations offered by the country station and the bush. It was all a matter of taste, of the talents and aspirations any particular individual possessed or lacked. The central point was that the men of 1788 made the first inroads, painful, tedious and exhausting, into the bush. Their successors carried forward their attacking initiative. Every decade saw the progressive urbanization of new generations of Australians. Melbourne – 'marvellous Melbourne' – led the way through the '80s. The proportion of inhabitants of the State of Victoria living in Melbourne jumped from just over 30 per cent to just over 40 per cent in that decade. From then on until well into the twentieth century, Melbourne, for reasons we will look at later (see chapter 13), seems to have had the greatest accumulation of talents among performers of music and the most discerning audiences. But it would not be long before Sydney caught up statistically – and as a 'market' for culture.

By the turn of the century, 40 per cent of all Australians lived in the capital cities of their States. It was a very high proportion, reminiscent of conditions in contemporary Germany, where historians have spoken of a whole generation 'rushing to town'. Did this encourage in Australia the rise of an urban proletariat such as could be argued to have come into existence in cities like Leipzig, Berlin or Vienna where peasant immigrants from the Eastern European countryside flooded in to eke out a bare slum existence eating black bread and margarine? Were the victims of Mr Wheelwright's vision of Empire really 'slaves' of this kind? Judged by the evidence, apparently not. As the land was cleared for grazing and farming, as mining went forward, as railways were built, housing programmes executed, manufacturing industries set up, vigorous competition for labour amongst employers ensued. In the burgeoning prosperity of the third and part of the fourth quarter of the century, wage rates stayed buoyant. Capitalists could afford to pass on some of the gains from increased productivity to large numbers of workers, and attract others into the stream of migration that led from the British Isles (and to a much lesser extent some other areas of Europe) to Australia. These benefits were more marked after the surplus labour from the gold rush had been absorbed.

This is not denying either the existence of social pockets of poverty or the problems of the aborigines. Readers of the letters, diaries and memoirs of rural Australian life will not have forgotten the presence on many a distant station of the aboriginal cattleman or tracker; he is often described and remembered by his employer and family with genuine affection and gratitude. Professor Sinclair comments:

> Rising primary production ... provided the basis for a wide ranging increase in real incomes which can be likened to an escalator on to which some overseas workers were able to step. It would therefore appear that

the economic development of Australia was making an important contribution to the sum of human welfare.*

According to A.R.Hall, author of an outstanding monograph on British investment in Australia, Australia's economic history was not shaped entirely inside Australia by Australians.† The flow of British capital made an indispensable contribution to Australian economic progress; most of all perhaps in the crucial phase of the 1880s, when a slackening of demand for capital by other borrowers coincided with a sharp rise in Australian demand. For the flow of these years was not merely a passive or automatic movement. The Australians were inveterate borrowers. Individual borrowers were joined by municipal and state, and later still by federal, public borrowers. The mixture of the two created a complex of investment mechanisms unique in the then British Empire where *laissez-faire* was at its height. Government decisions were not invariably wisely or objectively judged, but in general it seems that in the peculiarly difficult conditions of Australia, where the 'tyranny of distance' ruled all, the mixed public/private economy did help to stabilize and promote economic development from this time onwards.

Pioneers of private enterprise did much good (and some harm), Professor Shaw has written. Yet '... without government assistance, private enterprise could have done little'.‡

Marxists and counter-factualists (strange bedfellows) will no doubt continue to speculate on the alternative sources of capital to which Australia might have turned in the second half of the nineteenth century: it is difficult to imagine where they could have found it. Everything they could save themselves was lent. France was accustomed to lending overseas, but only in specifically favoured areas – especially to Russia. To imagine Australia being included in the investment map of France it would be necessary to imagine a massive remoulding of history – the occupation, perhaps, of the greatest island by, for example, la Pérouse or d'Entrecasteaux. Holland was under the French heel; her great days of foreign lending were past. America was herself still a net borrower. Dutch and French services having dried up, she was herself as dependent on Britain for capital as was Australia.

---

* W.A. Sinclair *The Process of Economic Development in Australia*, p. 114.
† A.R. Hall *The London Capital Market and Australia 1870–1914* (Canberra, 1963). It is extraordinary that this important contribution to international economic history has never been properly printed: it still appears in the form of a superior kind of typescript.
‡ A.G.L. Shaw *The Economic Development of Australia* (London and Melbourne, 1946), p. 185.

In the lending process, the choice of who should be borrower was a private, individual choice, not a government decision. The British Government did no more to guide investment towards Australia than to guide it towards Switzerland or Peru. Its job was to try and protect all parties concerned, so far as possible, against fraud. It was not government, but the self-governing, self-regulating market, supply and demand, assisted occasionally by a dose of inter-family sentiment, that ruled the movement of capital within the Empire.

There was only one serious snag in the whole process: that was the very ease with which money could be borrowed on the London market when conditions were favourable. When business was booming, when economic opportunity seemed endless, profits secure, losses unthinkable, yields from taxes buoyant, it was difficult for governments of all sizes and varieties not to see it as their plain duty to borrow at the going rate and be damned. In their euphoria they often forgot that rates of interest (fixed) which seemed entirely reasonable and payable in times of boom, would look usurious, outrageous and insupportable when times were bad. In the bright sunlight of the 1880s such melancholy speculations were too remote to be contemplated. In the bad times of the 1930s, they seemed to Jack Lang and Brian Fitzpatrick the inevitable consequence of imperialist finance capitalism and the flouting of the medieval usury laws.

7

'A RADIANT LAND'

'O Radiant Land! O'er whom the sun's first dawning fell brightest when God
said, "Let there be light".'

(John Farrell)*

'This was a Literary Period.'

(H.M. Green)†

Erasmus Darwin (1731–1802) was a great physician and botanist in
his day. He was also grandfather of Charles Darwin. He managed to
be something of a poet and a visionary, less afflicted by the unsmiling,
acidulous, dry superiority packed with guile that was the mark of some
of his academic offspring at Cambridge.‡ Undeterred by never having
seen Sydney, he determinedly provided a dream, in verse, to celebrate
Arthur Phillip's successful arrival in Australia:

> Where Sydney-Cove her lucid bosom swells,
> Courts her young navies, and the storm repels;
> High on a rock amid the troubled air
> Hope stood sublime, and wav'd her golden hair...

His grandson, who visited Australia in 1836 as tame naturalist aboard
HMS *Beagle*, on an epic journey round the world, found its flora and
fauna of absorbing interest. So odd and isolated did he find it all that
he began to wonder whether there had been not one Creator but two
– one for Australia and one for the rest of the world. Apart from this
eccentric attraction, he found his grandfather's vision singularly unful-
filled. Australia was dull, uninteresting, uninviting. New South Wales
(he conceded) might be an admirable place to accumulate a fortune,
'but heaven forbid that ever I should live where every man is sure to

* Bertram Stevens (ed.) *Anthology of Australian Verse* (Sydney, 1906).
† H.M. Green *History of Australian Literature* (2 vols, revised by Dorothy Green)
  (London, Sydney and Melbourne, 1984), p. 391.
‡ cf. Rupert Brooke.

be somewhere between a petty rogue and bloodthirsty villain'. When he finally left Western Australia for home, he managed to rise to the occasion with a few eloquent measures; but they were only dubiously complimentary: 'Farewell, Australia', he cried, 'you are a rising child and doubtless will reign as a great princess in the South; but you are too great and ambitious for affection, yet not great enough for respect; I leave your shore without sorrow or regret.'

Major Ross, Arthur Phillip's Deputy Governor, could have told the Darwins that it was easier to admire New South Wales from afar than from New South Wales. This was a view widely shared among its new settlers in the first half of the nineteenth century. The second half of the century saw a dramatic change of atmosphere and morale. The great 'gold rush' of the fifties was not wholly responsible for the decades of growing prosperity and development that followed; but it certainly initiated a totally new phase of Australian economic and social history, providing a firm base for a wide-ranging and profound cultural transformation. This superstructure was, if anything, more striking than the improvements in the purely material foundations of these years.

It was an achievement to which many sorts and conditions of men contributed: writers, poets, journalists, priests, bishops, explorers, archaeologists, anthropologists, lawyers, entrepreneurs, public servants, even politicians. Many of them, though not all, were immigrants attracted, directly or indirectly, by the upsurge in mining for precious and other metals. From this, as we have seen, other activities in manufacturing, trades of all kinds, banking and finance burgeoned and multiplied. Some were privately financed and developed; others were the work of the public organizations, local, municipal or state. The idea of what would later be called 'a public sector' was present from the very arrival of the First Fleet and even earlier. The creation of a nation frequently required, as Adam Smith himself had recognized, action by the state, temporary or more prolonged. The conditions in which Australia was created were such as to leave her inhabitants more free than, for example, Victorians in the mother country from the dogmas and prejudices of the *laissez-faire* economy which assumed the quality of a religion in many English minds until well into the twentieth century. The monster called distance was a tyranny that could only be held at bay, let alone conquered, by enterprise both private and public, working if need be in double harness.

Looking back from 1900 and later, Australians were to see a land and people bathed in a sunlit radiance that seemed, gradually, in a half century or so, to have encompassed all human activities, dispersing the

fetid miasmas and fogs that had enveloped the precarious earlier settlement of convicts, prostitutes, guards and warders, with curfews, flog-
gings, hangings, feuds, bushranging and general violence. The successor-
state was by no means perfect, nor is its literature necessarily a wholly
reliable reflection of its nature; but used with due reserve it can illuminate
the processes of social change which took place. They were indeed
remarkable. A new race of observers emerged to celebrate in poetry,
prose and paint the new Australia, its joys and beauties, its sunrises
and sunsets, its open life, sports, pastimes, customs, hospitality (above
all, perhaps), the patriotism of its people, their social progress, and their
religious beliefs. Even the aboriginals became the object of a new and
more understanding interest and concern.

Dorothea Mackellar's *My Country* is a naive but moving evocation
of the claims of the new land over the old to an Australian's affections.
Hers are fixed on the new, the old one left behind.

> I love a sunburnt country,
> A land of sweeping plains,
> Of rugged mountain ranges,
> Of droughts and flooding rains.
> I love her far horizons,
> I love her jewel-sea,
> Her beauty and her terra –
> The wide brown land for me.
>
> An opal-hearted country,
> A wilful, lavish land –
> All you who have not loved her,
> You will not understand.
> Though Earth holds many splendours,
> Wherever I may die,
> I know to what brown country
> My loving thoughts will fly.

Implicit in the poem is the conviction that a natural, simple emotional
loyalty to Australia and all it offers is essentially restricted to those who
live in Australia. Non-residents may aspire to membership of the fellow-
ship but are likely to achieve its true fulfilment only through personal
experience. This had been an underlying theme of mild controversy from
early days in Sydney. It had surfaced in differences between the merits
of Australian-born and immigrant youth – the 'sterling' and 'currency'
lads and lasses – between pro-emancipist and anti-emancipist enthusiasts,
most recently between the whole-hearted devotees of a purely Australian

Commonwealth and those who preferred to pay prudent obeisance to the appellate jurisdiction of the Privy Council in Westminster.

Art

A parallel conviction would grow that only artists born and bred in Australia were, in the final analysis, capable of interpreting Australia, its brown and sunburnt plains, its drought-seared river beds, its dotted scrub and thirsty paddocks in paint. The incompatibility of the European-born and/or trained artist and the disturbingly unfamiliar, intractable landscape has accordingly become the outstanding cliché of modern Australian art criticism. The early painters, whether they be Phillip Gidley King, third Governor, Thomas Watling, Joseph Lycett or J.S. Prout (to name only a few), all had their sights firmly fixed on Europe, its conventions, its climatic norms: they stuck to these in Australia, failed – in consequence – to notice the importance of aboriginal art, and generally failed to grasp the need to come to terms themselves with Australian conditions. They stuck to European models and techniques. They had technical skill. They were historically interesting but 'they signally failed to unlock the secrets of this [Australian] continent... There was nothing in their imported notions about art that fitted them to cope with the particular aesthetic problems set up by the appearance and "feel" of the newly-settled continent.'*

We shall return to these ideas and examine their claims to be valid generalizations later (see chapter 13). Enough here to say that while suitable concessions are made to a handful of artists (Martens, Glover, Piguenit, von Guérard, etc.), the obstinate proposition remains: they all represented an alien tradition which could only be imposed on Australian material at the expense of the true aesthetic satisfaction which can only come from an inner intimacy between artist and environment. Glover alone occasionally gets credit but largely because he points forward to later, modern schools of native Australian painting.

The growing number of Australian artists and growing output of Australian art as the nineteenth century progressed represented another tribute to the desire of the people to celebrate their faith, pride and joy in Australia and its scenery. All the artists who came forward from Governor King onwards were at one in expressing, in their quite different ways, what they thought of the homeland, its people, its vast natural beauties and social characteristics and peculiarities. Australian visual

* James Gleeson *Australian Painters* (Sydney, 1976), p. 17.

art, like other arts and activities, was part of the great outburst of enthusiasm that replaced the anxiety and bitterness of the early years. It was a form of national feeling but it was not nationalistic in any exclusive sense; indeed it usually overrode such differences of origin as existed. These have largely emerged in the retrospective analysis of the twentieth century. In reality there was no general 'progress' of art from the worse to the better. There were at any moment good artists and better artists. There was no Rembrandt or Velasquez; but one day, as the number of artists grew, there would be. For the time being, Australian artists glorified the beauty of their country. But they did it by means of techniques mostly acquired a long way from Australia.*

Poetry

The same was true of the poetasters. In early Australia poetry was an exotic growth. William Charles Wentworth, a remarkable man who was one of the small intrepid band who crossed the Blue Mountains, released the early settlement from its geographical bondage and later fought for an important measure of self-government, was educated at Cambridge. While still an undergraduate he came runner-up for the Chancellor's Verse Prize Medal (1823). His entry was a formal exercise in the classical style that owed more to the eighteenth than to his own century. *Australasia* offered up a prayer that:

> An Austral Shakespear rise, whose living page
> To nature true may charm in ev'ry age :–
> And that an Austral Pindar soar,
> Where not the Theban Eagle reach'd before.

Wentworth's hopes were premature. As Bertram Stevens explained nearly a century later,† conditions in early Australia did little to favour the cherishing of literature. The settlers were fully engaged in a hand-to-hand struggle with nature. There was no enlightened class of cultured people to provide an ambience in which letters could develop. Most of the inspiration came from overseas, from the old home country (Stevens could have said straight out, from Scotland and Ireland especially). Australia had not yet settled down to form 'any decided racial characteristics'; nor had 'any great crisis occurred to fuse our common sympathies and create a national sentiment'. There was therefore (in 1906) 'no great

* See pp. 212–15.
† Bertram Stevens (ed.), *Anthology of Australian Verse* (Sydney, 1906).

poet, nor ... any remarkable innovation in verse forms'. What had happened, he suggested, was that the old forms had been 'coloured ... and changed with the thoughts and feelings of a vigorous, restless democracy ... that they have an interest and a value beyond that of perhaps technically better minor poetry produced under English skies'.*

This was fair and apt comment, reminding us of the similar situation in the visual arts. Of the very earliest verse little or no trace remains; so that that strangely mingled compound of pomposity and humanity, Barron Field, Judge of the Supreme Court of New South Wales and a temporary immigrant from England, is often wrongly credited with the title of first poet of Australia. His claim rested on his *First Fruits of Australian Poetry*, privately printed in Sydney in 1819. Field was a friend of Charles Lamb who reviewed it in the London *Examiner*. Stevens' comment will suffice: 'one wishes for his sake that the verses were more worthy'.

The gold rush brought the first crop of poets, as well as diggers, to Australia. Among them were a few of note. Their focal point was Dwight's bookshop in Melbourne and they contributed mostly to that city's already famous newspaper, *The Argus*. For the most part they reflected past or current English fashions in literature. Adam Lindsay Gordon, descended from an old Scottish family, and educated at Cheltenham, Woolwich College and Merton College, Oxford, never lost the air of scholar and gentleman, even though he lived his life in Australia as horsebreaker, steeplechase rider, friend of jockeys and shepherds. His verse mixes horse ballads and romance. He always remembered England nostalgically:

> I remember the lowering wintry morn
> And the mist on the Cotswold hills
> Where I once heard the blast of the huntsman's horn
> Not far from the seven vills.

He still read his Horace by candlelight and owed much to Swinburne; but he became part of Australia, foreshadowing the bush spirit of Lawson, 'Banjo' Paterson and the later writers for the Sydney *Bulletin*. He was proud to have written verse that ordinary diggers and shearers knew by heart. In the late '60s personal tragedies overtook him, and he shot himself in June 1870. Amongst the younger writers he inspired was the immigrant Francis Adams (1862–93), who wrote two poems dedicated to Gordon. *Gordon's Grave* – not a very good poem – ends:

* Ibid., Introduction.

> This was a poet that loved God's breath;
> His life was a passionate quest:
> He looked down deep in the wells of death
> And now is taking his rest.

A chronic consumptive, Adams was obsessed by Gordon's suicide. *To A.L. Gordon* ends with the lines:

> As you have pondered I ponder,
> As you have wandered I wander,
> As you have died, shall I die?

He answered his own question: in September, 1893, he too shot himself. His prose writings, though uneven, are more important than his verse (see below pp. 153–64).

There are numerous writers whose verse celebrates the warmth and beauty of their emergent continent in suitably romantic or patriotic mood. One of the most distinguished was a Scot, Brunton Stephens (1835–1902). He arrived in Queensland in 1866 and swiftly set to work to maintain in his new home the reputation, familiar in his old home, of the civilized and creative civil servant. Dante was never far from his elbow in the government office in Brisbane where he presided. He had been in Australia only a decade when he wrote one of his best poems, an ode on *The Dominion of Australia: A Forecast, 1877*, which foretells the lustrous future awaiting *Australia Felix* when she becomes 'one Continent-Isle of Emerald':

> A gathering force, a present might,
> ... shall leap to light,
> And hide our barren feuds in bloom,
> Till, all our sundering lines with love o'ergrown,
> Our bounds shall be the girdling seas alone.

A score of versifiers of lesser talent than Stephens praised the rising natural and man-made glories of the new continent. They are not less touching for being sometimes gauche and stumbling in expression. For Ethel Castella (1861–1915), a Melbournian lady of Scottish-Spanish descent, Sydney was the successor of Venice and Florence:

> High headlands all jealously hide thee,
> O fairest of sea-girdled towns:
>
> Like Venice, upheld on sea-pinion
>
> Thou wearest, in sign of dominion,
> The zone of the sea,
> No winter thy fertile slope hardens
> O new Florence, set in the South!

Patrick Molony (1843–1904), a Melbourne physician of Irish descent, performed a similar office of commendation for his rapidly growing city in a warm ode to *Melbourne*:

> O sweet Queen-city of the golden South
> Piercing the evening with thy star-like spires,
> Thou wert a witness when I kissed the mouth
> Of her whose eyes outblazed the skyly fires.
> I saw the parallels of thy long streets
> With lamps like angels shining all arow

The gems and girls of Queensland stirred the pulse of Will Ogilvie (1869–1920), a roving Scot who filled in a break between Edinburgh and the United States droving and horsebreaking in Australia 1889–1901. In his *Queensland Opal* he caught the current Australian fashion for panegyric:

> Opal, little opal, with the red fire glancing,
> Set my blood a-spinning, set my pulse astir,
> Strike the harp of memory, set my dull heart dancing
> Southward to the sunny land and the love of Her.

There were others less fortunate than Miss Castella or Dr Molony; for example Dora Wilcox, a New Zealander who taught for some time in Australia. For some reason she removed to England where she found herself marooned in London, unhappily lamenting her fate and longing for southern haunts. She is not complimentary to the metropolis:

> This is not nature's City: I am kin
> To whatsoever is of free and wild...
> And London's smoke hides all the stars from me...
> Ah! what English nightingale,
> Heard in the stillness of a summer eve,
> From out the shadow of historic elms,
> Sings sweeter than our bell-bird of the Bush?

Miss Wilcox's homesickness amid London's teeming streets, grim grey houses and leaden skies where 'speech seems but the babble of a crowd, and music fails me' may not be quite the stuff of great poetry, but no one can doubt its sincerity. Nor, similarly, can we fail to be impressed by the very different poetic ruminations of a very different character who appears in Australian history in many different roles: Sir Henry Parkes, an English peasant turned artisan, emigrant to Australia (1839), politician, MP in Australia's first Parliament under responsible government, and several times Premier of New South Wales. Parkes was a consummate politician, a statesman even in spite of sometimes dubious manoeuvrings. Except that Parkes was tall and Lloyd George was short, the picturesque, commanding Parkes almost compels comparison with the Welsh wizard. The leonine head, the silver oratory, the magic each exercised over the rapt, enchanted audience; to say nothing of the labyrinthine complexity of their private lives, their love of pretty women and the confusion of their finances. All these they had in common. They also wrote their own speeches and loved great literature.

Parkes was also a very tolerable poet. Even in the thick of the political melée – his usual location – Parkes could turn aside and write a paean of praise, doxology, obituary or elegiac verse for a colleague, as he did on 6 November 1886, for Sir James Martin,* former Premier and later Chief Justice of New South Wales, in *The Buried Chief*:

> With speechless lips and solemn tread
> They brought the Lawyer-Statesman home:
> They laid him with the gathered dead,
> Where rich and poor like brothers come.
>
> He scaled the summit while the sun
> Yet shone upon his conquer'd track:
> Nor faltered till the goal was won,
> Nor struggling upward, once look'd back.

Again, this may not be the stuff of the greatest, or even great, poetry. What it conveys, and what Parkes unfailingly conveyed, was the sense of occasion. Australians were, before and after Parkes, often sadly deficient in their sense of occasion; but from his time onwards his example was there to remind them that Australia, proud, self-made, home-made Australia, from time to time needed, like all nations aspiring to greatness, a sense of occasion. Who could be bettered as its provider than this authentic man of the people, a peasant and poet who showed everyman the art of keeping up with, perhaps ahead of, his own upward progress?

But it was from Gordon rather than from the more traditional romantics studded with elusive references to Greek and Roman mythology that the verse revolution came. If – as it was claimed – every second person in Victoria could recite Gordon's celebration of 'the Wattle gold trembling 'twixt shadow and shine', it would be claimed that every second person in Australia knew by heart chunks of Andrew ('Banjo')

---

* J.A. Froude met Martin on his visit to Sydney. He was greatly taken by him: '... a stout, round-faced, remarkable old man': for Froude the personification of wit and a gently sceptical kind of wisdom. See Froude, *Oceana* (London, 1886), pp. 156–8.

Paterson's *Man from the Snowy River* and Henry Lawson's *Star of Australasia* by the 1890s. These ballads of the bush, popularized by the radical journal, the *Bulletin*, sang of the lives of ordinary Australians – cattle drovers, sheep shearers, land of rivers where grasses waved, hobble-chains rattled, the cattle lowed and the birds called; of men like Clancy of the Overflow, a shearer who had to get a letter written by a mate 'with a thumb-nail dipped in tar'.

> Our fathers came of roving stock
> That could not fixed abide:
> And we have followed field and flock
> Since e'er we learnt to ride;
> By miner's camp and shearing shed
> In land of heat and drought,
> We followed where our fortunes led
> With fortune always on ahead
> And always further out.

Their verse was coeval with that of Rudyard Kipling and possesses something of Kipling's cunning use of what appears to be direct, plain speech to describe plain, direct people doing plain, direct things. All were a healthy and welcome change from the emotional overheating of much nineteenth-century poetry. They made it seem artificial and sanctimonious. So Lawson, Paterson and the *Bulletin* went up in the cultural world of Australia, carried on the tide of a still fairly quiet wave of nationalism and egalitarianism. They still continue to do so (as Kipling's repute, once suspect to the liberal and left *avant-garde*, rises even higher in esteem in Britain). Paterson's verse transcended national boundaries: *Waltzing Matilda*'s Scottish tune is probably known to most people in the English-speaking world. Whether they know it or not (and most don't), its words describing swagman and billabong came from Paterson. Their moving authenticity, at once obvious and elusive, has played a role in establishing this old song as one of the world's most enduring and well-deserved favourites.

Writers

The versifiers give us one aspect of the emergent country and people. The prose writers give us a different, more extensive, more explicit account. Australia inherited a great tradition of natural English prose; prose born of letters written to families and friends was the basis of the prose of the historian, archaeologist, anthropologist, parson, novelist, explorer, and geologist. All these – Australian born or immigrant – contributed richly to the increasingly full descriptions of every aspect of the life of men as well as the flora and fauna of Australia. The Victorian world was not yet cursed with the problem of two cultures. Australians, like the British, wrote better prose in the pre-telephone age than they do in our age of mass communications. Some of the writers quoted below, women as well as men, will take their places in the history of English-spoken literature, as voices of a Golden Age no less than as celebrants of a new society. Without exception they wrote of Australia, land and people, *con amore*, unaffectedly, as watchers awakening to the unfolding potentialities of a vast continent, old as the world yet now for the first time revealed to Western eyes.

There is room here to sample the contributions of only a handful of the celebrants, some Australian by birth, others first generation immigrants, yet others passing visitors. Among the last was James Anthony Froude, a brilliant and deservedly popular historian and publicist who was later to be – somewhat unexpectedly – Regius Professor of Modern History at Oxford, a shrewd observer wielding a powerful weapon of literary style. Another was A.W. Howitt, a versatile scientist, scholar, bushman and explorer who arrived in Australia as a digger. His observations of the aborigines laid the foundations of Australian anthropology and his hyperactive imagination widened the whole character of that discipline. Along with Howitt we may place J.W. Gregory, whose *Dead Heart of Australia* established his reputation as a leading authority on the Central Australian desert, geologist of world repute and a brilliant writer. Also worth noting is Carl Lumholz, a Norwegian freelance anthropologist overflowing with perceptive, if unsystematic, observations of aboriginal life and customs.

There are contributions from three novelists/poets. Ada Cambridge was the wife of an emigrant Anglican parson. Her *Thirty Years in Australia* is a treasure house of highly articulate social, botanical and general observations; Mrs Aeneas (Jeannie) Gunn, whose affectionate and carefully observed stories of outback life brought her third prize (after Marcus Clarke and Rolf Boldrewood) in a poll carried out in 1931 for the best Australian fiction writer; Boldrewood (T.A. Browne, who borrowed his pseudonym from his model, Walter Scott) was a former grazier and squatter who turned from writing text books on scientific cattle- and sheep-raising to novels in serial form for Australian and English readers on bushranging and cattle rustling. They brought him wide fame, especially his *Robbery Under Arms*, highly regarded by Mark Twain and Rider Haggard as well as by most academic critics. His *Melbourne*

Memories (1884) describes that city in the 1840s with acute perception, very clearly articulated. Finally, there is a small group of clerks in holy orders (the church is still in this period a vital repository of intellect). The Bishop of Ballarat, the Right Reverend Thornton ('short, portly... with a lofty sense of his own dignity', as *The Australian Dictionary of Biography* puts it), was a capable synthesist and speculator on aboriginal anthropology. The celebrated war historian, C.E.W. Bean, and a handful of gifted journalists, Gilbert Parker and Archibald Marshall in particular, round off the list.

Ada Cambridge came to Australia newly married with her parson husband when she was twenty-six. She was to make her name as a versatile and imaginative writer. Today her novels and poetry are largely forgotten; but her remarkable descriptive powers and sharp observations are preserved in her *Thirty Years in Australia* (1901). It is full of incidents like this: 'They call these great creatures eagle-hawks, but they are wholly eagles... I have seen one swoop over a terrified flock, claw up a good-sized lamb and soar away with it as if it were a mouse.' Her husband's first parish church contained an unwelcome inhabitant in the shape of a snake which defied discovery. Eventually the parson found it asleep on the altar, bathed in the warm sun, asleep. 'So he hewed it in pieces before the altar as Samuel hewed Agog...'. Opossums came down the nursery chimney and smashed all they found.

> The lovely gabble of the cranes and wild swans comes back to me whenever I think of the place... in the elbow of the river at the corner of our paddock we used to watch for the platypus which had a home there....Four of these precious varieties we shot.... We are sorry for that now but we were proud of it at the time....

Not for nothing was Ada a Norfolk country girl, and Australia owes her a debt for her observant, gossipy diary.

Its debt to Carl Lumholz is greater still, for he was a professional, gifted with Scandinavian thoroughness. On the Diamantina river he talked with natives and whites of the great water-carrying frogs. Natives and whites used them as a source of drinking water in droughts. 'According to report, such a frog contains about a wine-glassful of "clear, sweet water".' J.W. Gregory, in his *Dead Heart of Australia*, was no less tenacious in his research on the Stony Desert of Central Australia. He describes how the South Australian police supplied dogs to the aborigines, not from generosity but to help them trace fugitives; for while the natives were adept at fleeing across the vast floor of closely-packed pebbles forming the Desert, dogs disturbed these pebbles and left clues for the police. Sturt, the explorer who first described the Desert as an ancient sea-bed, was wrong, declared Gregory. His view merely represented a 'habit so prevalent in the middle of the last century, of regarding water as the universal geological agent'. Gregory liked a good argument.

Water, and lack of water, naturally attracted attention. 'We are wont to think with awe of the Great Nile Dam', wrote Florence Gay in a piece on *The Irrigation of Australia* (1908); yet the new Tvqwool Gorge reservoir in Victoria would contain 200 times its volume of water. 'It is almost impossible to give an adequate idea of these projects – one is tempted to compare them with the titanic irrigation schemes seen by Professor Lowell in the Canals of Mars.'

Visiting travellers shared with denizens a sense of wonder over Australian resources of timber. This has been a source of controversy among historians. Sir Gilbert Parker in *Round the Compass in Australia* (1892) spoke in glowing terms of the qualities of *jarrah* ('one of the finest woods in the world'), the renamed *Karri*, gums and sandalwood: '... timber thickly set over 30,000 square miles of territory, and from it will come a great amount of wealth'. Piles in the Swan River made of it were as sound after forty years as when first put down. It was virtually indestructible. The Karri 'grows to an enormous height, rivalling the Gippsland and Huon Gums...'. Archibald Marshall, in his *Sunny Australia* (1911), added: 'many of the London streets are paved with them; they are invaluable for harbours dock, and pier work, and they are imported all over the world as railway sleepers.'

Bird life offered another fascinating topic of comment. The Australian magpie was a popular favourite with visitors. Their 'exquisite carolling in the early hours ... is the thing I remember best', wrote Ada Cambridge. 'There is no bird song in the world so fresh ... and never do I feel so much an Australian as when I go to the bush again and am welcomed by that fluting note.' Carl Lumholz agreed: there was nothing to compare with being 'awakened in the bracing morning air, before the sun is up, by the wondrous, melodious organ tones of the Australian magpie, "*Gymnorhina tibicen*"', as he added for good scientific Germanic measure.

Birds, sheep, cattle, the remarkable feats of the cattle drovers (one, as Sir Gilbert Parker discovered on the Darling, a former Fellow of St John's College, Cambridge); the night stillness of a camp in the remote bush when the camels had settled down and the embers were cold; 'the great umbrageous apple-trees ... covered with fruit of the finest size and quality'; ground so cumbered with peaches that it was scarcely possible to walk – these were some of the sights that greeted the sore, urban eyes of visitors. There was also another phenomenon which was to grow more important with time and the evolution of an Australian identity. This was sport: it impressed late Victorian observers in the shape of the horse – racing, riding, polo and buck-jumping.

'Horse-racing', wrote Florence Gay,

'is, and always has been, the natural sport... the racing instinct is in the blood. Youngsters riding to school race on their ponies; the loafers at the wayside shanties in the intervals of quoit-playing and haranguing on Social- ism, will pit their sore-backed nags against each other.'

The further she went into the interior the more completely she found the horse-race the reigning form of recreation. 'Where cricket and foot- ball are unknown, the settlers' horses provide the settlers' sport.' Much horse-racing was amateur. In buck-jumping, the amateur found no place. It was too dangerous. The buck-jumper was necessarily a professional, carefully trained: 'Generally,' Florence Gay observed, somewhat surpris- ingly, 'a man of fine and balanced character, as cautious as he is cour- ageous, gentle but absolutely determined... he has the utmost scorn for any careless or half methods.' Breaking a horse was a struggle for mastery between man and animal; it could be a life or death struggle.

Surf-bathing also had its death risk: sharks. But normally it was a light-hearted affair, as Arthur Adams noted in his *Galahad Jones* (1910). The girls were gay in their bright coloured Canadian costumes and ban- dannas. There were already 'young men who cultivated brownness... as a débutante cultivates her complexion'. Both sexes, it was whispered, used a special cream to put 'the brown bloom on bare legs and arms. For the dream of the surfer is to be brown.'

Other observers recorded their impressions of less tangible aspects of Australia and Australians: their courtesy, for example. Anyone who had knocked about the world (wrote John Foster Fraser in his *Australia*, 1910) was familiar with the 'brusqueness, nearing rudeness, of some democratic communities' – no names, no pack-drill. No people was more democratic than the Australians, but there was no rudeness: 'the quiet, dignified courtesy... was delightful to witness'. Fraser concluded: 'A beautiful land. I loved it. I loved the people.'

'The Australians', wrote another English visitor, Archibald Marshall, 'have a perfect genius for hospitality.' It was left to the Principal of the Brotherhood of the Good Shepherd, the Reverend C.H.S. Matthews,* to note 'The Beauty of Home Life in the Bush', where *'every girl [is]*

---

* Matthews *The Church in Australia* (1908, SPG).

a lady and every boy a gentleman in the poorest humpy'.

A little surprisingly, a number of visitors went out of their way to defend Australian speech. J.F. Fraser denied that all Australians spoke 'Cockney', and that when Cockney was spoken it was an inheritance from London. It was rather 'an independent growth, partly due to climate, but mainly due to carelessness'. This affected chiefly children and young women, rarely men or women of more mature years. The mature Australian was 'a particular clean speaker', without the slovenliness Fraser had noted in England. Even more surprising is that he was supported in his observations by J.A. Froude, who made a kind of 'State Visit', almost regal in its exclusiveness, in 1885. 'The first thing that struck me', wrote Froude, 'was the pure English that was spoken there. They do not raise the voice at the end of a sentence, as the Americans do, as if with a challenge to differ from them. They drop it, courteously, like ourselves.'

Others were equally flattering to the qualities of the Australian press. 'Nowhere in the world are there newspapers of more dignified, unpurchasable temper than the long-established, conservative journals of these five colonies' (Sir Gilbert Parker). Ada Cambridge, no recluse of the manse, had friends amongst the Melbourne press-men – the *Argus* and the *Age*. This latter (she wrote) was 'such a power in the State as I should think no individual paper was in any land, and the literary beauty and philosophical significance of some of its Saturday leaders have reached a level that would have made them notable amongst men of letters anywhere'.

Rather more surprising was her relationship with the Sydney *Bulletin*, and *avant-garde*, radical club if ever there was one. She describes a *conversazione* of the 'guild', as she calls it:

> Phil May (the great cartoonist) was a leading light of the society... the grimy and bedaubed plaster laughed with his conceits... Amongst them was a portrait of the then Governor of New South Wales, Lord Carrington, as an utterly disreputable vagabond... it was a focus of mirth the evening through. I wonder what became of it? It might have been disrespectful but it was a work of art and I think he who inspired it would have valued it as much as any one....

Ada was evidently a good mixer.

Music

Australia had not only art and literature, but also music. And music meant Melba; for Archibald Marshall, as for thousands more, 'the greatest of all living singers... born in Victoria'. She was at the end of a two-year visit there when Marshall visited her. 'Those were happy days... a great deal of talk and laughter, some heavenly music, reading and writing on the verandah... in a general way, the best of everything.' His most vivid recollection was sitting out in the garden on Christmas night. Madame Melba had had a record made of the chimes of Big Ben '... and it was beyond measure strange to hear those familiar notes – yet it was natural too, for English life wraps one all around in Australia and although you are farthest away from England in distance, you are never far away from her in spirit'.

Aboriginal Culture

Florence Gay's anthology, *In Praise of Australia*, which appeared on St George's Day 1912, contained a long section entitled 'The Black Man', devoted to the work of Australian and other writers who had dealt with the origins, customs, language, characteristics and beliefs of the aborigines. It would be quite mistaken to assume that no serious attention had been given to such subjects during the first half century after the settlement of 1788. Only the grossest ignorance can explain beliefs that the settlers were unconcerned about the native peoples they found in Australia, or did nothing to foster civilized relations with them. Since such beliefs do nevertheless persist, it should be stated again that Arthur Phillip's commission as first Governor included the most solemn instructions to conciliate them and foster amicable relations with them. These instructions were faithfully carried out by him and his successors. The halcyon years were short; the knowledge and experience garnered small. By the time of Macquarie and Darling, the aborigines, like convicts at one end of the scale and squatters at the other, were merely part of the exasperating, never-ending and apparently insoluble problem of law and order. They did not shine forth as part of the new and radiant Australia; but the reader browsing in Australian literature of the second half of the nineteenth and early years of the twentieth centuries cannot but be conscious of a change in attitudes. There were important positive efforts to identify the elusive aboriginal problem – their origins, way of life, grievances: to replace emotional by more objective standards of assessment; in short, to formulate criteria for their better understanding.

Basic to these was the mingled geographical and anthropological work of Lumholz, Wallace, Howitt, Calvert, Gregory, C.H. Barton and others. Huxley had suggested that the Australian aboriginal bore some resemblance to 'a coolie from the Dekkan of Hindostan'. Wallace strengthened the proposition that within the limits of time fixed by the existence of man, Australia may have been connected to the Asiatic land mass to Australia's north west. Its natives might therefore qualify for inclusion in the group of Caucasian peoples rather than as an unknown, degraded and barbarous race (admittedly, among the Caucasian lower orders). For good measure, A.I. Calvert added evidence which he suggested pointed to similarities between aboriginals and the Jews. Carl Lumholz added that much as the civilized Australian blacks like fat, they can never be persuaded to eat pork. 'There is too much devil in it they say.'

To these wide-ranging reflections, the Bishop of Ballarat (Samuel Thornton DD), in his *Problems of Aboriginal Art in Australia* (1903), added even more uninhibited suggestions. Was it not possible that amongst the cave drawings uncovered by Sir George Grey (the formidable, reforming Governor who retrieved South Australia from its early chaos) were *Christian* symbols? To say nothing of Tibetan or Buddhist? Was that cave drawing in South Australia not a well-executed representation of a Jewish seven-branched candlestick? Was it not extraordinary that in Ireland the Bishop had found an episcopal tomb exactly resembling a pattern in a mid-Australian cave? (Sensing perhaps that his imagination was straying a trifle freely, he had drawn the attention of the Archbishop of Canterbury to the phenomenon; to which the Archbishop had returned the prudent rejoinder that it was 'in a high degree remarkable and interesting...'!) Nor did the Bishop exclude language from his observations. Was it not 'singular almost to laughableness, that *cooee* should be so like the Italian *qui* and the Persian *koo*'?

That the Bishop was gifted with a fertile imagination is plain (imagination can be a dangerous quality amongst antiquarians). Yet the accuracy of his observations is not of first importance. His significance is in his passionate interest in the origins of the aborigines, particularly in their historic relationships with the extra-Australian world and the Caucasian, particularly Dravidian, tribes. However fanciful such reflections may sometimes have been, they had the major advantage of concentrating attention on the aboriginal peoples as an object of serious study.

The growing body of observers of aboriginal custom had to confess that in some respects their study confirmed the impressions of the early settlers that brutality of men towards women was a disagreeable feature of aboriginal social life. 'Alas!' wrote Albert Calvert, 'woman's rights are shamefully neglected and no one takes her part, whether innocent or guilty – the general principle being "If I beat your mother, then you beat mine; if I beat your wife, then you beat mine".' As against this, more careful observations seemed to exonerate the aborigines from the charge that their sexual relations consisted simply of unbridled concubinage (as some whites, including Lord Avebury, the celebrated banker and scientist-cum-anthropologist, had suggested). On the contrary, their marriage customs had much to commend them.

White ideas about aboriginal cannibalism were also substantially modified by observers like Lumholz, Howitt and N.W. Thomas. 'Various people have various modes of burial', wrote Lumholz. 'The Greeks cremated their dead; the Persians buried them; the Hindoos anoint them with a kind of gum; the Scythians eat them; and the Egyptians embalm them... we find all these modes represented among the Savages of Australia.'

There was general agreement that human flesh was nowhere a regular item of food. When it was eaten, the event was treated as a sacrament carried out according to strict rules (including precedence amongst the guests), and aimed at conveying the virtues of the deceased to the participants in the feast. White persons' flesh was not eaten. The natives complained of its salty flavour, which may have derived from white man's consumption of salt beef, bread and tea.

That their language was ingenious, as were their tools and contrivances – boomerangs, message sticks, stone implements – was not in doubt; nor their aptitude, up to the age of puberty, for acquiring a knowledge of languages other than their own. A new language was said to take two or three weeks to learn. One West Australian black (it was said) took five minutes to learn how to use a sextant; another learnt how to knit in five minutes. The aboriginal's ability to find and follow tracks surpassed that even of the North American Indians. A black tracker on horseback in the police could pursue and track at full gallop.

In his *Old Melbourne Memoirs*, Rolf Boldrewood recorded his high regard for the aboriginal police and their skilful actions against cattle raiders from their own people – a matter of controversy nowadays. Boldrewood was a former squatter, but a humane and generous one. He confessed he often had to smile when he heard 'some under-sized Anglo-Saxon, with no brain power to spare' asserting gravely that 'the blacks of Australia were the lowest race of savages known to exist'. On the contrary, he asserted, they were 'grandly formed specimens of humanity, dignified in manner, and possessing an intelligence by no means to be despised, comprehending a quick sense of humour, as well as a keenness of perception not always found in the superior races'.

Other squatters shared his respect for the natives. They appointed chosen best natives as 'kings'. In return for food, tobacco, woollen blankets etc. the 'king' would promise to keep an eye on his people and prevent them from damaging the white man's property. In her charming and touching story of *Bett: A Little Black Princess*, Mrs Aeneas Gunn describes Bett-Bett's uncle, who was such a 'king', and correspondingly proud of his office.

> He didn't have a sceptre – Australian kings never do; but he had what is quite as deadly – 'A Magic Death-Bone'. If you had been up to mischief, breaking the law or doing anything wrong, it was wise to keep out of his way; for every black-fellow knew that if he 'sang' his bone and pointed it at you, you would very quickly die.

So it happened that from impressions recorded by many very different observers, the aboriginals began to appear in many puzzlingly different guises – disconcertingly honest, maddeningly devious. 'It takes time to understand whether they are telling you the truth or not', wrote Lumholz, 'If you ask them questions, they simply try to guess what answers you would like and then they give you such answers as they think will please you. . . . Yet at other times they could be bluntly and disconcertingly truthful.' A squatter hunting wild turkey in the bush was asked by his black boy, 'Let me go ahead.' 'Why?' asked the squatter. 'I feel such an inclination to kill you' said the boy (he had served faithfully and capably for several years as a shepherd). Their curious sense of humour was renowned. Their war songs were bloody and murderous. Their strength and endurance in their natural environment was legendary, their bulldog courage indomitable. Away from their pathless woods and forest streams they were stranded as helplessly as fish out of water. When the remains of the once large Tasmanian native population was rounded up, and presented with Flinders Island (in the Bass Strait between Tasmania and the mainland), they slowly but surely pined away and became extinct by the twentieth century.

The Government of Australia, wrote Carl Lumholz, 'annually distributes blankets to the blacks on the Queen's birthday'. 'This', he added, gloomily but with a measure of truth, 'is the only thing the Government does for the blacks.' The new century was to put him in the wrong. At the instigation of the official Protector of Aborigines, the government bought some 850,000 acres of land in the Kimberley district as a reserve. Formerly the territory of three large squatters, it was stocked with 10,000 head of cattle and 38,000 horses. It was as much an act of desperation as of concern for the 'sacred duty' to provide for the blacks of which Lord John Russell had written to Governor Gipps nearly a century earlier. For the natives relentlessly went on spearing settlers' cattle and just as relentlessly the settlers wrought what they considered justifiable retaliation. The hope was that the reserve would prove self-supporting and a source of further recruits for bush tracking and the native mounted police. But it was far from being the end or solution of an insoluble problem.

Nevertheless, the years from the first gold rush to the Great War did see important changes in the nation's comprehension and treatment of the native problem. In Florence Gay's words, it had been recognized that the Australian aborigines were the living link between twentieth-century and prehistoric man – 'quite the most interesting nation on the Globe' and 'more allied to Europeans than many much more civilised negritic peoples'. Her hope that the remaining vestiges of 'Black Australia' might be preserved for a further short space also endured; but how that propitious objective might best be achieved was to lead to deep and bitter controversy.

Undoubtedly, the second half of the nineteenth century differentiates itself from the earlier, 'sordid' convict age. Its literature, art, science, music, poetry are still derivative, sometimes naive; except here and there in painting, there are few great or original creative artists or scientists. Yet everywhere there were stirrings of the creative spirit. Australians were beginning to take a pride in their new-found land and find joy and excitement in its possibilities. T.S. Eliot said a number of wise things on the importance of artists of 'the second order', of the need for poetasters to help create the environment in which genius of the first order could flourish: 'It is a perpetual heresy of English culture to believe that only the first-order mind, the genius, the Great Man, matters....'* It was not the least important function of this period of Australian history that it produced so much art of the top second-order, thus preparing the way for better things to come.

---

* T.S.Eliot *The Sacred Wood*, (London, 1982 edn), Introduction.

8

THE ETHNIC ORIGINS OF THE AUSTRALIANS

'Pommies and Paddies and Jocks are we.'   (*Old Bush Ballad*)

The official Commonwealth Bicentenary hand-out booklet for 1988 declares that Australia was 'settled by Europeans' in 1788, a mis-statement soundly rebuffed as 'a load of codswallop' by an indignant correspondent of *The Australian* on 27 February 1985. Australia (he correctly affirms) was settled by the British.

The incident symbolizes an inclination, natural enough but in recent years bordering on a dogma, on one hand to fudge the dominant role of Britain and the British in 1788; and on the other hand to try and deny that far the greater part of present-day Australians are of British (including Irish) descent. Earlier chapters of this and a hundred other books explain, but do not justify, a sense of guilt about certain aspects of Australia's history which seem to some to require the apologetic obfuscation of Australia's origins.

It is not even enough to say, with Dr Crowley, that 'British immigration substantially affected the character of the Australian people.'[*]

Better to affirm, straight out, with Dr Malcolm Prentis that: 'For most of their history the Australian people... were *made up* of British immigrants and their children; and that British immigration largely determined rather than just "substantially affected" the character of the Australian people.'[†] The English and Welsh (he concludes) account for about half of the population of Australia; the Irish some 30 per cent, the Scots about 15 per cent. Such figures cannot be more than estimates. The high percentage of Irish blood is probably correct; the stricter rules

[*] F.K. Crowley 'The British Contribution to the Australian population 1860–1919', in *Studies in History and Economics*, 1954.
[†] Malcolm D. Prentis *The Scots in Australia* (Sydney, 1983).

of the Roman Catholic Church against marriage to non-Catholics helped to keep the Irish more 'separate' as a demographic category. But even this was no absolute rule. Illicit relationships and human nature blurred the lines of almost everybody's genealogical tree. There was also, especially from the mid-nineteenth century, a statistically small but socially important inter-mixture of German, Italian and other European immigrants: this was to be of great importance in the development of viticulture, just as Cornish immigration was of great importance in the tin and copper mining industries in South Australia.

The Convicts

We shall return to the question of specifically Irish influences on Australian society later. For the moment it is enough to say that the largest category – the English immigrants – came from all parts of England but predominantly, in convict days, from London. The convicts of the First and other early Fleets were for the most part hauled out of the gaols of Newgate and other London prisons, and Norwich, Bristol, Lincoln etc., where they were incarcerated for mainly trivial crimes – petty theft, picking pockets and housebreaking – as well as some more serious crimes like forgery, extortion and fraud. Radzinowicsz* makes it clear that while the law ordained the severest possible sentences for a vast range of such crimes, the courts themselves habitually reduced the most stringent punishment allowed by the law to much more humane levels: in particular, to transportation. Hence the presence amongst the transportees of a considerable element of professional training and gentle birth and upbringing. Of these, Francis Greenway, architect of genius, sentenced for forgery, is the best known; but there were many, many others. They included, for example, John Frederick Mortlock, grandson of the Mayor of Cambridge, political dependant of the Duke of Rutland and creator of a bank which became an early and successful branch of the Barclay chain. Other relatives were learned Fellows of Cambridge Colleges, Knights of the Shire, and wives of Bishops.† In 1843 Mortlock was sentenced to transportation for burning down one of his uncle's houses and for the attempted murder of another uncle in Christ's College, Cambridge, of which he was a Fellow. Mortlock was in fact a fairly harmless but deluded character, who spent

---

* *History of English Criminal Law*, vol. I, *passim*.
† See A.E. Clark *Cambridge to Botany Bay: A Victorian Family Tragedy* (Cambridge, 1982).

the rest of his life trying to establish his right to what he regarded as his large share of the family fortune. Amongst his employers, companions and friends in Van Diemen's Land and Norfolk Island was another Cambridge graduate, Mr Mummery (in Mortlock's own words, 'a queer little man in Holy Orders and less than five feet in height'). He had been transported for theft and now, with his wife, kept a school for thirty boys where he had Mortlock as assistant. 'I was' (wrote Mortlock) 'one day helping a gang to unload a ship; on the next, behold me, cane in hand, installed in the Headmaster's awful Chair.'

Oxford, like Cambridge, had its quota of representatives. There was, for example, Henry Russell, recommended, unsuccessfully, by the Chaplain-in-Chief for pardon: he was seconded by the Proctor of the University of Oxford: 'Russell' (he said) 'has been an industrious man in the Colony.'

Mortlock in his *Diary* confessed he did not hear of any military or naval officers, barristers or doctors of medicine amongst his 'society', but it could at least boast 'two protestant clergymen (one a doctor of divinity), several solicitors (one of them an ex-mayor) and a number of Chartists'. To these, later, was added an ex-MP, William Smith O'Brien, an Irish Nationalist whose private house may still be identified at Port Arthur.

The convicts were, in truth, a mixed bag – quiet Scottish prisoners of conscience, truculent Irish political rebels, naughty, adolescent boys training as apprentices in socially useful trades, 'gentleman' labourers, skilled tradesmen gone astray, etc. To Greenway, Sydney will always owe an irreparable debt for its finest historic buildings. Simeon Lord was a rough diamond but a man whose enterprise brought him wealth, reputation and ultimately membership of the Bench. When Andrew Thompson, nurtured by Arthur Phillip, died, he was mourned by Governor Macquarie as a 'highly esteemed good friend' and supplier of 'superior and judicious advice'. The majority of the convicts were a poor lot but, unlike Tennyson's 'poor', they were not 'in a loomp' all bad. Mortlock was amongst the less talented; but of his breed harmless. He spent the last years of his life still in hot pursuit of the crock of gold which had eluded him since his transportation. He died, back at home in Cambridge, in 1882. His last, crowning work of fiction was his Will. This was printed and published. It solemnly and charitably disposed of all the property and money which he – but no one else – still believed to be rightly his to dispose of.

Scottish Immigrants

Not many of the 15 per cent of the Scottish element were to be found among the convicts. An Australian saying is that 'the Scots own all the land, the Irish own the pubs'. Academic sympathizers with the Left have sometimes even ruled out the Scots from the Australian working classes. There was, on the other hand, a far larger percentage of Irish than Scots amongst the convicts and the poor.

The Scots (their critics have often urged, in a way resented by some patriotic Scots) were mostly eminently 'respectable'. They were tough, hard-working, and accustomed to austerity, living, as they had long done, on herrings and oat- or wheat-cakes. For centuries they had emigrated and settled in lands faraway and near: the ubiquitous Scottish engineer was only extrapolating an ancient trend. In Australia their early occupations were often humble – but pointing upwards. Highland shepherds were far from affluent at home; transported to Australia, their skills, toughness, and economy of life often led to wealth as pastoralists and squatters.

However, it was not only in the country and the bush that they made good. In city, town and village the Scot was to be found, as merchant, lawyer or teacher. He took, everywhere he went, the ancient Scottish faith in education. Johnson's reproof to Boswell, – 'No, Sir, the noblest prospect to a Scotchman is the road to England', was early extended to include the road to Australia (as also to Canada). Education (and method) took Scots to be the founding fathers of the Australian press – the *Sydney Herald*, the *Port Phillip Herald*, the *Geelong Advertiser*, the Melbourne *Age* – all were founded or developed by Scots.

At all social levels, but especially in the ranges between middle and top, Scots were to be found. Resolutely they marched forward:

> A race unconquer'd, by their clime made bold,
> The Caledonians, armed with want and cold.

John Dunmore Lang

Scottish, but not only Scottish, emigration would have been less notable than it was without the formidable energies of one of their number who personified many of their positive, to say nothing of some of their negative, qualities. The Reverend John Dunmore Lang (1788–1878), Doctor of Divinity, remains as highly controversial a character in the age of the Bicentenary as he was at the Centenary. To assess the nature of the thirty large volumes of his writings is itself a task that calls for a scholar equal to the author in industry – and perhaps confidence in his own judgement (and rectitude). Lang still awaits an authoritative biographer. His *Reminiscences of My Life and Times*,* begins: 'I was born in Greenock, a seaport town in the West of Scotland, on the 25th of August, 1799. My excellent mother... had dedicated me to the Christian ministry from birth.' He arrived in Sydney in 1923. His 'ministry' entitles him to the distinction of being the founder of the Presbyterian Church in Australia; he was also the most important single figure in the organization of immigration into Australia. For the rest, his life was a long series of quarrels. Before his Church was complete he was already embroiled in excruciating rows with his colleagues and congregation. Wherever he went he left behind a trail of vituperation and abuse of which he was the exponent *sans pareil*. After one quarrel with a Presbyterian colleague he sat down and wrote his enemy's early epitaph in twenty-nine pages. It ended with an assurance that 'it was from no want of inclination but simply from sheer inability to carry it along with him that he left behind him the whole of this most unclerical hoard of 13,000 pounds'.

Upon Caroline Chisholm, a practical, warm-hearted woman, mother of a large family, who devoted herself to the rescue of young women immigrants (especially from Ireland), he poured out the vials of his most savage wrath. To Earl Grey he wrote to warn him that he, and the Lord Lieutenant of Ireland 'were merely the dupes of an artful female Jesuit'. Mrs Chisholm (he declared) was 'silently subverting the Protestantism and extending the Romanism of the colony through the vile, Jesuitical, diabolical system of mixed marriages'.

Yet Lang worked for some better causes – the ending of transportation, the institution of manhood suffrage, land reform, a national system of education and responsible government. Above all, he made no less than nine tedious, arduous voyages to England (and Scotland) and two to America to promote emigration to Australia. In this great cause, he talked and lectured interminably, wheedling money out of governments and the pockets of the rich, stirring up sympathy for the poor Scots, and fomenting suspicions that the poor but papistical Irish were getting away with a better deal.

His friends, such as remained, paid tribute to his heroic efforts; these included Sir Henry Parkes. But many others thought differently: he was 'a noisy liar... mischievous, meddling, unprincipled... a foul-mouthed slanderer'. His carelessness over money landed him in gaol for the first

* Edited D.W. Baker (Sydney, 1972).

time; gross libel on a fellow Scot and future Premier of New South Wales (Alexander Stuart) sent him back for six months on a second sentence of a false allegation of 'malice prepense of the foulest character imaginable ... and a degree of low-bred brutal malignity worthy of only an incarnate demon'.

Rogue, slanderer and unchristian ruffian though he was, this giant and prophet embodied some of the sturdy Caledonian qualities that carried some of the emigrants to Australia from poverty to substantial squatter and business wealth. In his dedication to political and religious causes good and bad (including recurrent bouts of republicanism), Lang bears some resemblance to the Reverend Ian Paisley. There is no doubt he thoroughly enjoyed the polemics that flowed freely from his poison pen, to say nothing of the hundreds of thousands of miles of free travel that came from the pursuit of his ambitions. He was (writes the editor of his *Reminiscences*) 'a born tourist who experienced a continual delight in travelling ... had he been born a century later Lang could obviously have made a comfortable living writing travel books for a generation of trippers.'* The idea is plausible; but Lang was in reality a figure not of the future but of the past: a past not of Calvin but of his successors in whose capable hands Calvinist doctrines became mean and malevolent, and his crusades turned into witch-hunts.

'Caledonia Australis'

Lang's role in the promotion of Highland emigration has recently been told with an eloquence rare in modern Australian historiography and with impressive detailed research by Don Watson.† *Caledonia Australis* was the name that suggested itself to Watson's principal actor in his drama, Angus Macmillan. He was a Highlander from the Outer Hebrides who migrated and prospered, a loyal British Scot, twenty-eight, short and grim, racked with home-sickness and anxiety when he left home for New South Wales in 1837. A year later he was exploring the area between what is now Melbourne and the Monaro Plains with a small party of companions and trackers. Beyond a large river they named the Mitchell (after another Scottish relative of Lachlan Macalister, a Highland emigrant and soldier in a Highland regiment who had prospered mightily since his arrival in 1817), Macmillan sighted a land,

---

* Ibid, Introduction.
† Don Watson *Caledonia Australis: Scottish Highlanders on the Frontier of Australia* (Sydney, 1984).

itself low lying, but with high mountains to the north west and lakes stretching towards the sea on the southern aspect: '... it put me', he wrote, 'in mind of the scenery of Scotland more than any country I had hitherto seen, and therefore I named it at that moment, "Caledonia Australis"'.*

In outline, Watson's story begins with the Highland 'clearances' that followed the 1745 rebellion, leaving an already distressed area in a worse condition than before. Emigration followed: first a trickle, then, by the 1830s, running at 4,000 in a decade. The potato failure of 1846 destroyed the source of more than three quarters of the food of the Highlanders and Islanders. Emigration – to somewhere – became essential. This was where Lang came in. There followed the explorations of Macmillan and others. Amongst the others was the Count Strzelecki, a resourceful Polish émigré who saw the importance of good public (and private) relations for an explorer. He crowned his exploration of the mountains by naming Mount Kosciusko after his national patriot. His carefully nurtured relations with Governor Gipps finally cemented his claim that he, not Macmillan, had discovered what Macmillan had called 'Caledonia Australis': henceforth it was discreetly and officially named 'Gippsland'. A KBE followed in due course.

Macmillan's life became steadily more tragic. He, who had done so much for the aborigines, became (according to Watson) the central engine of their destruction. Yet he was a sincere professing Christian with many acts of philanthropy and mercy to his credit, to aborigines as well as to local Highlanders in distress. His death was the tragic climax of his decline. It was said officially to have been caused by endocarditis; rumour had it that it was drink or suicide.

Don Watson commands a genuine eloquence, a compelling style that combines passion and compassion. It is not so clear that he commands judgement to match. *Caledonia Australis* crams too much into a relatively small space – the Highland 'clearances', the potato famine, the transportation of Highland society, the story of the Highland Scots in Australia, the life of Angus Macmillan, his conflict with Strzelecki, the war between the whites and Kurnai tribes in Gippsland – all this is too vast a task of research and judgement.

One of Don Watson's weaknesses is that he does not pause to ask what would have happened if 'capitalist greed for profit' had not created the possibilities for the transport of food – more food from better farming – and people from areas of disaster to areas of promise

---

* Ibid.

and plenty. The human tragedies of Skye and Barra, as of Gippsland, were it is true, real tragedies, but the essence of tragedy is that no party to it is wholly right and none is wholly wrong. It is not to be 'explained' in terms of economic abstractions and blanket condemnations of 'capitalism' – whatever that may mean.

Less doom-laden impressions of the Scottish immigration may be drawn from other clan and family records. Anne Fairbairn paints a very different picture of white–aboriginal relations in her account of the Munros and Reids, in *Shadows of Our Dreaming* (1983); Steve Fairbairn's *Fairbairn of Jesus* (see below, pp. 233–5) takes a robust, high-spirited and unrepentant view of himself and his ancestors – John Fairbairn of Berwick, sheep farmer, and his son, George, who came to Australia by free passage as 'a shepherd'. By 1870 he was grazing several million acres and claimed to be one of the only four Australians who owned over a million sheep.

It was on the achievements of Scots such as these that the promoters of the Highland Emigration Society built their hopes. They were not disappointed. Between 1852 and 1857 they brought out nearly 5,000 emigrant families. The Queen and Prince Consort headed a list of subscribers which included three Scottish dukes, Members of Parliament, clergy, Mr Rothschild and scores of others. At the Treasury, Sir Charles Trevelyan breathed zealous enthusiasm and pushed the business on, prophesying that 'in five hundred years time there will be aristocratic families of the great Australian Republic who would boast that they could trace their ancestors in the Highland Emigration Book of 1852–3'.

Aristocrats or not, Scots of distinction in high places appeared much more rapidly than Sir Charles allowed. Three early Governors of New South Wales – Hunter, Macquarie and Brisbane – were Scots. Out of a total of forty-eight colonial premiers between 1856 and 1900, twelve were Scots; 29 per cent of Victoria's MPs, 19 per cent of Queensland MPs and around 25 per cent of members of New South Wales's Legislative Assembly were Scots. The first Governor of the Federal Commonwealth (1901–3) was Lord Hopetoun, formerly Governor of Victoria, and an inveterate Scottish golfer.

Irish Immigrants

The Irish immigrants were in every respect different from the English and the Scots. In the beginning they came as political deportees. From 1791 their numbers increased. They were (writes Marjorie Barnard) 'ignorant, credulous and truculent'. And, the (usually genial) Governor

Hunter wrote:

> so turbulent, so dissatisfied ... so extremely insolent, refractory, and trouble-
> some that without the most rigid and severe treatment, it is impossible
> for us to receive any labour whatever from them. Your Grace will see the
> inconvenience which so large a proportion of that ignorant, obstinate and
> depraved set of transports occasion in this country. . . . *

The Irish cauldron bubbled until 1804. There were escape parties (one
set out hopefully for China guided only by a drawing of a compass),
intrigues, plots, secret signs and passwords, nights of terror. Then, in
1804, at Castle Hill, Paramatta, the powder keg blew and a full-scale
rebellion broke out. Like its minor predecessor, it was pathetically incom-
petent and easily suppressed. After that the Irish lost heart; but wherever
there were Irish, there were always imagination, fantasy and excitement.
They brought colour even into the drab world of convict life. Where
they were not under lock and key they formed the spearhead of the
bushrangers. Some bushranging was harmless Robin Hood practice;
other manifestations were brutal and vicious. In recent years the figures
of men like Ned Kelly and Matthew Brady have become the centre of
an Australian cult, especially among Irish hero-worshippers. Their support was ill-deserved. Kelly, Brady and their like were brutal ruffians,
who murdered civilians and police – mostly Irish like themselves – without excuse, scruple or mercy. They have been grossly overvalued.

Fortunately, they were not representative of the Irish of Australia as
a whole. The Irish, were, it is true, poor: their standard of life was
low, as it was in Dublin, Liverpool and Glasgow. It continued low
because their religion and almost total lack of even the most elementary
education kept them poor and illiterate. Their poetry and music lived
on, here as elsewhere, by oral tradition. Little of it was written down.
Yet the flame of Irish national feeling was kept burning. Waverley Cemetery, Sydney, has an arresting monument to the 'men of '98', replete
with embossed heads of the Irish nationalist leaders and inscriptions
in Gaelic. Some of this feeling surfaced violently in 1854 on the 'Eureka'
section of the Ballarat goldfield. According to Raffaelo Carboni, an Italian digger there, this was a 'stronghold of the Irish diggers ... a rowdy
mob'. It was a bad time. Nearly 30,000 hungry immigrants had entered
Australia from Irish ports in the previous year. The famine since 1846
and O'Connell's political campaigns had fanned hatred of England. It
was an age of societies for Australian independence (even J.D. Lang
had stomped the goldfields stirring up support for a republic!)

* Barnard *History of Australia*, p. 236.

Apart from a certain amount of Chartist calls for 'responsible government and land reform', the miners had more pressing local grievances.
These centred around the difficulties and expense of obtaining licences
to dig, and were compounded by the tactless handling of crime and
disorder on the goldfields by the local government, which was ignorant
of the causes of the deteriorating situation. Sir Charles Hotham, the
Governor of Victoria, was an upright but authoritarian Royal Naval
officer who had neither the ambition to be Governor nor the diplomatic
talent to carry out his job. Least of all did he understand that the Eureka
field had a predominantly Irish labour force.

On 29 November, there was a meeting of the so-called Reform League.
Some 10,000 diggers attended. It was an intensely hot day and the proceedings were not cooled by the presence of grog sellers plying the
speakers on the platform with the contents of black bottles. Hearing
news that tempers were rising dangerously, the Roman Catholic Bishop
of Melbourne and other clergy rode for Ballarat to try and calm the
rising passions of the mob. They found that some 800–900 men had
already dug themselves in behind barricades. About half were Irish. They
were armed and led by two pikemen, Michael Hanrahan and Patrick
Curtain.

Nevertheless, by Sunday, 2 December tempers seemed to be settling.
All but about a hundred Irish had left the site, discouraged by their
prospects. Then in the early morning of 3 December, between 3 a.m.
and 4 a.m., a military contingent was ordered into the diggers' camp.
Before any shot was fired by the military or police, the insurgents opened
fire. In the exchanges of the next fifteen minutes, one soldier was killed
and a number wounded. Thirty-four diggers were killed or wounded;
of these, twenty were Irish.

The Governor's action was strictly legal, but it would better have
been avoided. The diggers' action was illegal, but it was understandable
that in a tense situation tempers flared out of control. 'It is', writes
C.H. Currey, 'the Irish stand in the affair ... that lends particular significance to the *émeute* and gives coherence to the drama in which it was
the central act.'* The Eureka 'Stockade' was a horrifying and alarming
incident, but not otherwise of any great significance in Australian history.
No jury could be found which would condemn the rebels. A Commission
was set up – it would have been in any case – which recognized the
need for a reformed licensing system. Peter Lalor, the Irish leader of
the Eureka diggers (a graduate of Trinity College, Dublin), went back

* C.H. Currey *The Irish at Eureka* (Sydney, 1954), p. 87.

into Victorian politics. He ended his career as Speaker of the Victorian Parliament, an office he discharged with great distinction – and punctilious attention to parliamentary discipline.

A high proportion of Australians of Irish origin remained poor and often illiterate. Many would remain so until Roman Catholic Schools were funded like other schools in the twentieth century. This change was the greatest achievement of Archbishop Mannix of Melbourne, who saw that education, or lack of it, was at the root of the Irish problem. Nevertheless, along with many other material improvements, there were social improvements in the conditions of some of the Irish after the mid-nineteenth-century. In the great cities especially, a middle-upper class emerged. A number of its more prominent members surface in contemporary news and popular literature. In Bertram Stevens's *Anthology of Australian Verse* (1906) sixty-five poets are represented. Nineteen are wholly or partly Irish; fourteen are wholly or partly Scottish; one is Welsh; the rest are English or not attributable.

One remarkable Irishman in public life was W.B. Dalley, Attorney-General and acting Premier in the Stuart New South Wales Government in the 1880s. J.A. Froude saw him in action and visited him: '... a short, thick-set man of fifty or thereabouts, with strong neck, large head, a clear steady eye, and firmly shaped mouth and chin. The face was good-humoured, open, and generous. The directions which I heard him giving were quick but distinct, no words wasted... evidently a strong man, but perhaps generally an indolent one... except on extraordinary occasions.... He was a Roman Catholic, but a Catholic of the high cultivated and liberal type of which Cardinal Newman is the chief living representative. He was also a fine Italian scholar, collector of pictures, architect, a widower still living in the shadow of the death of a much loved wife.'

Froude's visit coincided with England's self-created troubles in Egypt and Gladstone's sacrifice of General Gordon. There was therefore every excuse for Australia to leave the mother country to stew in her own juice. However, Australia, much to the surprise of Lord Derby, the Foreign Secretary, and hardly less of Sir Henry Parkes and many others, did not stand aside: she offered to send an 'auxiliary force' to help out the British. The offer was made by Dalley, an Irish Australian, acting in his capacity as Deputy Premier. Even more remarkable, he was supported by large numbers of fellow Irish, headed by Archbishop Moran, the Catholic Primate of Australia, who 'gave a hundred pounds, as an example and instruction to the Irish'.

Among the writers and poets who illuminated the nature of Australia and embellished the culture of its society were a number of Irish origin.

The most talented was probably Bernard O'Dowd, whose example was held up to many aspiring young Irish. O'Dowd, it has been perceptively said, 'wove into the rhythms of verse the thought of a complex and swiftly changing age'. More lyrical and light-hearted was Patrick Molony (1843–94), a leading physician in Melbourne, poet and *bon viveur*; he was the best describer of the joys of life to a civilized Irishman in the 1870s: '... a drive into the country behind a good spanking horse, a good cigar in my mouth, a bottle of whisky under the seat and that girl in red from the Gaiety by my side'. Characteristically, his medical practice receded in size and importance as the years passed. So (sadly) did the Gaiety girls; writing and philosophy occupied more of his time.

On board the SS *Australasia* that took Froude from England to Adelaide, he met an 'unmistakable Irishman... in the unmistakable Irish costume, coat-seams gaping, trousers in holes at the knees, battered hat, the humorous glimmering in the eyes'. He told, with unmistakable vivacity and pathos, his life story: briefly, in Ireland he had won 'fixity of tenure' only to have 'thim banks' take the skin off his back. 'How many hundreds of thousands of his countrymen', Froude reflected sorrowfully, 'will travel the same road?'

Lest it should be assumed that all the Irish bound for Australia travelled the same road, however, it is well to ponder the remarkable story of the Duracks, Costellos, Tullys, Connors, Docherts, Guilfoiles and others.* From 1853 to 1950, fifty descendants of John Durack, of County Galway, settled in Australia. They took up (i.e. pegged out for renting), along with even larger holdings by their partners of the Irish family of Costello, 17,000 square miles of pasture. By 1842 they had huge enterprises at Goulbourn (New South Wales), West Australia and the Victoria River district of Northern Territory, south of the Joseph Bonaparte Gulf. From their original disembarkation, this fertile, indomitable family had multiplied, intermarrying with other Irish families – the Guilfoiles, Scanlans, Costellos, Doyles, Murphys, Brogans and others. Their activities as graziers, wool and meat producers, miners etc. were spread all over this vast continent.

As soon as land could be freely 'selected', Patrick Durack could hardly pass an unclaimed block of land without 'taking it up' for himself, or for a relative or friend, be they already neighbour or still living in Galway or Clare. In 1863 he wrote to an old friend in Ireland of 'a smawl block' of forty acres near Goulbourn available to anybody

---

* Their remarkable story is vividly told in Dame Mary Durack's *Kings in Grass Castles* (London, 1959), its authenticity underscored by the labours of Professor Geoffrey Bolton.

who is not minded to stop or frikened to blister his hands.... So the selection is yers John if ye like to come.... Enclosed find 10 pounds for part passage... and if ye decide not to come keep it for the help ye have all been to poor old grandma... God rest her soul!*

On their trek in 1879 to Kimberley they drove 7,250 cattle and 200 horses for 3,000 miles. It took them two years, putting men, women, children, aboriginal trackers and stockmen to unbelievable tests of endurance, but eventually founded a chain of properties and a dynasty that drove a vast business in Australia and exported as far as the Philippines and South Africa.†

The claim has been made, and widely accepted, that Australia stands at the end of a great Irish 'chain of being', beginning with the Irish convicts of the First Fleet, the Irish rebels of Castle Hill, the Irish working class, the Trade Unions and the Labour Party.‡ This is a not altogether implausible proposition and has certainly made a wide appeal to the kind of people – and these form a sizeable proportion of the population of any country – who like poking about in search of quick, ready-made solutions for difficult, even obstinately insoluble, problems, like the so-called 'identity' of Australia and Australians

This particular version of an 'Australian legend' has been equally vigorously challenged. Dr Prentis has described it as a new-fangled, exaggerated historiographical invention; a kind of left-wing, 'Whig interpretation' of Australian history.§ This is fair comment. That the Irish have made an outstanding contribution to the emergent Australian national character goes without saying: the organization of labour, internally and politically, owes an enormous debt to them. With the reform of education, the nature of their influence has changed, perhaps even grown, even as their ethnic isolation has waned. But throughout much of Australian history, popular opinion has confused an admiration for courage and independence, and sympathy for the underdog, with hero-worship of the gangster. The same instinct that found high merit in Ned Kelly found it in the bankrobber, the horse-thief, the city thug, and the 'larrikin'.

Cyril Pearl has observed in his colourful *Wild Men of Sydney* (1958) that the 'larrikin' was an organic element of Australian life; with 'his

---

* Durack *Kings in Grass Castles*, p. 81.
† Durack *Kings in Grass Castles* and Geoffrey Bolton 'Gold Discovery1851–1880 and Ireland' in *Ireland and Australia*, Colm Kiernan (ed.) (New South Wales and Ireland, 1984).
‡ See Russell Ward *The Australian Legend* (Melbourne, 1966).
§ M.D.Prentis *The Scots in Australia* (Sydney, 1983).

round soft hat, his blatant neckwear, his tight-fitting bell-bottomed trousers, his high, cut-under heels... cheeky aggressiveness, contempt for authority, strident masculinity', he possessed some disagreeable, unacceptable ingredients that are still part of the Australian make-up. They were precursors of the 'spiv', the 'wide boys', the 'bikies' and the football hooligans who are still a social plague in Australia (as in Britain and other places).

Pearl's story (as his blurb rightly says) is one of 'corruption, blackmail, and moral degradation which outmatches Tammanay Hall at its worst'. Throughout its obscene texture of crime the Hibernian threads are close-knit, ugly and unmistakable. Not the least ugly was 'Paddy' Crick, the 'licensed larrikin' of Australian politics who held the record for his number of expulsions from the Legislative Assembly. The principal figure and organizer in this incredible story of violence, perjury and corruption died of drink to the tune of praise from the Irish-born Premier of West Australia, Scadden ('His personality will be missed by whole classes whom he befriended'), while another Irish friend, Mr McLoughlin of Boulder, West Australia, on behalf of the Industrial Workers of the World, lamented his death as a heavy blow to 'the toil-stunned multitudes of Australia'.*

These ugly aspects of Irish Australia did exist; but they should not be exaggerated. They are offset by quite different Irish activities. In other, upper reaches of society and politics, Irishmen of high talent and reputation gradually seeped into prominence. The first six speakers of the Victorian Legislative Assembly were Irish, two of them Protestants. Sir John O'Shanessy, a Roman Catholic, was three times Premier of Victoria between 1857 and 1863; another, Sir Bryan O'Loughlin, was three times Attorney-General and led a ministry in the early 1880s. The Irish also account for four Australian Ministers in the 1930s and 1940s, and the internationally famous Australian artist, Sir Sidney Nolan.†

Dr David Fitzpatrick (of Trinity College, Dublin) has put the Irish legend of Australia neatly into proportion. The Irish immigrants did not come from the most afflicted areas of the old country. They came from areas that were neither specially poor nor specially prosperous. Although many remained poor, there were few barriers to assimilation in Australia of those who were prepared or competent to move upwards. There were no Irish ghettos. And in spite of priestly doubts, many Irish girls attracted English and Scottish husbands. Thus there were, after intensive Irish immigration ceased after 1890, few Australians who were

* Cyril Pearl *Wild Men of Sydney* (Sydney, 1958), pp. 239–40.
† See Geoffrey Bolton in Colm Kiernan (ed.) *Ireland and Australia*, p. 37.

wholly Irish; equally, there were few who were without some Irish blood.* The ethnic Irish consciousness did not disappear, but it was to weaken, especially – ironically – after Archbishop Mannix succeeded in his plan to obtain state funding for Catholic schools. To be of Irish origin did not mean automatically opting for a republic, or opting out of military service in 1914 or 1939. Nor was there any particular association between trade union extremism and Irish sentiment, or any special Irish representation in the ranks of the revived, narrow-minded Australian nationalism of the 1970s and 1980s. This seems to derive from a mixed collection of fanatics and impressionables who are not peculiar to Australia. They are peculiar everywhere. They represent, not the progressive manifestation of conscience, but a reaction against the inevitable, and to them frightening, international interdependence of our age.

9

VIEWS AND PROSPECTS OF AUSTRALIA IN THE EIGHTIES

'The inhabitants of Victoria and New South Wales are as completely subjects of the Queen of Great Britain as any of ourselves. . . .'

(J.A. Froude)*

In the 1880s and 1890s, Australians were – though they did not know it – at the end of nearly half a century of unbroken prosperity and social progress. Into this temporary twilight they advanced, pretty content with their domestic situation, grazing and droving their stock, exporting their wool, importing – mostly from England – the needs of their rising standards of living, mining an increasing range of metals, precious and base, laying railways, building cities. The goings-on in the outside world bothered them little. In 1885 Australian troops were sent to the Sudan, dividing opinion, though not very sharply. The Australian soldier was to earn further laurels in South Africa (1899) and in the Boxer Rebellion in China (1900).

A conference of the states at Sydney in 1883 entered a protest at rumours that the United States was threatening to extend the *diktat* known as the Monroe Doctrine to the Pacific; few Australians, however, were much bothered by this. Even Papua roused positive interest in only one Australian Premier; but neither in New South Wales nor in London did Henry Parkes's grave protest against the German threat to New Guinea cut any ice. In the end, Bismarck edged his Machiavellian way through to 'a friendly understanding'. In Queensland the Premier, McIlwraith – a man of determination – and in London Lord Derby, Lord Granville and the whole amiable Foreign Office establishment stood helplessly by while Germany filched the northern part of New Guinea. Queensland carried on the administration of the rest of New Guinea on behalf of the other Australian States. The whole awkward incident

* *Oceana* (London, 1886), p. 191.

was then put on one side in a tacit agreement that while everybody carried some responsibility, nobody was really to blame. Australia returned to her own business. Britain resumed a questionable role in relation to the Empire; but questions continued to be asked and things were never quite the same again.

Meanwhile, Australia was visited by two English travellers, totally different in age, temperament, education, background, career and ambition. James Anthony Froude (1818–94) 'secured' for himself

> in the closing years of my own life ... a delightful experience. I have travelled through lands where patriotism is not a sentiment to be laughed at ... but an active passion ... where I never met a hungry man or saw a discontented face ... the gold with which the earth is teeming converts itself into farms and vineyards, into flocks and herds, into crops of wild luxuriance, into cities whose recent origin is concealed and compensated by trees and flowers – where children grow who seem once more to understand what was meant by 'Merry England'.

Shorn of the colour and Victorian rhetoric of which he was past master, Froude was saying that he had visited Australia and New Zealand, sailing by way of South Africa and returning by way of the Pacific Islands, Canada and the United States: a journey lasting in all some two years. His voyage ended as it had begun – in his own word, 'brilliantly'. Throughout, Froude remained his usual ebullient, talkative, sociable self. In spite of his advanced age (to which he made continued reference – he was in fact sixty-seven), his mind was clear and his eye bright, missing nothing. He was renowned for his wit and style in conversation. Wherever he went he found, by accident or design, fascinating company, usually well-placed and well-to-do. He made it his business to do justice to them and to himself. His manner was that of the man of the world, of Oxford, the Church (for which he was intended, but had himself rejected), of the London clubs, of publishing and writing circles, of Westminster politics, of the drawing rooms of the rich and grand. Yet Froude was more than a fluent and sociable talker. He was the close friend of that most difficult of critics and historians, Thomas Carlyle, and of Matthew Arnold, Charles Kingsley and all the literary lions of his day. He had shocked and shaken contemporaries on a number of occasions by abrupt, forthright and disconcerting declarations of his heretical departures from orthodoxy in theology, history and politics. He was probably the most popular and widely-read scholarly historian of his day.

By the time he wrote *Oceana or England and Her Colonies* (1886), recounting his world voyage in the two previous years, Froude's political and historical philosophy had clarified and matured. Under the influence of Carlyle, in the light of the events in South Africa and the economic tide in Europe – symbolized by the 'Great Depression' of the 1870s and the growing rivalry of Germany – he had become convinced of the folly and futility of the doctrines of current liberalism. Free trade, *laissez-faire*, popular democracy, Gladstonian anti-imperialism and industrialization were merely leading Britain into dust and disaster. They had destroyed all hopes of ideals and quality in men. In his historical writings on the Tudor age, he was half returning to a Carlylean world of heroes and heroism. Politically and economically he saw Britain's salvation in renewed and strengthened ties of blood, trade, alliance and understanding with her colonies. This was the leitmotiv of his thought, talk and speeches as he went on his travels to and round Australia.

It may, at first blush, seem odd to pair off this bright and successful ornament of English intellectual and political society with a relatively unknown journalistic nobody struggling to earn a living in Grub Street or its Sydney equivalent. Francis Adams's *The Australians: A Social Sketch* (London 1893) was written some four or five years after Froude visited Australia. Its material had appeared as articles in the *Fortnightly Review*. The author took the proofs back from Australia when deteriorating health sent him back to England; the dedication – 'To My Australian Friends – So Many, So Dear' – was written at Christmas, 1892, in Cairo, as he passed through Egypt. His ideas are examined later in this chapter.

Froude's targets were to be Australia's growing cities, Melbourne and Sydney especially, as the centres of government for its dominant States, Victoria and New South Wales. As he approached Adelaide, his disembarkation port, he set out his philosophy of *Oceana*, James Harrington's dream of a perfect commonwealth, a destiny reserved for 'the Scotch, English and Anglo-Irish' nations. Folly had lost America to the English; now there was a great conspiracy to regard South Africa, Canada, Australia and New Zealand as also destined to be lost – but this time thanks to the obstinate, unchanging wisdom of 'economic science'. The world's great workshop would defy competition with the weapons of cheap labour and cheap coal. With world markets conquered by the laws of competitive efficiency, what need for *colonies*?

But in this England designed by the economists and politicians, what would be left for the ordinary people, after the rich had subtracted their 'pleasure grounds and game reserves'? Nothing but towns, crowded with the workmen who were there to create the wealth. Froude's picture of the future England – creeping miles of dreary suburbia, dirty streets, stinking sewers, drink shops, slums and disease – competed well for top marks in nastiness with the nightmare visions of Marx and Engels.

What crime and folly! Even now (cried Froude), intelligent opinion was rebelling against these monstrosities of the politicians and exponents of the dismal science.

> It begins to be admitted that Canada and South Africa and Australia and New Zealand are members of one body with us ... with a free flow of our population into them, we might sit secure against shifts and changes ... the Australian, as a consumer, is more valuable to us than the American. Other nations press us with their rivalries. Expenses increase, manufacturers languish or cease to profit.

And so on.

Such was the political vision in Froude's mind as he approached Adelaide. The following months were dedicated to describing the natural beauties and resources of the world's greatest island, the economic and political opportunities offered by a closer union with its political leaders, peoples and markets. It was a vision neither Liberal nor Tory in terms of party policies as they stood. Both, Froude believed, were wrong. He was a radical, not in the Chartist or socialist sense with a capital 'R', but a patriotic yet international radical with his roots in a British 'Commonwealth'.

Froude passed his few days in Adelaide in deliberately modest political silence. His vision of the future was clear; how it was to be achieved, he freely confessed, was a closed book to him – as yet. He was abroad to try and find answers to his own questions. His business was to listen. On the other hand he lost no time in putting his considerable descriptive talents to work on the natural and man-made attractions of Colonel Light's elegant city: 'Adelaide is already a large child for its years. Its streets are laid out in anticipation of a larger future – broad, bold and ambitious. Public buildings, law courts, Parliament House, are on a grand scale. Churches of all denominations are abundant and handsome....'
He was delighted by city and people – and resources. Burra's great copper mine might be worked out but agriculture, arable and grazing, was expanding and prosperous. Given only a mountain reservoir, 'the plain of Adelaide might be as the Gardens of Ephraim'.

Adelaide's relatively new vineyards provided him with a bottle of excellent Australian hock, bright and pleasantly flavoured. Its abundant oysters and crayfish were delicious; its public gardens a delight, replete with large magpies singing with a low, crooning, melodious gurgle that enchanted many a visitor from overseas. A laughing jackass fascinated him even more, particularly when it boldly drove off an intruding cat. A smelly pond and animals' instincts were less attractive – did they remind him of the politicians at home? If so his eye was quickly diverted by the brilliant wealth of the oleanders, jasmine and passion flowers, and the avenues of dense evergreens – Froude loved and understood gardening. But already it was time to sail for Melbourne.

At first sight, Melbourne impressed him less than Adelaide. It had grown prodigiously, so much so that it bore the marks of haste. The streets were good, the great buildings – Town Hall, University, Parliament, banks, exchanges, superb shops 'gorgeous as any in London or Paris' – splendid; but alongside you could see 'houses little better than sheds'. On the other hand, wealth was visible everywhere, and ambition and self-confidence too.

Froude was the guest of the Governor of Victoria, Sir Henry Loch, a hero of the Chinese War in which he endured the agonies of a Chinese prisoner-of-war camp. A great personality, he had enlarged and beautified the Governor's residence – at his own expense, and it had left him in comparatively reduced circumstances. He was, when Froude met him, up to his eyebrows in a storm over Germany's implication in the affairs of New Guinea. The dispute was warm; worse still, sentiment in Melbourne seemed to be directed, as much if not more against England, and Lord Derby in particular, as against Germany. Froude was not against a political row: he had provoked (and survived) many at home. But he had no wish to spoil his imperial tour by provoking controversy in Melbourne. His concept of 'Commonwealth' did not, in fact, embrace New Guinea. It was not worth fighting for or against. The row, he felt sure, would blow over. He was right.

Off he went on happier errands: to inspect the Municipal Gardens (better kept than the Governor's – Froude was quick to seize on the unusually weighty role of the 'state' in Australia) and the Law Courts (which reminded him of the Four Courts of Dublin), to watch the young ladies of Melbourne energetically playing tennis, and to note the profusion of Victoria's fruit orchards, so great as to bear down and break the branches and leave them lying strewn on the ground with rotting fruit. As for Victorian society, '... party followed party, and it was English life over again ... all was the same – dress, manners, talk, appearance.... They are closely united; they are ourselves.'

Through the Governor he met James Service, the Premier of Victoria, at dinner 'and liked him well ... a spare, lean man with a high, well-shaped forehead ... a manner quiet but dignified; a mouth that indicated a capacity for anger if there was occasion for it'. Mr Service foresaw an Australia of fifty million people within half a century if things continued as they were going. He looked forward to Australian independence – but not yet. In the meantime he hoped England would grow more conscious of the value of her colonies. He deprecated (as did Froude) the language of English Liberal politicians favouring 'Separatism'. If there was too much of it, it would spread to Australians. He resented the way they talked about 'Australians' as if they were just another collection of foreigners and not members of the same family.

Froude was right in his estimate of James Service. Deakin later described him as 'a sturdy, stiff-necked, indomitable, canny Scot'. He had a record of shrewd parliamentary wisdom, and he was by nature a conciliator – not least between capital and labour. Many observers have underrated him; not Froude.

Politically speaking, Froude was much in agreement with all this. Somewhat reluctantly he dragged himself away from politics and went on exhausting tours of the Observatory ('very impressive'), museums, galleries, libraries (ditto, but in the end, so rich and profuse in *objets* of every kind as to leave him bemused). The mighty organ in the great Concert Hall ('as large as the Free Trade Hall at Manchester') impressed him enormously. The organist gave a recital in the afternoon two or three times a week, and 'workmen, workmen's wives and children, ladies and gentlemen, all sorts and conditions call indiscriminately to listen. ... I have rarely heard any organ-playing more severely grand.'

Again reluctantly, off he went once more, this time to Ballarat to see the gold fields. He felt only moderate enthusiasm, but 'in this, as in many other things, I was to find myself mistaken'. Even the mines, with their now colossal investment in great machines and plant, could not fail to impress. Best of all were the journeys through the surrounding countryside with its vast forests of pines, eucalyptus, magnolias and fig-trees. Trees, vast trees, were everywhere, growing like vegetables to heights much greater than the size of trees in England and in a tenth of the time; they grew everywhere – 'in yards and courts, streets and squares, out-topping the chimneys'.

Hardly less wonderful was the reception Froude's party received. At 'Erceldoun' they were entertained on the vast estate by a company of high spirits and intelligence to match.

Good pictures hung round the rooms. Books, reviews, newspapers – all English – were strewed about the tables – the 'Saturday', the 'Spectator' ... the contrast between the scene which I had expected and the scene which I found took my breath away. Here was England renewing itself, spontaneously, in a land of gold and diggers, a land which in my recollection was a convict drain. . . . These were the people whom our proud legislature thought scarcely to be worth the trouble of preserving as our fellow-subjects. It seemed to me as if at no distant time the condescension might be on the other side.

Wherever they stopped to change horses the same experience repeated itself: 'groups of gentlemen were waiting with preparations of fruit and champagne . . . we might have floated in champagne, they were so liberal to us'. The farms were fertile and prosperous, the farmers courteous and independent. Froude could not avoid the thought that perhaps his 'Commonwealth' might form itself in ways he had not before contemplated.

The [English] landed interest itself – gentry and all – will perhaps one day migrate *en masse* to a country where they can live in their own way without fear of socialism or graduated income-tax, and leave England and English progress to blacken in its own smoke.

Such gloomy thoughts were put aside to make way for a last farewell dinner given by the leading citizens of Ballarat. From this further Australian treat Froude eventually escaped ('deafened by the noise, fainting with the heat, wearied with the endless talk of gold – and if truth be told – a little overfilled with champagne'). He was, however, cheered by one new discovery. The Australians in one respect (he found) differed from 'our cousins west of the Atlantic'. The American 'puts you through a catechism of interrogatories. The Australian talks freely, but asks few questions, and does not insist on having your opinion of him and his institutions – a commendable feature in him.'

On to Bendigo, to Sandhurst, to Mount Macedon and another collection of country houses. These were the properties of Sir George Verdon, the popular agent for Victoria in London, a Mr Ryan, 'an Irish gentleman of considerable fortune', and others of that persuasion of the fortunate, well-to-do and intelligent who seemed to grow as part of the scenery wherever Froude set his foot. These were the people he describes best: Froude did not take any greater satisfaction from dwelling upon slums than from dwelling in them. He does, however, offer a glimpse of a sad aboriginal settlement near the famous vineyard of a Swiss winegrower, Monsieur Castella, of whose excellent wines he partook.

The poor creatures were clothed but not in their right minds, if ever minds they had possessed. The faces of the children were hardly superior to apes, and showed less life and vigour. The men threw boomerangs and lances for us but could not do it well. The manliness of the wild state had gone

The slight physique, the quizzical eye, the iron will: Francis Wheatley's portrait of Captain Arthur Phillip, RN, shrewdly suggests the leading traits of his character.

The Captain Matthew Flinders memorial window in Donington Parish Church, Lincolnshire. Flinders is flanked by his two fellow-explorers and close neighbours, Joseph Banks and George Bass.

3. The ruins of the former penal colony at Port Arthur, Tasmania, with the convict-built church in the foreground. The whole of this bold (and notorious) penological experiment, which lasted from 1830 to 1878, is being steadily and faithfully restored.

4. A family of New South Wales natives engraved by William Blake after a sketch by Governor King. King, like many of the officers of the First Fleet, showed both curiosity and sympathy for the natives.

5. Governor Lachlan Macquarie by John Opie. In his twelve years in office Macquarie extended the settlement, initiated a building programme and gave great impetus to convict emancipation.

6. St Matthew's Church, Windsor, regarded by many critics as the masterpiece of the numerous creations by the architect Francis Greenway, who was originally transported to New South Wales as a convict in 1814.

7. Gold discovery transformed Australia. No one recorded the social changes more vividly than Samuel Thomas Gill, who settled in Adelaide in 1839.

8. Nellie Melba, the Melbourne girl of Scottish origins, succeeded Patti as the leading operatic soprano of her day. The unique quality of her singing can still be detected even in the primitive recordings made in the 1920s.

9. Percy Grainger, the master of folk music, conducting the band at the Kneller Hall Military School of Music in 1957: 'highly gifted, handsome and half mad'.

11. Steve Fairbairn, the famous oarsman, painted by D. B. Quinn: 'an extraordinary man, and a great Australian'.

10. Eugene Goossens (right) with Arturo Toscanini. As conductor of the Sydney Symphony Orchestra and director of the music Conservatorium, Goossens raised musical standards in Australia to unprecedented heights.

12. Elaborate cast-iron-work – 'Sydney lace' – was a popular feature of urban architecture in Australia in the second half of the nineteenth century, and is now being carefully restored and preserved.

13. Sir Henry Parkes, Premier of New South Wales five times between 1872 and 1891, by Tom Roberts (1894). This is probably Roberts's best portrait.

14. One of the paintings of the great spectacle of Sydney Harbour by Conrad Martens (1801–78). Martens was part-English, part-German, pupil of Copley Fielding and topographer to H.M.S. *Beagle*.

15. *Spring's Innocence* by Norman Lindsay (1937). Nothing brought this versatile artist more admirers among the avant-garde, or more enemies among the 'wowsers', than his lush, exotic paintings of the female form like this one.

16. *Melbourne Burning* by Arthur Boyd. This great modern Australian artist conveys the sense of cosmic horror as few have done since the medieval primitives.

17. The great bridge, the spectacular Opera House, the towering sky-scrapers – Sydney is today one of the world's most exciting cities, and symbolizes the new economically and culturally expansive Australia.

out of them and nothing had come in its place, nor could come. One old fellow had been a chief in the district when Mr Castella first came to settle there. It was pathetic to see the affection which they still felt for each other in their changed relations.

Then back to Melbourne where Froude stayed in the Melbourne Club surrounded by the very considerable hum of conversation of the members on the subject of New Guinea, Germany and England; on the second day of his stay came news of the fall of Khartoum and the death of Gordon. 'With singular unanimity the colonists laid the guilt of this particular catastrophe at the door of the Liberal leader. Surely he could not survive?'

'Upon the King – all falls upon the King' was Froude's – for once – relatively charitable response; but, on further reflection, he was inclined to agree. 'He [Gladstone], after all, is personally responsible, more than any other single man, for the helpless condition into which the executive administration of the English empire seems to have fallen.'

With difficulty he tore himself away from thoughts of Gladstone (for indeed the Prime Minister's malign influence was becoming an obsession with him), to consider better, more agreeable and, fortunately, nearer matters: in particular the 'exceptional quality' of the principal men of Melbourne, loyal to the English connection, reliable and facing a brilliant future. Froude's only doubt related, again, to opinion in England: '... if our relations are left undefined, and separatism is spoken of as a policy which may be legitimately entertained, they may be capable some day or other of rash acts which may be irreparable'. For the Australians, he did not doubt, were 'impulsive, susceptible, easily offended ... '.

He then went on, by train, to Sydney and New South Wales: less progressive, more conservative, than Victoria. His first duty on arriving in Sydney (as of every properly instructed visitor) was to pay proper tribute to the truly exceptional beauties of Sydney Harbour. This he did in his usual handsome style. Next, somewhat unusually, he had to turn to problems of money; for a somewhat special reason.

He had, with his usual care, arranged his arrival hoping to stay with the Governor of New South Wales (Lord Augustus Loftus). Unhappily, His Lordship was away in the mountains. Froude was therefore met by Sir Henry Parkes, former Premier and now in temporary retirement: '... a tall, fine, hale-looking man of seventy, warm and generous in manner and most anxious to be of use ... '. Alas! here came a snag. In the question of Australian help for the British in Egypt, Sir Henry had taken a line diametrically opposed to that taken by Mr Dalley (see p. 137 above). The possible alternative host was a friend of Parkes, also in opposition to Dalley. In this *impasse*, lodgings were recommended in Macquarie Street ('the Park Lane of Sydney', as Froude aptly described it).

Enquiry unfortunately revealed that the price for a sitting room and two bedrooms was fifteen pounds a week. 'A modest price, admittedly', wrote Froude, 'though at first startling. Wages in Sydney are twice what they are at home; and most other things are in proportion. What in England costs sixpence, in Sydney costs a shilling; money is twice as easily earned, and the result to residents is the same in the long run. I, however, had not come thither to earn wages double or single, and 15 pounds a week was beyond me.' This unexpected impact of the Australian cost of living sent him off to the Australian Club, just off Macquarie Street. There he found the prices more moderate and the entertainment and company everything he could desire; all in close proximity to all the celebrated beauties and practical facilities of harbour and city, amongst the Sydney citizens. These struck him as having

> ... contracted from the climate something of the character of a Southern race. Few collections of human beings on this planet have so much to enjoy, and so little to suffer; and they seem to feel it, and in the midst of business to take their ease and enjoy themselves.

Verily, great and wonderful changes had been wrought in New South Wales since 1850. Froude revelled in the natural and human luxury of Sydney – the 'soft beauty' of the harbour, the gorgeous colours of the public gardens with their exotic birds and curious animals. He dined aboard HMS *Nelson* as guest of the Australian Admiral Tryon and his officers, discussed the problems of naval finance, manning and discipline in relation to an Empire Commonwealth, and gossiped with the most eminent of Sydney's notabilities – Sir James Martin ('irresistible') and the Deputy Governor of New South Wales, Sir Alfred Stephen (kinsman of Sir James Stephen), 'a bright-eyed, humorous old man', over eighty but still full of force. He had been brought up in the Clapham sect, had himself (he recollected) once boxed Sam Wilberforce's* ears for impudence, and remembered how his great-uncle, unable to bear 'the intolerable nonsense talked by old Wilberforce', broke a couple of eggs on his head. His beliefs and habits delighted Froude: they chimed in so exactly with his own. He had broken with the Claphamites. ('He disliked especially the irreverent acquaintance with the intentions of Providence to which conventionally religious people pretend.') After all this,

---

* Samuel Wilberforce, Bishop of Oxford, and adversary of Charles Darwin.

this 'beautiful old man' left the party, to set off for Melbourne, the prospect of a 400-mile journey bothering him as little 'as if he had been starting on his first circuit'.

On other days Froude explored the city and port, now grown rapidly with the aid of 'capital frightened away from England and Ireland', which was flowing fast into Australia, much (he thought) invested in house property in Sydney. A friend of his was making 6 per cent net after all expenses and the property 'must inevitably grow more and more valuable'. More than Adelaide and Melbourne, Sydney had grown *ad hoc*. The houses of the well-to-do were solid and well-looking: the working labourers, by contrast, were housed in sheds 'made of mere boards and corrugated iron, slatternly slums, without any of the plantations and flowers' he had seen in Melbourne.

Sydney was fascinating, but exhausting: 'Late hours, fine cookery, and agreeable society are very pleasant, but less wholesome than one could wish....' There was one other drawback – mosquitoes. What rabbits were to the farmers, mosquitoes were to Froude. They made his life a perfect misery. They added to the restlessness that was overtaking him. It was soothed, but not wholly cured, by a visit to the Governor, Lord Loftus, at his country residence at Moss Vale. He was cheered to find him encouraged by the dwindling influence of the 'Separatists' in England, whose ambition to ditch the colonies had held sway too long.

Back in Sydney he had one more long talk with Mr Dalley. They did not find it difficult to agree on the importance of more, and more urgent, policies to unite and develop an imperial federation. Not the least important move must be to restore 'the English flag' to Australia – 'the one subject [on] which Mr Dalley seemed to speak with bitterness'. It was, he said, English officialdom which had 'for some reason unintelligible to the ordinary mind' insisted that the colonies should use their own flag, and not the English. Froude shared Dalley's indignation to the full:

> Those who are talking and writing so eagerly now about a confederated empire should insist at once, and without delay, that when any colony expresses a desire to fly over its ships and forts the old flag of England, neither childish pedantry nor treacherous secret designs to break the empire into fragments shall be allowed to interfere with a patriotic and honourable purpose.

Froude left Sydney with only one reservation about its people. They were courteous, energetic, attentive to health, sanitation and engineering;

they displayed a growing taste for art and creative aptitudes in painting, engraving and the like. They had one good poet – Gordon, 'an inferior Byron ... desperate, dissipated, but with the gleams of the most noble nature'. But these, in the last analysis, were matters of pleasure or material comfort. Otherwise, like a large part of the civilized world: 'they have no severe intellectual interests. They aim at little except what money will buy: and to make money and buy enjoyment with it is the be-all and end-all of their existence.' On this sombre note, and dispensing only some not very practicable proposals for constitutional machinery to further the federation of the colonies, he departed for New Zealand.

Neither Froude's ideas nor his style brought him many laurels in Australia. The trend of the times was more towards domestic than imperial federation. Such Australians as read *Oceana* were as likely to be put off by his apparent preoccupation with those in high places as attracted by his praise of Australia, its natural beauties and the attractive qualities of its peoples. In England, his reception was also muted. He seemed to many – they were quite correct – to be neither Liberal nor Tory at a time when party allegiances were beginning to harden into irreversible dogmas. His vision was noble and is not less so for proving only very partially attainable. His assessment of the men in high office he met and talked with – Dalley, Service, Martin, etc. – was sound. The goodwill that runs through *Oceana* is undeniable. His account goes a long way to explain how English Liberal pedantry wounded Australian susceptibilities to an extent that has never been quite forgotten or forgiven. At the very least, Froude did no harm; at best, *Oceana* remains on record as a warm-hearted, spontaneous tribute to a new country and a new people, written without condescension or pomposity. If its proposals were – as he himself admitted – vague, they were intensely felt and held with deep conviction. A practised politician or a professor of constitutional law might have spotted more of the pitfalls facing *Oceana*; it is unlikely, however, that they would have injected into it a fraction of the feeling it was given by Froude.

Francis Adams

'Feeling' was one of the qualities shared by Froude and our other observer of Australia in the 1880s, Francis Adams (1862–93), who lived there from 1884 to 1892. Like Froude he came from a family background of professional stock, but unlike Froude's, it was partly Scottish. His education, unlike Froude's, was patchy and irregular. Cursed with tuberculosis, he could – again unlike Froude – be rancorous, abusive, jealous and in every way difficult. Such moods alternated, according to his state of health, with interludes of rhapsodic charm and affection. He was romantic and impressionable, and he was sometimes almost able to do justice to his aspirations in writing; but as we shall see, not quite. His poetry was anaemic, and his prose too often became the victim of his unstable emotions and broke up into almost unintelligible fragments, lacking cohesion, syntax and even grammar.

In spite of this, his account of *The Australians** is frank, shrewd and colourful. Not all his biographical sketches were fair, or even humane. He had a flair for the prophetic, which happened to turn out accurately on McIlwraith, but missed the mark badly on Samuel Griffith, whose high promise he failed totally to discern. James Service he underrated as much as he overrated McIlwraith. Adams had strong instincts about individuals but they often overpowered his judgement. He was powerfully attracted to individuals whom he felt he resembled. In his inconsistency he strongly resembled Archibald, creator of the *Bulletin*, whom he warmly admired and for whom he worked. Archibald was also a brilliant neurotic. His leftish, folklorish philosophy was socialist, anarchic and republican. He boycotted the centennial festivities of 1888 because he hated the convict system (long since dead, but not for Archibald). In his fifties he went hopelessly mad, but recovered some years later to enjoy a rich, socially and aesthetically ambitious old age.

It is difficult to imagine two more strongly contrasting personalities than Francis Adams and Froude. Adams was young, passionate, radical, but often confused. His eloquence is often the eloquence of Hyde Park Corner, not infrequently libellously frank, verging from time to time on the incomprehensible as his syntax disappears with a shriek. Was this simply the shock of recognizing a society and culture which seemed (to Adams) to have eluded the understanding of both English and Australian observers? Or was it, perhaps, the feverishly overheated temperament of a consumptive, driven on by the fear that it was already almost too late, running anxiously to declaim his revelations to the world? Whichever it was, *The Australians* is the work of a minor Victorian prophet, confused, labyrinthine, disordered, but never without a kind of fire in his belly.

Froude's *Oceana* may be uncomplimentary to English governments, and political and economic theorists and practicians at home, but it was only uncomplimentary or pessimistic in moments, permissible for

* (London, 1893)

an oldish man tired by too much travel, too much company and too many champagne dinners. Froude enjoyed life, company, people and new scenery. His smooth descriptive prose and the witty conversation for which he was renowned were the rewards he had won by overcoming his original shyness as a young man.

Adams, in *The Australians*, reveals an observer and writer still entangled in a never-ending search for a philosophy of history, politics and society, and a simultaneous quest for an adult mode by which to articulate the elusive flow of ideas which teemed out of his imagination. Strangely enough, in spite of the gulf that separated him from Froude, some of their perceptions of Australia and Australians are not so far from each other. (See below, p. 155.) Adams' essay on Gordon – poet of the bush – and Marcus Clarke – prosifier and gambler of the city – is typical, in its mingled clumsiness and perception: significantly, for it was the bush where he sought and found the true heart of Australia. Gordon was his hero, the key to the younger Australians and the age of colonial democracy. Yet the essay, with its ready-made literary epitaphs on Musset, Baudelaire, Leopardi, Heine, Clough, etc., never rises far above clever schoolboy stuff. His poetry is similarly jejune and adolescent. His best efforts were to be achieved elsewhere, in his observations of contemporary Australian society. Usually tinged with the scepticism and bitterness which masked his nature, they are always worth reading. They make useful comparison with Froude's almost euphoric impressions of Australia and its people; and his basic optimism as to their future in the world.

I do not know whether Adams ever met Froude. It seems unlikely, for neither in Australia nor their native England did they seek to mix in the same circles. Froude was not a snob; he simply found his natural habitation in, or next to, the corridors of power, wealth and influence, where he was at ease in Zion. Such visits as Adams may have made to those regions were distressingly disturbing to him. He disliked most of the inhabitants, and lacked both the social grace to conceal his feelings and the sense of humour or wit that might have enabled him to squeeze some malicious amusement out of the *haut monde*. He simply viewed it all with surly distaste.

Included in his disapproval were in fact, Froude himself, *Oceana*, and a number of the important personages (for example, Sir Henry Parkes) on whom Froude had expressed all too rash and generous opinions. Amongst the culprits for perpetrating the fatal lack of mutual understanding which Adams identifies (correctly) as being the gravest danger to their future relationship, Froude is accorded a high place: he had misled

'the Anglo-Australians of London' into believing *Oceana* to be 'a historical record'; 'Englishmen' (wrote Adams) 'lost their heads over the Contingent [for Egypt] and the imaginary denizens of Mr Froude's *Oceana*;
the Anglo-Australians followed suit.' More specifically, Froude had
encouraged readers to suppose that *Oceana* had writers on a par with
its other wonders. In consequence, Gordon had suffered, while 'a throng
of mediocrities' monopolized attention, and so on.

None of these allegations by Adams holds water. Froude had been
pretty fair in his judgement of Gordon. He had said little or nothing
in favour of the poetasters of the traditional 'Anglo' school. Adams'
remarks must be explained either by carelessness or perhaps by jealousy
– natural but unattractive. What, at a distance of a century, is remarkable,
is how often Adams found himself in agreement with Froude's ideas
about Australia whenever he chose to discuss those aspects of Australian
life on which Froude had touched a few years earlier. Thus he ordains
that 'the only possible union between Australia and England, which
shall contain the elements of solidity and growth, is one based on the
principle of "Alliance not Dependence"'.* Yet Froude had gone at least
as far as this, perhaps even further, by proposing for Australia, if need
be, 'a president elected by the people' as the pivotal alternative to a
governor appointed by the Crown.

Froude had glimpsed only one deficiency in Australia: what he called
a 'lack of severe intellectual interests'. Life consisted of the pursuit of
money and the pleasures money could buy. Here, as far as one can
judge, Adams was of precisely the same mind. One whole chapter (3)
of *The Australians* is devoted to expanding precisely Froude's theme.
'Disinterested study' is unknown; by 'education' is understood only
'primary education'; universities are merely 'examining bodies'; 'history'
is identified with religion and therefore excluded from the curriculum;
'the sense of poetry of the past and the solidarity of the race is rapidly
being lost to the young Australian'. To the outer world, the average
Australian is 'either indifferent or hostile'. 'Importations' from foreign
lands are resented; in spite of this, European trivialities of fashion are
welcomed in a country created by 'muscle', the pick-axe and the shears.
Yet the result is that the two great classes of capital and labour are
ranged in the bitterest hostility. Cliques everywhere monopolize the political power in the capital cities. To own *land* is 'the thing'. 'Of intellectual
life, any more than spiritual life, there is little or none, and the social
life suffers accordingly.' (Could Froude have said more?) For Adams,

* Adams *The Australians*, pp. 6–7, 98–100. Froude, *Oceana* 1886), pp. 195–6.

the one really talented and original outcome of the Australian press was the *Bulletin* (to which of course Adams was a contributor), but even *its* literary criticism was that 'of clever, sixth-form schoolboys and imperfectly-educated pressmen ... '. Again, Froude could not have said more. 'It [the *Bulletin*] is the only mouthpiece of originality in Australia.' Only in Sydney had the 'narrow-minded and insignificant horde' (of old English officialdom from convict days) allied with the big squatters ('the pure merinos') to build a university imitated from the old Oxford model. Australia's spiritual companion and guide was the ignorant and superficial 'pseudo-intellectualism of the cleverer journalists': ' ... it would seem as if one could not but conclude that "Culture" at the Antipodes is in as bad a way as "Society". The rest was all opera-bouffe and football matches.'

There was only one saving grace to the crude provincial hedonism of Australia and that was music, which was popular in both Sydney and Melbourne. According to Adams, 'in neither case is the article in demand very elevated; but one is grateful nowadays to find average people really liking anything'. Who was the bigger snob – middle-class Adams or upper-middle-class Froude? It is sad that Adams did not live to hear Melba.

The most readable of Adams's chapters are those given over to describing the different groups in society: leading politicians ('the Men of Mark'); the squatters; the selectors; the bush people; and, finally, the villains of the Land Question. The topics handled seem to be in order of ascending importance. For example, few of 'the Men of Mark' seem to be more than corrupt and fraudulent dummies.

Take, first, that 'memorial of the past', Sir Henry Parkes, 'the only Australian name ... in anyway familiar to the general run of Englishmen'. Adams does not disguise his distaste and distrust of that 'Aristophanic Cleon ... large and gross in build, with a great mass of white hair ... a piping treble ... the tedious vulgarity of the rhetoric ... egotism as empty as ... oppressive. Of late ... often feeble and languid ... the not unpathetic image of a big, sick anthropomorphoid ape.' Yet a born fighter, of superb courage, 'he survived a Moscow and eluded a Waterloo'.

Then there was the 'shrewd, antique sagacity' of Mr Service, 'the canny, senile Scotchman'; Sir Graham Berry, 'the little ex-grocer and violent cart-spouter'; Mr Groom, 'the eternal apostle of shopkeeping respectability, despite the most untoward early accidents ... '; Mr Pattison, 'the Mount Morgan millionaire, who stepped from behind his butcher's block into power and place'; and numerous others. Adams' most concentrated venom is reserved for Sir Samuel Griffith, the son of a Welsh

... lower middle class, little dissenting minister [himself] terribly wanting in frankness and generosity ... power is his only lust, variety his only weakness ... this cautious, cold-blooded lawyer ... committed to the most incommensurable schemes of what, even in Australia, is called out-and-out Socialism.

Adams clearly regarded him as dangerous: not least to the one politician for whom he professed high regard: Sir Thomas McIlwraith, Premier of Queensland, and for Adams, 'the only public man in Australia ... one could call great'. It is a good sketch of the hero of the New Guinea crisis – clumsy in person and speech, hesitant and stuttering on his feet; when seated, with 'the stolid passivity of an Indian idol cut in bronze ... the hawk-like eyes glancing and penetrative'. He had 'the element of the miraculous ... Caesar had it; Napoleon had it ... they knew what it was to risk all and win by risking'. For Adams, McIlwraith was Australia's man of the future; but 'what will local politics, business complications and the savagery of the climate do with him' before he could come to power? His presentiment was, again, uncannily correct.

Among non-politicians, he sought in vain for great men. The sheep millionaires might graze hundreds of thousands of sheep over millions of acres; they were still dull men. The Great Strike and conflict with the shearers might make them more interesting in five years' time. Among the journalists, only Archibald of the *Bulletin* had true genius. The rest had become mere business managers. So he comes to the land and the bush; to the squatters, selectors and shearers.

The 'squattocracy' he saw in sad retreat, ruined by reckless overstocking of their pasture, equally reckless expenditure, and finally by drought. The old profuse hospitality, the hunts and dances and four-in-hands were now only a dim tradition: the squatter-kings were no more. Their land had passed to the banks and syndicates. These were now the bosses. If he was worth keeping, the one-time proprietor might be kept on as a manager. A few lucky ones survived by turning themselves into urban capitalists, chairmen of companies, or politicians. The unlucky rode round their former properties as agents, 'morose and surly'. The bush, droughtland, was a cruel place.

'Pastoralism', Adams concluded, 'can now be made to pay on a vast scale, but the chances of failure keep growing steadily greater than those of success.' Added to the natural hazards of grazing were now the 'hot fits and cold fits of elation and panic that periodically afflict the capitalistic "bosses" in town'.

His generalizations were sound. A century after he wrote, the control of the great cattle empires of Northern Australia was concentrated in ten great companies. Some were very old: the Australian Agricultural Company, for example, owning 55,000 square kilometres and over 200,000 cattle, dated from 1824. It is a public company. The Kidman Holding Company is a mere century old; it owns 117,000 square kilometres (as large as England) and grazes 120,000 cattle. It was founded by a remarkable entrepreneur, Sidney Kidman.

Kidman saw that the secret of success was water supply. He sited his cattle and sheep stations on three great West Queensland rivers which caught the floodwater from the northern catchment area. It turned arid wasteland into bush grazing, bright with clover, saltbush, blue bush, cotton bush and cane bush herbage – a colourful, fattening paradise, the best in Australia. All in all, ten great companies, private and public, now graze well over a million and a half cattle on 130 stations, covering nearly half a million square kilometres. They produce vast quantities of beef for domestic consumption as well as a large export trade for overseas.

Even less happy than the fate of the squatters was that of the 'selectors', the sad creation of much legislative effort which since the mid-nineteenth century had aimed to break up the vast rural empires of the squattocracy. This attempt to form 'what used to be called in England a yeoman class [of small farmers] ... has utterly failed'. In Queensland, where the Act of 1884 permitted the selection of farms of 160 acres, and where the land was rich, there were barely any takers. The condition of the small cultivators in Australia seemed worse than that of either the four million peasants of France or of the petty English farmer.

> Both have enough to eat and to clothe themselves and reasonable pleasures of social life. Neither is afflicted with that dreadful isolation which makes of so many selectors' hours intensified, if more vulgarised and depraved samples of life drawn with a pen of fire in *Wuthering Heights*.

The average selector's existence was spent in the exercise of unremitting and monstrous toil. The best were driven down into the shearing class, the worst 'dip into wilder trades and risk the gaol ... of culture and refinement, so feeble and jejune a growth in the richer and better-educated folk, there is in them no trace whatever'.

In their state of transition, they could not profit by the ideas of 'union combinations' and socialism, which were helping to regenerate the shearers. The wretched 'selector' had nothing but a savage malignancy for 'the unions': he would rather throw in his lot with his hereditary enemy – the squatter – than admit the equality of the new democracy. Adams drew a parallel between the selectors and the 'mean whites' of the southern states of America who had supplied the rank-and-file of their armies to Jefferson Davis and Lee.

The conclusion – for Adams – was plain to see: there was no room in Australia for a class of pastoral *tenuiores*.

> There is no room for any class intermediate between the large wool-growers and the shearers.... The trend of things is relentlessly towards huge monopolies of capital and labour, and these petty intermediate classes, striving to combine a little of both are foredoomed to failure and ultimate extinction.

So to 'the Bush people', the one powerful and unique national type yet produced in Australia, and the *'fons et origo* of the New Race'. They had some features in common with the small squatters, managers and selectors, but the resemblances were slight. It was 'in the ranks of the shearers, boundary riders and general station hands that the perfected sample [of the bushman] must be sought'.

The society of the bush had changed out of all recognition since old colonial days. Wire fences had ended the old romantic pastoralism with its shepherds, abiding in the fields, keeping watch over their flocks by night. The shearer could no longer be classed with the woebegone, happy-go-lucky swagman or sundowner, spendthrift, profligate, mortgaging future earnings to buy liquor, living from day to day. 'The Shearer of today ... arrives on a horse, leading another, and with a bank-book in his pocket ... a member of a union.' He has political views. His letters and newspapers await him at the 'sheds' in which he works nomadically but regularly. The political discussion of the shearers was 'astonishing in its earnestness ... showing a grasp of general principles and their application to the questions of the hour ... '.

No politician had yet emerged who could hoodwink the bushmen. They it was who had made the 'Queensland for the Queenslanders' cry into a triumphant movement, and halted the invasion by the Chinese Coolies: ' ... today the cry of Australia for the Australians [white!] owes to them its widest and deepest national application'. So far the electoral law had thwarted their aim of political solidarity; but ' ... now, direct representation embraces the theory of applying their socialistic ideas to the framing of laws and they are determined to try it'.

Even to contemplate this bush society was to be dazzled by its mingling of all the social virtues – charity, kindliness, fearlessness, courtesy, neighbourliness etc. – that shamed not only urban Australians but the English back home. Among their sometimes odd collection of qualities, Adams made observation of one that was perceptive and indubitably correct.

'The love of music seems innate in all Australians and its future effect upon the nation is incommensurable.... If you ask these [bush] children to sing, they stand up, with bright unabashed faces, and warble like birds.'

His romantic vision finally outrunning the abilities of prose to encompass its glories, he fell back on quoting in full the *Sick Stockrider*, a poetic invocation of the spirit of the Queensland shearer and drover. It had then just appeared anonymously in the *Bulletin*. (It was later to be acknowledged as the work of Andrew ('Banjo') Paterson.)

The heroes established, Adams passed on to the villains and their plots, in other words, the landlords and their plans for an increased population to keep the cost of labour cheap. He started with the agitation for responsible self-government in Western Australia. This in turn prompted all the

rich, colony-trotting lords and capitalists ... Lord Brassey [the railway tycoon] ... the late-lamented Duke of Manchester, and the late-lamented Lord Carnarvon [an ineffective former Colonial Secretary and dupe of Germany in the business of New Guinea] to doubt how the inhabitants of that area (more than 16 times the size of England and Wales) could be trusted to look after such a vast territory.

Had Lord Carnarvon ever told anybody that while Colonial Secretary he had purchased the lease of 64,000 acres of the best land in Australia for one penny an acre, with option to buy, whenever he chose, at two shillings and sixpence an acre? Did not the late Permanent Under-Secretary of State, Sir R.W. Herbert, do exactly the same and forget to mention the fact? What of the three others who carved parcels of up to 145,000 acres apiece on similar terms? To say nothing of partnerships and companies which, all told, owned two and a half million acres, culminating in the two giant land-grabbers – one company (unnamed) owning four million acres, and the Union Bank of Australia owning just under eight million acres. Nor did Western Australia suffer alone: in Queensland, four private owners commanded some three quarters of a million acres. In all (Adams alleged), two million acres of Queensland were owned by fifteen land-grabbers.

The result? By strange accident, railways, though state-owned, 'have a habit of running into the estates of these millionaires'. The land on either side of any railway rose swiftly and steeply in value from the day the railway received parliamentary sanction. All this unearned increment, millions of public money, had quietly slipped into the pockets of the great landowners. Thus Australia was rapidly becoming the land of a handful of millionaires and a helpless, subservient class of 'mean whites'.

So far, the argument, though extravagant and of doubtful accuracy, held together: it pointed to the emergence of the Shearers' Union as the vehicle of moderation and reason in the corrupted world of Sir Henry Parkes's politics. But at this point everything fell to pieces. Union indecision and weakness in New South Wales and Victoria, and a corresponding violence and over-confidence in Queensland, had led to total rout in the Great Shearers' Strike. The consequence was 'a complete upset of social balance', with disagreeable results. The capitalists provoked the strike 'and from the impartial point of view, they did so justly'. They were able, in spite of labour scarcity, to round up enough men to replace up to 50,000 shearers! Yet 'the average Australian has the good sense to thoroughly believe in a free and independent labour', and knows that neither freedom nor independence could be maintained for a day without the aid of unions.

Bewildered (as well he might be) by these quantitative economic and social problems and his self-contradictions, Adams leaves the bush and returns to the less complex pleasures of politician-bashing (English politicians especially) and the denigration of imperial 'or any other sort of federation' that attributed any power or significance to Gladstone, Disraeli, Salisbury, Bright or any other party hacks who ran the meaningless game of politics for the witless mother of nations. England was 'a little foggy island in the North-West of Europe completely occupied with her own affairs'.

Had he been less preoccupied with utopian dreams and (like Froude a few years earlier) more interested in the price of his hotel room, Adams might have concentrated his attention on the policy of immigration and the fall in wages which had accompanied the end of the Great Boom and the collapse of the Great Strike. Instead, he fell floundering in a welter of wild denunciations, rantings and split infinitives, all in the style of the short punch-sentence later popularized by Lord Beaverbrook and the *Daily Express*.

Nevertheless he managed to retain some of the prophetic perception which, at his best, was his outstanding quality. He stuck to his point that the capitalists' victory in the strike would tend to bring about or underpin what they had denounced as the certain consequence of a union victory – conditions of monopoly. Second, since Australia was innocent of the kind of prejudice against labour that existed in England, the pressure of public opinion would be towards conciliation and compromise.

Social reform would be resumed. Third, if further bitterness and protracted contests could be avoided, the chief energy of labour could be transferred from the unions to the houses of assembly and operated there by their representatives.

Like most philosophers, idealists and prophets, Adams was at his best when he stood a respectable distance from the problems he tried to solve. He was stronger on principles than on their execution or administration: for these his talents were nugatory. Like most journalists, he reflected the ideas he picked out of the air, or more particularly the gossip and argument he heard in the office of the *Bulletin* and the circles of its contributors and sympathizers. He described himself as 'a party-less man'. It was an apt description, but the reasons for it being so were not what he thought they were. He was partyless not so much because he rose above party, but because he was unable either to analyse, or even face, the realities of political life.

Adams differed from Froude, in that the latter knew and accepted his limitations as an operator in the real world. He stuck to principles and rhetoric, and avoided talking about things he did not feel he understood. The major difference between the two men as historical witnesses is that Froude was preoccupied with the Anglo-Australian political relationship; internal development, political, economic or social, ran a poor second to external relationships and sentiments. Hence his title, *Oceana*. Adams was obsessed with the social, internal, evolution of his *Australians*. His stay in Australia was longer than Froude's. Had his health been better he would probably never have gone back to Europe. At sixty-seven, Froude was still the (almost) indestructible tourist, quick of wit, keen of vision, his antennae sensitive to every change in the environment in which he happened to be moving. Adams was essentially the recorder of the stuff of politics round the parish pump – a vast parish, an important pump, but in spite of all, a parish pump. Which is what, in many respects, Australian affairs were to continue to be.

Typical of Adams's inconsistencies is the reversion, in his post-script to *The Australians*, to Lord Carrington and the Anglo-Australian relationship. Elsewhere he had expatiated on the futility of the English politicians whose arrogance and ignorance of Australia had wrought such havoc on the relationship with a young nation struggling, against all odds, towards a more democratic and egalitarian future. In the last few pages of his post-script he suddenly discovers a 'solitary exception' to his excoriating judgements: it was Lord Carrington, Marquess of Lincolnshire, thoughtful, generous and wise, and backed by the experience of five years' residence in Australia as Governor of New South Wales.

Carrington, and Carrington alone, had discovered that 'the idea of Nationalism – a very different thing from Separatism – is growing and increasing in Australia'. Five 'happy years' had taught him that 'the people of Australia ... ask that they should be under no more restraint or control by the Governor, as to purely local affairs, than the people of England are by the Crown'.

Here, suddenly, was a man of candour and intelligence, the most successful of Australian Governors, a man whose loyalty to England and the Empire was 'beyond all question ...'; yet he challenged both Tories and Liberals in their autocratic policies which resembled English policy towards Dublin more than it approached a true concept of Commonwealth. Both parties (he said) were sadly to seek. Yet it was not too late: there were those (like himself, and Adams) ready to work in harmony with the times, 'poor, partyless individuals', who were ready to accept a compromise between Disraeli's jingoism and Gladstone's *laissez-faire*. Why couldn't the 'Colonial Question' be put outside the narrow sphere of English party politics? He ends with a 'dream of the solidarity of mankind'; without this, the English nation was doomed to condemnation for all time.

By the end, the dream had dissolved into misty generalizations and nothingness. Francis Adams had scored his points; the first priority was a united Australia, united in itself and against its external enemies. England could survive, provided it recognized Australia's right to an egalitarian and democratic future, led by its noblest elements – the bushmen. This was the radical stuff of the *Bulletin*. Adams had neither time nor, perhaps, stuffing to advance further. He committed suicide in London in 1893.

Froude, meanwhile, had reached home, to be invited in 1892 by Lord Salisbury – it was a Crown appointment – to accept the Regius Professorship of History in the University of Oxford, an invitation he accepted.

In Australia, conventions and referenda between 1887 and 1899 had revealed a clear trend towards moves to unite the separate states into a single federation. The Act, when it came into being on 1 January 1900, was based on the firm understanding reached between the states that they would yield to the federal government only the powers they were willing freely to yield; what they chose to withhold they withheld. As an eminent Australian historian wrote:

The Australian democracy chose its own men from its own ranks and set them to build for it a constitutional house to dwell in. Nearly all the leaders of the Convention were native born, and had been schooled in their own land. All were of British origin. Amongst the fifty names of the members, not one is of foreign derivation.*

Within the new federation, important domestic developments continued. The economy slowly recovered from the effects of the depression, droughts and rabbit plagues of the '80s and '90s. Labour and unions continued to organize themselves for the transfer from industrial issue status to full parliamentary representation. By 1914 the Labour Party was ready to take power, on the eve of the outbreak of the greatest war the Empire had ever faced.

In a sense, the course of events justified the concerns of both Froude and Adams – the first for the continued solidarity of the British Commonwealth of Nations, the second for the continued social and economic progress of the States of Australia towards self-governing democracy and a more equal society of men and women.

The name of Francis Adams was forgotten by most people both in Australia and Britain. Froude, continued, from his Chair at Oxford, to charm and impress most of his readers and listeners. Only a relative handful of pedants complained of his habitual inaccuracies, and he was recognized as being in the ranks of the true scholars.

Froude's ideas on imperial relationships may have been cloudy and confused. Nevertheless they helped to reflect the gradual change that had overtaken many thinking peoples' notions in the 1870s and 1880s. His precise contribution to the continuation of the process cannot be quantified, but that is no reason to underestimate the effect of his advocacy. The fatalistic ideas of the 'separatists' had been starkly set out by Frederic Rogers (later Lord Blackford), Permanent Secretary of the Colonial Office in an autobiography. Rogers saw the basic duty of the Colonial Office to be to preside over the demise and dissolution of the Empire. His remarks provoked the explosive Chief Justice of Victoria, George Higinbotham, to compare the Empire to the Athenian Republic, of which it had been said that it was in reality governed by a poodle; the poodle belonged to the courtesan of the tyrant; the poodle ruled the mistress; the mistress ruled the tyrant.

> The million and half Englishmen who inhabit these colonies, and who during the last fifteen years have believed they possessed self-government, have really been governed ... by a person [he might have said poodle] named Rogers. He is the Chief Clerk in the Colonial Office ... he inspires every minister who enters the department, year after year, with Colonial Office traditions, Colonial Office policy, Colonial Office ideas.

* Ernest Scott *A Short History of Australia* (Oxford and Melbourne, 1947), p. 404.

Froude cannot be credited with the extinction of this Colonial Office 'Yesministerism'. But he certainly gave heart to those who opposed it. Without him and those he helped to turn away from separatism, the growing aspirations to domestic unity in Australia might well have been accompanied by greater Australian scepticism about the merits of remaining inside the Empire; for the following decades were to uncover new strains and stresses on what Henry Parkes had called 'the crimson thread of kinship'.

10

AN EVOLVING RELATIONSHIP 1900–18

'Commonwealth ... will give to them ... in their corporate unity, a freedom of development, a scale of interests, a dignity of stature, which alone and separated they could never command.'

(*Herbert Asquith*)*

The Australian settlement had never from the beginning been a place of unbroken harmony, peace and sweet reasonableness. Its quarrels were not solely the consequence of the 'tyranny of distance'; after all, relations between the nations who lived cheek by jowl with one another in Europe were hardly a model of concord. The peace had been more often disturbed by rifts within the lute – convicts against free settlers, 'currency lads' (Australian-born) against 'sterling lads' (English-born), squatters against 'selectors' and vice-versa; the Irish against marines. Governors were invariably unpopular, not only with those they were supposed to govern but with their masters in London. Marcus Clarke, better known as the author of the famous convict novel *For the Term of His Natural Life*, predicted that the Australia of the future could be cut in half across the middle, the southern part a Republic, inhabited by a race of men 'fretful, clever, perverse, irritable ...'.

Nationalism

There were already many such men about by Clarke's day; they included the redoubtable Dr John Dunmore Lang. He, like many others, took it for granted that the separation of Australia was predestined. In his book, *The Coming Event*, he wrote in 1871 to Earl Grey, the Secretary of State 'I assure you, my Lord, that ere very long a President of the United

* From his speech in a House of Commons debate on the Australian Commonwealth Bill (1900).

States of Australia will be knocking at your door.' Two years earlier the conservative *Sydney Morning Herald* had written: 'We have never doubted that Australian independence is among the things to come.' But the major problem faced by the 'Separatists' in Australia was defence. How would the colony cope with the tremendous burdens and risks by themselves. Would they not, asked George Higinbotham, 'be a helpless prey to any European power that might choose to pick a quarrel?'* This alone gave pause to men of reason.

In the 1880s Britain's bungling over New Guinea provided ready fuel for the founders of the 'Republican Union' (1884). George Black, one of the founders, pinpointed the human target: Queen Victoria. Was she not a German and the spear of all other Germans who were steadily encroaching everywhere in the Pacific and the Eastern Seas? 'We knew', wrote Black, 'that the Royal children were first taught to speak German, that seven of the nine married petty and impecunious German princes and princesses – all paupers on the People's Purse.' Behind the demagogues there were always enough discontented Irish to raise a cheer for a Republic and home rule for Australia. At the other end of the political scale, loyal empire men were understandably embittered by Her Majesty's Government's refusal to allow colonial governments to fly the British flag.

The economic depression and strikes of the 1890s added yet more fuel to the fire. The radicalism of the *Bulletin* reflected more than J.F. Archibald's neurotic anti-British hatred. Like another popular journal, *The Hummer*, it was the mirror of the discontents of the shearers. *The Hummer* was first published by the Shearers' Union in 1891 and was peppered with such republican prayers as: 'let Young Australia snap the chain that binds her fair young form to the dying leper of Imperialism.'† But as Blainey adds: 'Few Victorians in the 1890s thought the "leper" was dying: even fewer thought it was a leper.'‡

Nationalism could (in Blainey's phrase) take negative or positive forms. The republicanism of Archibald, the *Bulletin* and the Shearers' Union was negative, and it was still a sectarian minority manifestation. The positive version was growing. Australians visiting Europe began to return 'home' to Australia, sure with relief to be back in a country they understood and loved better than the land of their fathers, now remote and strange. This 'positive' nationalism began to show up in many of the

---

* E.E. Morris *Memoirs of George Higinbotham* (Melbourne, 1895).
† Geoffrey Blainey *Our Side of the Country: The Story of Victoria* (Melbourne, 1984), p. 135.
‡ Ibid, p. 135.

fin de siècle landscape paintings, prolific at that time. The Australian scenery of Buvalot, Streeton, Tom Roberts and the so-called Heidelberg School (the name came from Heidelberg, overlooking the Yarra Valley in Victoria where they painted) can be identified as belonging to a particular genre, and it seems that an 'Australian School' was, at that time, certainly in the making.

There was too a distinctively Australian architecture. The Melbourne architect Nahum Barnet predicted in 1882 that a native style would arise in 'Sunny Victoria'. A few years later it came. The so-called 'Queene Anne' or 'Federation' style was executed in 'largish red bricks, orange tiles of terra cotta first imported from Marseilles in about 1886, a hipped roof with golden and occasionally a squat spire ... a kangaroo or emu, griffin or dragon, all of red clay, perched on the end of the gables...'.

Until 1914, such villas multiplied in Melbourne. They were even more abundant westwards in Perth, 'bringing a touch of the flamboyant Mediterranean to many sandy Perth streets'.* Sydney in the 1880s underwent its own version of an Australian renaissance which swept away the sheds, huts and slums which had cluttered up areas like Paddington. Small firms, builder-developers, rebuilt a large area, still as picturesque as anything to be seen in English 'Regency' towns and far superior to late Victorian development of the same date. Rows of well-designed two- and three-storey houses, modest but elegant, with simple, well-designed doors and windows, balconies fronted with decorative, cast iron 'Sydney Lace', compose whole tree-lined streets redolent of Aix-en-Provence. Nor are the shopping streets of that date to be despised. Like some of the dwelling houses they are decorated with pediments from which rise moulded vases and figures of great variety, occasionally luxuriating into elaborate neo-Gothic castellations. Today, reflecting the sun from their pastel-coloured surfaces – greens, pinks, yellows and beiges – they are a unique manifestation of the quiet, positive, creative nationalism of the 1880s.

So the nation grew and flowered until 1914. Now and again the general peace was shattered by a rustle of indignation, as a tactless Minister of the Crown put his ministerial foot in it. This happened in Queensland in 1888, and again in South Australia in 1890, when the Colonial Secretary proposed for Governor a *persona non grata* with local opinion. The upset was sharp but short. Thereafter it was agreed that the sensible

* Ibid, p. 133.

and courteous procedure was to make sure before any name was put forward that it was acceptable. Similarly, an incoming Colonial Secretary in a new government of 1907 reached agreement with France about the New Hebrides without telling the Commonwealth Government. The gaffe was rectified when the British Government explained that the culprit minister was a new boy who had overlooked the established convention of discussion with the Commonwealth Government on occasions when their interests were involved.

So it went on until 1914. The local politics of federation were highly charged with drama: but the action was contained on the Australian stage. This was all the easier because after 1900 the new constitutional arrangements coincided with a considerable degree of economic recovery. On the land more intensive and diversified forms of farming came into vogue. Wheat farming led, the successful product of a combined group of improvements – new strains of seed, new fertilizers, new methods of rotation of fallowing. William Farrer named his new variety 'Federation', an appropriate label to indicate his place in history. With wheat came also butter and dairy products, meat and fruit. Together they spelt exports; and exports spelt ocean-going ships and – after some trial and error – practicable refrigeration and agricultural and food processing that actually worked.

The growth in the new wave of exports was achieved with little resort to new capital investment. They utilized railways, harbours and housing built out of the capital investment of earlier decades which up to 1900 had not been fully employed. Local manufacturing industry benefited by a new federal tariff of 80 per cent imposed in 1908. Victoria had long since enjoyed a tariff on imports (the result not least of an unprecedented newspaper propaganda campaign against free trade dogma led by David Syme, proprietor of the Melbourne *Age* in the 1860s). The overall result of the 1908 change of Australia to protection was that Victoria's industry got lower protection, while other states got higher protection. The results were debatable. Opponents said (some still say) Australian industry became less efficient, less competitive, labour and capital more complacent; supporters felt industry received a valuable incentive. The argument continued. But, following the Disraelian doctrine (which combined doubts about the value of colonies with a conviction that imperialism should pay its way), British imports into Australia enjoyed a preferential rate. Simultaneously the removal of inter-state tariffs stimulated internal trade and industry.

From 1906 the Australian balance of payments improved. This made it possible to pay off most of the debts still owed to overseas creditors since the black days of the 1890s. As the newly federated states moved into the second decade of the twentieth century, so immigration of men and money went on apace. In the three years before the First World War the annual number of immigrants increased five-fold. The annual borrowing of capital (almost entirely from Britain) was £7 million: down to 1910 capital had left the federation at about the same rate in repayment for old debts or the excess of imports over exports. The economic climate was thus set fair: and the result was a resumption of capital borrowing – this time, without any doubt, on Australian initiative.

This was an important phase in the Anglo-Australian relationship. It has often been portrayed by left-wing economists as one dominated by ruthless bankers and moneylenders of the City of London, forcing their services on the Australian borrower, public and private, on usurious and manifestly unjust terms.

The fact is that the capital borrowings of the pre-war years – largely public borrowings – were inspired entirely by Australian authorities for the benefit of Australian enterprise. There was no persuasion or pressure from London capital lenders; the terms were regulated simply (and as usual) by market forces. Australia now needed a fresh injection of outside capital; her balance of payments put her in a position to borrow; Britain was able to lend; the result was a 'division of labour' within a well-established system of trade and money, and one which was to the mutual advantage of borrower and lender. The rate of economic growth recovered, housebuilding was resumed, and workers surplus to the needs of declining industries (like copper and gold mining), as well as newly-arrived immigrants, were able to move to areas of new industries needing labour; for the most part at wages high by any standards, and under improving conditions beneficial to labour and employment.

The anti-imperialist 'analysis' of the school of Fitzpatrick, Wheelwright, Dunn, etc., tends to be unhelpful and misleading. The borrowing and lending was a mutual convenience – to Australia it was necessary for economic growth and social progress. The war was to interrupt the process – but only interrupt, not conclude it. After 1918 the building of railways and houses was resumed. The Australian partner offered preferential treatment to imports of British manufactured goods. British Governments gave special priority to the renewed flow of men and money to help Australia to resume its rural and urban development, but thereafter it was to become progressively more difficult to maintain the rate of real economic growth. It was clear, nevertheless, that the 'separatism' of the Gladstone era was at an end.

The First World War

Meanwhile, the character of the First World War itself introduced new complications into the Anglo-Australian relationship. Australians had not forgotten the German occupation of a large part of New Guinea a quarter of a century earlier. In the twentieth century they viewed with some anxiety the expansionist ambitions of the new Germany. The German naval programme especially was one good reason why a combined naval programme was worked out. It provided for one fast, heavily-armed battle cruiser and two smaller cruisers for Australia. The battle cruiser, HMAS *Australia*, arrived at Sydney in 1913. The problem of military defences had been settled since 1909–10 when federal government had accepted (and implemented) the principle of compulsory military service.

When war finally broke out, both the Labour Party and its opponents were fully agreed that Australia would share fully in the British war effort. By November, the Australian cruiser *Sydney* had sunk the German raider–cruiser *Emden* after a running battle of over four hours. By 1915 the Australian army was in Egypt in full training, and fighting off the Turks in an action which saved the Suez Canal. Then, in April, came the grimmest test of the First World War: Gallipoli.

Gallipoli

Churchill was the principal architect of this characteristically daring strategic concept. On the Western front, there was total deadlock. Some new enterprise was needed: if the Dardanelles were forced, and Constantinople captured, the Black Sea could be opened and effective sea communication established between the Western allies and Russia, with great mutual advantage. In the vast operation planned to execute this daring enterprise, the Australian and New Zealand troops stationed in Egypt were to play a vital role. Their telegraphic name: Anzac (Australian and New Zealand Army Corps), was to earn them an heroic but tragic place in history. The story has been told a hundred times. Here it is only necessary to state the basic facts as briefly as possible and record the effects of the campaign on public opinion.

Of all the controversial episodes of the 1914–18 war, none has been the subject of so much bitterness and misunderstanding as Gallipoli. From the start, the struggle against the Turks was gruelling, bloody and unsuccessful, the slaughter, suffering and heroism beyond belief. From April until December, the carnage continued. After an assessment by Lord Kitchener, Minister for War, the Allied decision to evacuate was taken on 9 December 1915. The total evacuation was completed just before Christmas.

Estimates of the casualties on both sides are varied and often unreliable. The most recent and reliable figures, by Robert Rhodes James, author also of the best most recent book on Gallipoli, are as in Table I.

Table I. The Gallipoli Casualties

	Dead (known)	Wounded; unaccounted for
British	25,254	
Australian	7,594	
New Zealand	2,431	Total c.220,000
Indian	1,718	
French	10,000	
Total	44,997	

The total Allied casualties are estimated at 265,000 killed or wounded (the corresponding figure for the Turks is 300,000, of which a high proportion were dead). Within this shocking total of killed and wounded, the Australian sacrifice – 27,954 killed or wounded – represents a terrible proportion. Before Gallipoli, the 'Poms' had sometimes been inclined to regard them as an undisciplined rabble of loud-mouthed hell-raisers. They returned with an unlimited admiration for their incredible bravery under fire. There was a similar change of view by the Aussies of the British. As one wrote in his dug-out: 'I do not suppose anything could be more different than the British soldier and the Australian. But they are both quite unbeatable.' C.E.W. Bean, in his *History of the Australians*, likewise expressed deep admiration of the British soldiers at Anzac – and Bean was, as Rhodes James has said, the 'authentic voice of Anzac'.

At the time, as A.B. Facey recorded in his uniquely fair and honest account, people in Australia 'were all a hundred per cent behind the war. They were all sad about what was going on in Gallipoli, but the feeling was to send more troops to help. They'd have sent everyone they could get hold of to help....'* Later on, of course, there were bitter recriminations; Churchill especially, as the major architect of the Galli-poli strategy, received the heaviest share of the blame. Yet, in the end – and to a considerable extent because of Gallipoli – the Allies won. The Turks came out of the holocaust with awed admiration for the

* A.B. Facey *A Fortunate Life* (Victoria, 1951), p. 2.

Allies. (In the Second World War, Turkey, though under tremendous pressure, remained neutral, but pro-Allied. British and Anzac visitors to this day are warmly welcomed in Turkey, especially in Gallipoli.)

Nor were the terrible sacrifices at Gallipoli wholly wasted – as is often alleged. As the first combined, amphibious operation in history, its immediate failure was deeply studied, especially by professional military planners in Britain. Its lessons (Rhodes James has written) 'ensured the triumph of D Day in 1944'. (Rhodes James's history of the campaign, *Gallipoli*, was used as a textbook for the execution of the Falklands operations in 1982.)*

Unfortunately the rise of the Australian film industry has been the occasion not only of some fine creative work in the cinema, but also of some grotesque mangling of history. In the film of *Gallipoli* (as in *Breaker Morant* and, strangest of all, *A Fortunate Life*) the authors seem determined to do their best to poison their history in favour of popular and profitable entertainment. The *Gallipoli* film (again, Rhodes James's words) is 'a travesty of what occurred in the terrible charge of the Light Horse at The Nek; this had nothing to do with the British landing at Suvla; it was to assist the New Zealanders on Chunuk Bair'. In spite of all the work of Charles Bean, Rhodes James and other meticulous scholars, Australian and British, the mass media entertainment-mongers seem determined to ignore the heroism and comradeship shown by Australians, New Zealanders and British on the Peninsula, not to mention the Indians and the French. (From May until August, 1915, the brunt of the attack all fell to the British and French at Helles, with enormous casualties.)

A.B. Facey's moving autobiography is too gentle and fair-minded to give the mischief-makers and Pommie-bashers much scope. But even in *A Fortunate Life*, it is noticeable that the producers took special care to quote him as saying 'we all thought that the whole Gallipoli Campaign was a mistake, and a terrible, unnecessary loss of life'. Facey's view was not an unnatural one for a private soldier who had just been through hell and came out with a shattered leg and his nerves in pieces. Nevertheless, in the 1980s a different view is perhaps possible. But neither this, nor Facey's numerous friendly references to the British, receives very much attention.

Nothing is more contemptible than the pseudo-statistical games in which the dead heroes of history are used like counters on a phoney chess-board designed to prove that your own side was braver or cleverer

* I am indebted for much of this information to R. Rhodes James's articles in *Quadrant*, June and July 1985 (Sydney).

than the other. But it is undeniable that the kind of misrepresentation that unhappily characterizes the popular versions of Gallipoli has left many Australians with the belief that the battles of Gallipoli were solely fought by Anzacs. Others have gained the impression that if foreign forces were present, then their contribution was negligible. Even historians and biographers have been persuaded to go along with such views. Norman Lee, in his biography of John Curtin, writes (of Gallipoli and the Greek campaign of 1941) 'both were devised by Churchill and both were carried out *largely by Australians many of whom were killed*'.*

That Churchill was responsible for the conception of the campaign is indisputable, but the responsibility for its adoption and execution lay not with him but with the Allied High Command and the Allied Governments who were the political masters. When it became apparent that Gallipoli was a disaster, there was an ugly rush to find a scapegoat: Churchill was the obvious candidate, and the blame continues to be laid at his door – despite all the evidence. Yet if Gallipoli had succeeded there would have been an equal clamour to stake claims for the honour of its parentage.

The British, as Rhodes James has remarked, have not joined in this competition of mutual denigration with the Australians. Lloyd George described the Australian General, Monash, as the most resourceful and able officer in the Great War. Charles Bean, the finest contemporary historian of the campaign, would have been angered by this cheap form of patriotism. Let us leave the last word to Robert Rhodes James: 'Had Bill Slim been alive ... we would have had a memorable explosion which would have sent all concerned scurrying for cover; and I would not care to be in their shoes when they meet him in Paradise.'†

Later Campaigns

The Australian forces, morale and technical experience raised rather than lowered by their crucifixion at Gallipoli, went on to distinguish themselves heroically in two other vital centres of operations. On the Somme, under Monash, their task was (with the British on their left, Canadians on their right) to break through the centre of the seemingly impregnable German defences. They succeeded, though again at the cost of very heavy casualties. In Palestine, under General Chauvel, an equally brave triumph – the capture of Damascus from the Turks – was achieved

---

* Norman Lee *John Curtin, Saviour of Australia* (Sydney, 1983), p. 97 (my italics).
† 'The Mystery of Gallipoli', *Quadrant*, June 1985.

by the Australian light horse and camel corps. The final verdict on the Australian military contribution to Allied victory may be left to the French Marshal Foch: 'From start to finish they distinguished themselves by their endurance and boldness. By their initiative, their fighting spirit, their magnificent ardour, they proved themselves to be shock troops of the first order.'

Not least surprising to an outsider was that all these important interventions in imperial and world history took place under an Australian Labour Government or (in later stages) a para-Labour Government. Its permanent central dynamo was a Labour political leader, like Lloyd George a Welshman by origin; W.M. Hughes, a fiery patriot. Hughes became Prime Minister of Australia in 1915. He remained in office until February 1923 – but only at a price. The price was a split in the ranks of his own Labour Party and his virtual expulsion from it, carrying his supporters with him.

Hughes's outright espousal of total conscription caused one of his Labour colleagues to accuse him of 'the blushless impudence of Iscariot'. The 'little digger' was more than a match for this kind of abuse: 'I did not leave the Labour Party', he declared, 'The Labour Party left me.' Deaf, dyspeptic, increasingly gnome-like with the years, Hughes was indomitable. He fought for what he believed to be right – regardless of party politics.

It was not the first nor was it to be the last time that the fragile unity of the Australian Labour movement was to be fragmented. Hughes was a man of swift and sometimes violent decision; his methods evoked equally violent response from his enemies. He had come up the hard way. He was a man of the people, originally an immigrant hand on one of the Fairbairn sheep stations. (See p. 234.) Deeply patriotic, he tried to convert Australia by referendum, to the idea of conscription. Twice the battle raged; twice he lost. But Hughes survived. On behalf of Australia he signed the Treaty of Versailles. He secured mandates for the Australian administration of German New Guinea and Nauru; thus the defeat of McIlwraith over three decades earlier was avenged.

No tangible recompense for the human sacrifices of war can ever be possible; but Hughes was at one with the majority of the Australian people in his devotion to the cause of victory in what was seen to be a war for human freedom and democracy. To this end, Australia provided well over 300,000 soldiers, sacrificed 60,000 dead and 167,000 wounded, at a total cost estimated at nearly one thousand million pounds. It was a prodigious effort. Since arguments used to justify it were shortly to come under heavy fire (and still are under heavy fire), it is important to realize how Hughes and those who agreed with him saw Australian intervention in the First World War.

It was not merely a sentimental act of support for Great Britain herself. Britain was seen as a principal participant in a war for freedom and democracy against the enemies of freedom and democracy. As Hughes, and probably most other Australians, saw it, Australia did not merely align herself with Britain, but with the Western Allies – France, Italy, Belgium, later the United States – even with Russia and Portugal. A victory for Germany, the Austrian Empire, and Turkey not only would have destroyed Western democracy, but would have destabilized political and economic relations the world over, including the Mediterranean, the Middle East (including the Suez Canal), Africa, Asia and the Far East. Australia would have been amongst the victims.

To some contemporaries, this view seemed exaggerated or incomprehensible. To their present-day ideological descendants it still is.

11

CREDITS, CRISES AND CRICKET
1918–39

'The memory lingered ... the outrage remained ... in growing scepticism about the imperial heritage and its value and values.'*

Even before federation it had become clear that Australia was developing an economy with features unique in the English-speaking world. The chief one was a combination of private and public investment as instruments by which Australian land and resources could be expanded and exploited: in short, a mixed market system, heavily dependent on external borrowings at both private and public levels; British capital was the major support. Population growth, both by natural increase and by immigration, made for an enlarged and increasingly complex economy. This had raised living standards for Australians of all kinds: rich, middling and poor. It had also made the Australian economy more vulnerable – or at least made it seem more vulnerable. Better communications, more literacy, more newspapers, greater consciousness of the *possibilities* of better things – all these were to make Australians more aware of the scale of the disasters that smote them in the *fin de siècle* – drought, rabbit plague, price fluctuations, strikes, etc.

Australia survived the lean and hungry years. Some banks had gone broke, but banking practices survived, bankrupt banks recovered, new ones rose to replace the old. Both the great pastoralists and the small farmers suffered, as classes, but as a profitable activity farming went forward; gold mining declined but mining of other minerals and metals increased. After 1918 the mixed economy came back into its own. Successive British governments moved in to promote emigration and to help resume the programme of extension of agrarian development. This called for private and public response in Australia: but public response was

* 'Bodyline ... End of the Age of Innocence', leading article, *Sydney Morning Herald*, 18 December 1982.

now the more important, for railway building was traditionally a state enterprise. Now the Federal Government was also involved, as, for example, great irrigation schemes and tariff adjustments were seen to be crucial if Australia was to catch up after the interruptions of the war years. Regionally, the south-east (New South Wales and Victoria) went ahead fastest in rural expansion, followed closely by South Australia. Manufacturing industry expanded round Sydney and Melbourne, probably helped by the new tariff arrangements of 1920. Urban expansion continued, Perth (Western Australia) now growing fastest of all.

Like the United States and Europe, Australia felt the shock of the post-war inflation (1919–21) and the even more violent shock of the slump of 1921. The price of Queensland beef for export dropped by more than 50 per cent in early 1921. Thereafter, trade, agriculture and industry all picked up gingerly until 1927–8. From then on the signs and portents were threatening – unemployment rose; investment, productivity and exports all began a downward slide. Things got worse as Australia began to feel the effects of the world depression of 1929. The particularly serious consequences for Australia were accentuated by the increasingly unfavourable balance of payments combined with the existence of a large bill for the interest payable on the foreign loans that stood unredeemed, a forbidding monument to Australia's traditional dependence on borrowed capital. As export prices fell (in parallel with prices everywhere) it became more difficult to meet the national bill for interest payments; the disappearance of overseas confidence made it impossible to borrow more money to bridge the gap between solvency and insolvency.

From this disastrous mess, Australia extricated herself by a number of desperate measures. Import duties were raised and the Australian currency devalued. These moves helped, respectively, home manufacturers (by reducing foreign competition) and exporters (by lowering the cost at which foreign customers could buy Australian goods). The effects of the other major federal intervention (the so-called 'Premiers' Plan' of June 1931) remains a matter of controversy among the experts. The Plan was essentially a bankers' plan. Its emphasis was on cutting down public spending. This it did. Did it stimulate recovery by making Australian production costs more competitive, or did it over-deflate the economy all round and make recovery longer and more difficult? No clear answer has been given; but by mid-1932, and for a variety of reasons, there were signs that the worst was over. Depreciation of the currency raised the price of gold and helped a strong recovery of the Western Australian gold producers. Wool exports began to improve, partly for the same reason, partly through economic recovery in the European wool markets. Government subsidies and other forms of assistance helped manufacturing industry at large to start moving again.

Many Australians suffered by reason of serious unemployment, or lower wages and incomes, and through the lower levels of consumption which affected trade and especially the small shop-keepers in the cities. On the other hand, the great gains in living standards of the 1850–90 period were not permanently lost. Between 1932 and 1939 substantial recovery was visible on all fronts – investment, employment, wages, consumption. 'The depression of the 1930s, like that of the 1890s, proved to be no more than a pause in the long upward movement of output in Australia.'*

In one respect, nevertheless, the effects of the crisis of 1919–32 are apparent in the long term, even though indirectly. British loans to Australia had brought undreamed-of expansion to rural Australia. Without them, there would have been no railways, public utilities, irrigation schemes, etc.; or they would have come much later and with greater problems than was the historical case. The world crisis produced a specifically Anglo-Australian financial crisis which was finally resolved by a scheme for converting existing loans into new ones at lower rates of interest in 1932–3. In conjunction with the changes in economic policy this eased the acute financial crisis between Australia the borrower and Britain the lender. But in the course of the negotiations, and for reasons unrelated to affairs of agriculture, trade, industry, banking or any other conceivable economic element in the crisis, Anglo-Australian relations received another shock. It was not administered in Chancelleries, Treasuries, Government Offices or Parliaments: it all happened on the Australian cricket grounds.

1932: Was That Cricket?

'If I had my way', declared Mr Hawke, the Australian Prime Minister, in January 1984, 'I'd certainly introduce cricket into China and the Soviet Union. I think that if we could make them play cricket we'd have a much more likely chance of a peaceful world.' Had he forgotten that in the 1930s there seemed a real chance, during months when Whitehall, Westminster and Canberra held their breath, that cricket was about to destroy, if not world peace, at least the peace of the British Empire?

Less than a year after he spelt out his peace programme, the Australian

---

* W.A. Sinclair *The Process of Economic Development in Australia* (Melbourne, 1980), p. 211.

press would describe in 1985 the gala dinner which capped a memorable evening for 500 people gathered at the largest hotel in Adelaide. It was to celebrate a week's Test Cricket at the Adelaide Oval and the great game's

> romance, lore, poetry and pure traditions ... the room, bedecked with flags of the cricket-playing nations, was filled with warmth and great affection ... the spirit of the night was overwhelming, touching everyone who was privileged to be there, to salute the ground and great men who have enriched its history and traditions.... Tales, true and apocryphal, were spun throughout the week. It was a time to laugh and cry, remember and reminisce ... for touching and caring, a time to toast anyone and anything at any given moment and to remember mates who now play their cricket at a higher level.

It only remains to note that the most honoured and interviewed guests present were a handful of old English gentlemen, survivors of the 'bodyline' test matches of the early 1930s.

Let us lift our eyes for a few moments from these scenes of goodwill and marvel at the change that has come over the Anglo-Australian cricket scene in fifty-two years. In 1933, by the end of the test season in Australia, the press had taught half Australia to regard Douglas Jardine, the English captain, as a fiend in human shape, a Machiavelli whose bottomless intrigues and machinations had turned cricket from a harmless game into a diabolical form of warfare against Australia, and the peaceful cricket grounds of Sydney, Melbourne and Adelaide into battle grounds whence the cries of the injured and the howlings of the outraged spectators on the Hill were wafted over the air for all Australia to hear. Police precautions were on a military scale.

With Jardine at the centre of the storm was Harold Larwood. A simple Nottingham miner, Larwood, together with Voce, another Nottingham miner, was accused of hurling down, at unbelievable speed and with consistent and deadly accuracy, deliveries of exceedingly hard cricket balls, said to be aimed at the *bodies* of the Australian cricketers. And aimed to maim if not to kill. Larwood in particular became a second monster in the Antipodes. Later he recounted his memory of a visit to an Australian theatre. Sitting near him was a child. After gaping at him for some time she turned to her mother and said innocently, 'Mummy, he doesn't look like a murderer.' Had she been reading the grisly forensic anecdotes of the (literally) unspeakable Herman Diederik Johan van Schriekhaven, alias Jacob Larwood, with whom Harold was perhaps confused by a bewildered public?

In self-defence, and no doubt to supplement the earnings of a professional cricketer (in those days by no means princely) Larwood set out his own views on the Anglo-Australian crisis. *Bodyline* (June 1933), with its foreword dated 8 May 1933 by Douglas Jardine, seems to be the one book on 'bodyline' out of scores which nobody nowadays reads. Was it a piece of ingenious and disingenuous propaganda ghosted for him by some anonymous hack? Or was it the spontaneous response of a straightforward sportsman and ex-miner who honestly believed that he had been misjudged by both the larrikins on the Hill and the Australian Board of Cricket?

I suspect that most people nowadays who might take the trouble (and it is considerable) to find the book will prefer it to the carefully-structured and (mostly) specious arguments of journalists and television script-writers with their eyes on the circulation or the ratings over half a century later. The central question remains: did Larwood deliberately bowl *at* the batsman? Harold's answer was a firm no. Very few fast bowlers playing in test matches today could say the same. They are supported by the armoury of body pads, helmets and face visors now universally used by batsmen and by the serious, possibly fatal, injuries which without them would be the certain feature of any test cricket match in the 1980s.

Whatever the name, be it bodyline or bouncers, deadly, murderous cricket has come to stay.

Harold was not in the end the prime target. The deepest hatred of the anti-bodyline party was reserved for Jardine. In their way the 'Bar-rackers' (Larwood always ennobled them with a capital letter, like 'God') understood Larwood. They were rough and open: so was he. It was Jardine they couldn't abide – smooth, unflappable Jardine, shining with public school, upper-Pom polish, devious as only the English uppercrust could be: false, fishy, faithless. For the Hill, Jardine was Albion, and as perfidious as possible.

They were quite wrong. Jardine was not English. He was a Scot. And a more Scottish Scot never walked. Second, and perhaps more serious, he was a Wykehamist: and a lawyer. He had all the cool of his school, to say nothing of New College, Oxford, of the NSW Scottish Land Agency and of the Australian Scottish Agricultural Company (both of which he was Chairman of). In short, if Jardine was not an Australian, he had many of the ingredients that went to make an Australian. There must have been more than just malice against Don Bradman to keep Jardine in comfort in Australia. Perhaps it was a dour Scottish sense of humour. In his foreword to Larwood's book, he wrote: 'it is curious to think that had you been playing for Australia you would have been the most popular man in Australia'.

As for the fundamental question – did Harold bowl to hit the man or the wicket? – Jardine produced what seemed to be the short, conclusive answer.

> More than half the thirty-three wickets you took in the Test Matches were clean bowled, or its equivalent leg before wicket – 18 to be exact. This, on the perfect and toned down wickets of Australia where numbers one to seven in the batting order are less frequently clean bowled than in England. *If this isn't bowling at the wicket I don't know what is....*

Jardine went on to quote the authority of M.A. Noble, the former Australian captain, in support when he summed up Larwood's performance: 'It is all humbug to say that his tactics were unfair or that he bowled at the man instead of the wicket. He didn't. I could see no difference in his methods from those he used during his previous visits.'

This was Harold's own line. So far as the recollections of an inexpert schoolboy are of any value, they tend to support the pro-Larwood party. I can remember watching Larwood bowling at Trent Bridge, his home ground. I still have a vivid memory of that long, loping, beautifully-rhythmical run and the final delivery, an almost invisible cannon ball, deadly accurate and – this was the remarkable thing – consistently accurate.

Not all those English observers nearer to the heart of things were with Larwood. The other fast bowler of 1930 was the great Gubby Allen, one of the wise heads of cricket, later Captain of England and later still Chairman of the England Selection Panel and President of the MCC. Gubby, more diplomatic than Jardine, was never in favour of bodyline. In its full Jardine manifestation there were seven men on the leg side and up to five behind square leg – something that would be impossible after the change in cricket laws which prescribed a maximum of two men behind square leg. Gubby Allen objected to bodyline under these conditions. 'The batsmen were left with no stroke at all. If it had continued it would have destroyed the game.' And it was 'the game' – their game – that people like Gubby Allen and others in the English team like Freddy Brown, Ames and Wyatt cared about. They were quite right. The combined spectacle of fast bowlers and tortured batsmen weaving and ducking did not make for large, happy cricket audiences.

Nevertheless, though they agreed that the great Don Bradman was the fundamental *raison d'etre* of the new attacking strategy, they always maintained that bodyline had grown out of the developing problems of the early thirties as Jardine and others patiently tried out new strategies against the Australian batting superiority. It was never planned consciously as a theory or practice of violence to the person of the bats-man. The two notorious balls from Larwood which hit first Woodfull and then Oldfield were not (Allen himself is categorical) bodyline balls. There were balls which fell a little short and lifted because of the uneven bounce of the wicket.

In the 1980s, bowling bouncers is a normal part of the test bowler's repertoire, probably to the detriment of the art and craft of good cricket and stroke play. It threatens cricket with monotony for the audience and lethal violence for the batsman. But now and again, a cricket pitch will itself produce a natural and very dangerous bouncer, regardless of the intentions of the bowler.

Undoubtedly these were among the considerations pondered by the cricketing community in England and Australia in the 1930s. And even-tually they prevailed. But the defeat of bodyline was not achieved solely on the cricket grounds of Australia or England, or in the Committee Rooms at Sydney or Lords. The spectacle of mounted police riding up and down the serene precincts of the Adelaide Oval, red-bricked and ivy-walled, keeping back thousands of infuriated spectators who were trying to invade the arena and attack Jardine's team – such nightmares were enough to keep awake many whose concern for Anglo-Australian relations were far wider than the good health of sporting events. They included businessmen and bankers, diplomats, demagogues and Cabinet Ministers, like J.T. Lang and Jimmy Thomas.

For the near-tragedy of bodyline did not stand alone. The metamor-phosis of a friendly, subtle, sleepy game nurtured on English village greens and in quiet pubs over cheering glasses of warm beer, into a bitter source of international hostility was itself mysteriously related to the larger tragedy of economic depression and political frustration which settled on the world in the late 1920s, and led, directly and indir-ectly, to the Second World War. In spite of the vast distances which separated Australia from the original centre of this cosmic disturbance in North America and Europe, and the comforting sense of isolation in which Australians often lived, Australia was, willy-nilly, in the firing line. Australia's problems were essentially part of the problems afflicting the rest of the world.

Political Chaos and International Debt

Australia, remote as she was geographically, was hard hit by the contrac-tion and disequilibrium which afflicted international trade relationships everywhere. Her exports – wool, wheat, metals and minerals – were all under severe pressure in world markets. But such external dislocations were compounded by another circumstance which was peculiar to Australia and her relationship to England.

In the palmy days of Australian expansion down to the 1880s, and again after the recovery from the depression of the 1890s, British capital had poured into Australia to finance private, public, municipal, state and finally federal economic development. Neither the growing popularity of socialist doctrines nor the increasing coherence of political parties labelled 'labor' (spelt in the North American mode) and of trade unions largely run by radicals of Celtic origin, had made the slightest dint in Australia's determination to put on speed and hasten the process of economic and social growth by the same means which had promoted it since 1788. Capital-rich Britain had been the source not only of the money but of a great part of the necessary manufactures – iron, steel, coal, tools and all the needs of everyday life – which had brought Australia into being. By the end of the nineteenth century, Australia was the leading overseas borrower from Britain.

As the borrowings grew, so did the burden of interest payments from Australia to the lender. In good times there were few problems. The development of trade, private industry and public utilities like railways were seen and felt to be the means to wealth – and a wealth ever more widely spread about society at large. In bad times the picture was less clear. The burden of the debt was felt as a dead weight and the clamour against 'foreign capitalism' became increasingly acceptable not only amongst the unemployed, but even amongst middle-class shopkeepers and tax-payers feeling the pinch. The unrestrained public investment of the 1920s came home to roost in the Depression of the early 1930s. In the prevailing confusion and near panic, the entire system of capital borrowing from Britain suddenly ceased to be the beneficial and benevolent miracle it had once seemed to be. Suddenly it was an intolerable burden, a millstone and a crime.

The noise and violence of the 1930s was in part the consequence of the victory of 'labor' in 1929, and that was the consequence of the deepening world depression. The new Government, under Scullin, faced problems which it could not diagnose, let alone solve. Its helpless thrashings and gesticulations were only symbolic of a universal confusion that gripped Australia. A Federal Labor government fought with State Labor governments, both fought with the bankers; British bankers fought with Australian bankers; Australian bankers fought with Australian bankers. Scullin fired his own Treasurer, but restored him before he had been cleared of criminal charges.

The Federal Prime Minister was simultaneously locked in violent quarrels with J.T. Lang, Premier of NSW, who saw himself as a man of the people, a proletarian figure whose efforts to encourage public enterprise and ministrations to the needy and underpriviliged aroused less gratitude from his supporters than opposition from the predominantly moderate 'labor' supporters for whom 'Langism' seemed to be the same thing as Red Communism. There was even a semi-fascist organization calling itself the 'New Guard' whose members saluted one another and saw themselves as the protectors of traditional values opposing the disloyalty of Lang. While Labor Party fought with Labor Party, Lang fought with everybody including himself; his inconsistencies were unlimited. (He was one of the few Australians in favour of a European Community.) One day he was in favour of repudiating the vast debts, domestic and external, piled up through the insouciant years by the premier states; the next day he was against repudiation.

So it went on. In the middle of the chaos there arrived in Australia, on the invitation of the Federal Government, an expert financier and leading adviser of the Bank of England, to discuss the dangerous mess into which Australia's public finances had fallen. His name was Sir Otto Niemeyer. It was hardly a name to inspire confidence amongst Labor supporters or indeed, in times when everything German remained suspect in Australia, amongst any sizeable body of Australian patriots.

The *Labor Daily*, the voice of the NSW Branch of the Australian Labor Party, did not wait for any lapidary statement from the great man himself before making its opinions public. It launched itself at once into hysterical denunciations of the visitor which were as characteristic of Goebbels as of Marx.

'This sublime impertinence of the lately-arrived emissary of Capitalism abroad – Sir Otto Niemeyer – who comes here to tell us that human misery – life even – is as nothing compared with the necessity of providing the London Jews with their fat rake-offs, passes our understanding . . . our financial straits are wholly due to debts incurred in participation in a war which had nothing to do with us, really. He who would suggest that Big Money should cut off some of the profits is labelled a mad man – a repudiationist. NO! The worker, his wife and his children, must starve.'

J.S. Garden, the powerful Secretary of the Labor Council, gave his warm support. Niemeyer (he cried) wanted a 20 per cent cut in wages. Garden's response was to threaten total repudiation. There would be no payment for 'the Shylocks of London if they will not agree to fund the debt free of interest for 5 years'.

The voice of Labor will be immediately familiar to anyone who knew the Germany of the 1930s. Today, after the revelations of the Nuremberg trials and a half-century in which anti-semitism became the dirtiest word in the language, most people have forgotten – few perhaps have ever known – that the word 'Nazi' (as it came to be known in the English-speaking world) meant National *Socialist*. Many Nazis sincerely believe that they were both Nationalists and Socialists. So did the anti-semites and Nationalists of the Left and Right in the 1930s. Distinctions between Nationalism, Fascism, Communism, Socialism, even Liberalism were paper-thin down to 1939. Jews and capitalism were well-chosen targets and the far Left was as ready as the Right to shoot at them.

In his own newspaper, the *Century*, Lang repeatedly represented Niemeyer as the silk-hatted City financier smoking a large Havana cigar in order to concentrate the sinister forces of his mind in oppressing and extinguishing the Australian working man.

It was all the cheapest and most distorted demagoguery. Niemeyer was not a city gent. He was a civil servant in HM Treasury, educated impeccably at St Pauls and the University of Oxford. In the course of time, Montagu Norman, the Governor of the Bank of England, had managed to attract him away from Whitehall to the Bank where he needed all the economic and financial talent he could muster to cope with the complexities that beset the world's currencies, and sterling in particular. Niemeyer, diligent, clear thinking and of proved integrity was just the man that Norman was looking for. Niemeyer became a Director of the Bank and one of the inner circle of advisers closest to the Governor. Unluckily, his economic theory was as classically orthodox as his education.

Why should this mantle of diabolical evil have fallen on his unfortunate shoulders? One possible answer is that there is more than a suspicion that some Australians, like a number of non-Australians, confused him with another contemporary international figure of more than shady repute, Sir Basil Zaharoff: variously known as *der Mann in dunkel* (the man behind the scenes), the armaments king of kings, the pedlar of death, etc. Confusion deepened when Zaharoff was knighted for his services. Were his services performed in his role as armaments king? Or spy? Or capitalist? Or political adviser? Or did he simply pay for his title? Some little confusion was after all pardonable. Both Niemeyer and Zaharoff had foreign names. Both were given to long journeys into remote parts of the world – like Brazil and Australia – on missions said to be financial and therefore mysterious, if not sinister. Both were commonly said (though untruthfully) to be connected privately with

Rothschilds as agents for protecting and extending their interests overseas.

The fact that there was no similarity whatever between the characters or activities of the two men did nothing to clarify the situation. To Lang, Niemeyer and Zaharoff, if not identical, were out of the same basket and that was good (or bad) enough to be going on with.

Niemeyer faced other problems besides being the prophet of the doctrines of orthodox economic rectitude. These were bad enough. Suggesting as they did financial retrenchment and a general pulling-in of belts all round, they stuck in the gullets of Premier Lang and his followers on the Left. Worse, the messages he brought from London on behalf of the Bank, which were supposed to soothe and alleviate Australia's economic sickness, contained no acceptable remedy for Australia's problem. On the contrary, they were most clearly (for Lang at least) the result of the insensitive brutality of British Government policy. This it was which created the insupportable burden of interest payable on Australia's debt to Britain, including the debts piled up in the First World War specifically to help Britain and not Australia. It mattered not to Lang that the Federal Government of Australia failed to share his views.

Worst of all, the unfortunate Niemeyer insisted on conveying his sermons on economics and finance at enormous length to his Australian audiences and with a rigorous dogmatism which reminded them too often and too clearly of his combined Teutonic and Whitehall origins. Of all his shortcomings, this was his most serious. He was a ponderous bore.

It was all too much for J.T. Lang. Putting aside the doubts which had led him to dither for a long time between repudiating and not repudiating the public debt owing by NSW to London, he finally decided – to repudiate. This not only shook the conservative business community to its foundations; it forced the Federal Government to reassure London at once that they would honour the debt. Proceedings were at once instituted to recover the money needed from the NSW Government. This led to a run on the State Savings Bank by panic-stricken depositors. A defiant Lang in turn proceeded to withdraw Government funds from the banks and refused the Commonwealth Government access to the Treasury of NSW. Thus at one blow he defied both the Federal Government and the High Court of Australia.

The end was not far off. In May 1932 Lang was summoned to Government House by the Governor, Sir Phillip Game, and sacked for 'pursuing illegalities'. With remarkable lack of fuss Lang gave in. The Governor and the ex-Premier came out of the front door, shook hands and Lang departed. However disappointing for the journalists (who hoped for a much bigger row) it was perfectly characteristic of Lang's engaging inconsistency. Elections followed and a new government was formed.

Montagu Norman to the Rescue

All this was strange enough but what followed later in 1932 was even more strange. And it all centred round a figure as remote, mysterious and controversial as Niemeyer or Zaharoff; this was the Governor of the Bank of England himself, Montagu Norman. Thus far, in the imaginations of those Australians who were sufficiently interested in public finance and banking to know anything about him, Montagu Norman had played a role compounded of Ebenezer Scrooge and a pantomime Wicked Uncle. Even Joseph Lyons, the Federal Prime Minister, had been haunted by the fear that 'obduracy in London', by which he meant Montagu Norman, would provoke a new wave of what he called 'Langism'. Rightly or wrongly – and perhaps he was right – Lyons shared the belief that there was a widespread mood of resentment in Australia against the amount of money that Australia had to pay Britain annually in interest on the debt at a time when the balance of payments was heavily against Australia. As the old Rothschild family motto ran: 'private lending brings little gratitude and public lending no friends whatever'. This seemed to be amply borne out by the course of Australian history. Yet except for France, who lent on a vast scale to Russia but hardly at all elsewhere, there was no other source of capital for a national borrower except England (and Scotland) in the nineteenth and early twentieth centuries. And British lending meant British goods. Without British money and goods there would have been no First Fleet, no money to fence the sheep and cattle stations, build great cities, prospect for gold, iron, coal or any other minerals, build railways or the Sydney Harbour Bridge.

Of all the many ironies that adorned the history of an ironically-minded people, the opening by J.T. Lang of Sydney's great bridge (financed by British capital and built by a Scottish construction firm and Dorman Long, Britain's largest constructional steel company) was surely the most remarkable. Nor was it merely that his cutting of the ceremonial ribbon was interrupted rudely by a mounted officer in uniform from the Governor General's Escort who galloped forward and slashed at the ribbon bellowing that he was opening the bridge on behalf of the decent and respectable citizens of the state. The offender was Captain de Groot, a member of the 'New Guard', and he was quietly removed. Lang then cut the re-tied ribbon in the name of all the people of New South Wales. The bridge remains: a monument to British engineering skills and British willingness to lend abroad. Motorists still pay a toll to pass over it.

The confused absurdity of Lang's own position was sufficiently clear to most people to reinforce the feeling in financial circles and the Bank of England that to reduce the terms of the Australian loans was not only very difficult but unjustified. Was not the beneficence of the whole financial process crystal clear to Australians as well as to the British lender? Had it not brought about the largest and most spectacular demonstration of its virtues, now crowned and graced by the blessing of its noisiest and most obstructive opponent?

So far as Montagu Norman was concerned, at least a year or two could be allowed to pass before any action seemed necessary. It was therefore autumn 1932 before nervous Australian observers suddenly saw a light at the end of the tunnel. Supporters and critics of Australia's dependence on English capital were alike surprised to see that the figure holding the lantern of hope was the Governor of the Bank of England himself. At a stroke Montagu Norman underwent a sudden change of mind, heart and costume. No longer Wicked Uncle, he was now seen to be waving the wand of the Fairy Godmother and offering welcome gifts. Suddenly, and for reasons still far from clear, the Bank of England proposed an Australian conversion loan at a reduced rate of interest. This, at one stroke, eased, indeed revolutionized, Australia's position as a borrower on the London market. Even S.M. Bruce, the Australian financial adviser in London, was puzzled. (Bruce, a leading member of the Melbourne Club whose slogan was 'men, money and markets', had been leader of the Country Party and dominated politics for some years in the 1920s as a right-wing prime minister. His strongest suit was finance but he had been defeated in the election of 1929 and, as one observer had put it, gone abroad to London 'on a well-deserved holiday to study economic conditions elsewhere'.) If Bruce could not understand Norman's startling move, nobody else could. But what matter?

The new loan was a huge success. Heavily over-subscribed, it swept up to a premium without delay. The City entered a euphoric state, which was to continue throughout the following year. The London financial press and the City at large underwent a total sea-change towards Australia, its economy, its prospects and everything Australian. Why did the leopard change his spots? One can only guess.

Montagu Norman was the most intriguing character ever to rise to high office in the Bank of England. He was as far removed from the image of the banker as a desiccated human calculating machine as could be imagined. He was, on the contrary, a neurotic, hypersensitive intro-vert, subject to strange and unpredictable change of mood for which he himself could find 'no reasons, only instincts'. He was generally believed to be remote and intimidating, certainly he had a temper, being apt to fly into ungovernable rages. Whilst in one of these rages, he hurled an ink-pot at a dutiful member of his senior staff. But, despite all this, he had his strengths and was not a man to yield to fear of Australian or any other public opinion of his policies, nor to any sentimental–charitable feeling on behalf of public borrowers in Australia (or anywhere else).

One must speculate further. For it was doubly fortunate that the public passions unleashed by Jardine and Larwood were paralleled by a transformation of the whole political atmosphere in Australian political circles towards London. Almost overnight the lowering City grotesques conjured by Lang and 'Langism' were transformed into benevolent, avuncular figures: the old Victorian relationship seemed to have returned.

Why was Norman suddenly converted to conversion? By the 1930s the nature of his philosophy and his life's ambition were clear; he was convinced the central banks' bankers of the world could offer it salvation from the follies of governments, politics and politicians. Lurking behind this, in the deeper recesses of his mind, were memories of his deeply unhappy childhood at home and the misery of his boyhood at Eton. He was the scion of a fanatical cricketing family for whom cricket was life. He had come to loathe the very name of the game which had imprisoned him and made his young life totally wretched. His attitude towards test matches, whether in England or Australia, was that of the cricketing widow who sees her husband wrenched from her bosom daily in the cricketing season by the prospect of bat and ball, sandwiches and beer.

Norman's financial instinct was that economic recovery, and with it lower rates of interest, was indeed round the corner. The rational evidence of this had yet to be revealed. But his instincts could for once be used to offset the developing Commonwealth conflict which was rooted in the most loathsome of sports. The game that had destroyed his childhood seemed to be about to destroy the Empire. This was a situation in which the head of the central banking system of the world could, by a justifiable intuitive process of anticipation, once more unite in true amity and prosperity an Empire distracted by the idiocies of sport. Such reflections would certainly have been deeply pleasing to the Governor of the Bank of England. Was it not sweetest revenge – as well as good finance – to salvage peace and Empire while flanelled fools beat one another into the (cricket) ground with bat and ball?

The course of negotiating such intuitions did not (if recent speculations are correct) run smooth. After the third test – when Woodfull and Old-field were struck – the Australian Board of Control cabled the MCC, accusing the English team of being 'unsportsmanlike'. The MCC, deeply offended, offered to cancel the rest of the tour. The Chairman and moving spirit of the MCC, 'Plum' Warner, simultaneously appealed to the British Government's representative in Canberra to try and persuade the Australian Cricket Board to withdraw their charge of unsportsmanlike British tactics.

What happened next must be largely surmise. It will probably never be known what, if anything, passed between our man in Canberra and the Federal Prime Minister. But Mr Lyons seems to have intervened with the Board of Control: at least, on 1 February 1933, the Chairman of the Board sent a telegram to its secretary. It ran:

> Prime Minister interviewed me today. Stated that British representative had seen him and asked him to get us to withdraw word objected to. If not likelihood of England pulling right out. If we do withdraw has no doubt attack will be modified. *Government afraid successful conversions endangered.*

When the Prime Minister was later asked about rumours that he had intervened in the cricket dispute he laughed them off. One way or another, the cricket crisis had been averted though bad feeling continued. Sales of British goods in Adelaide (the scene of the test) fell and Australian wine was said to have become unpopular in Britain (though in the high noon of 'Emu' red there could have been other explanations of its declining reputation than disputes over cricket). What seems reasonably established is that the Federal Government was worried that the cricket fracas might upset their negotiations in London with the Bank of England: but whether their anxieties influenced the Australian Board of Control remains unknown. Equally, it is not known whether Montagu Norman was even interested in the antics of the cricket managers. It seems doubtful: if he was, he certainly did not allow them to affect the course of policy on the conversion loan.

'Bodyline' in Retrospect: the Wider Implications

'Bodyline' can now be seen in focus. It represents an important stage in the growth of sport mania and mass hysteria whipped up by the press. It was a step in the brutalization of cricket, though in perspective a small step. Australians protested violently and the English moderates, led by 'Plum' Warner, Gubby Allen (himself at least as fast a bowler as Larwood), and a number of others, did their best to modify the tactics exploited by Jardine.

The Australian response was to do their best to stiffen the aggressive qualities of their own bowling. Australian cricket authorities declined to limit the number of 'bouncers' a bowler might deliver in an over. (This was the English solution.) Meanwhile, in the 1980s, the whole scene has changed. In successive test match series, first against the West Indies (in Australia), then against New Zealand (in New Zealand), Australian cricket suffered an almost total collapse. This time it could not be blamed on England, who suffered a similar fate in the Caribbean.

Jardine and Larwood always stoutly maintained that Larwood never bowled at the man but at the wicket. In the course of half a century since the 1930s, such old-fashioned inhibitions have gone to the wall. Cricketers everywhere have become accustomed to the idea, exemplified most clearly, ruthlessly and unrepentantly by the West Indies, that lethal bowling is the quickest and surest way to victory. The winning team should contain at least three or four fast bowlers banging away continuously at the batsman's body, destroying not his wickets, but his confidence. The final result can only be to create a game that is not a game but a form of organized violence that will end by becoming as boring for the spectators as it is lethal to the batsmen. That Australian cricket is in tatters can be attributed to no single cause or person or episode. Everybody has been to blame – cricketers, cricket organizers, umpires, spectators, commercial exploiters of the spurious merits of the one-day game, newspaper cricket correspondents ... but, most of all, the malaise is the responsibility of the mass media. It is their hacks who have repeatedly exploited and exaggerated any violence or conflict incidental to sport as a form of mob entertainment.

In a strange, bizarre conjunction, journalism, television and film-making have used human gullibility to swell what began as harmless pastimes and social needs into festering cancers of hatred. This happened in 1932–3; but the political effects have been exaggerated – again by the media.

The *Sydney Morning Herald* has a claim to the attention of serious readers. Half a century after the Anglo-Australian cricketing crisis of 1932–3, the *Herald* printed a celebratory series of articles on 'bodyline' (omitting any reference to Larwood's book or Jardine's introduction to it). They were (said a fervent leading article) 'a part of the story of the evolution of the Australian society and of its search for identity'. The story ended – conclusively – with the attempt, by 'the cricketers of England, land of hope and glory ... to demolish Bradman by brute force. ... The psychological shock was profound....' Class divisions were suspended while 'thousands saw their Australian heroes ambushed and assaulted'. According to the *Herald*, the memory lingered, resulting in 'growing scepticism about the imperial heritage and its value and values. Bodyline ... brought to Australian self-consciousness a new element of separateness....' The article (dated 18 December 1982) was entitled: 'Bodyline – the End of Innocence' (that is, 'bodyline' had ended, exactly fifty years earlier, the alleged age of Australia's 'enslavement' to British influence in all forms – political, economic, financial, cultural, etc.).

Even if the 'enslavement' had ever existed – and by 1933 only a minority believed in it – the *Herald*'s article itself admitted that 'the outrage was not long loud'; it remained only in 'growing' scepticism about the imperial heritage. No doubt the editor was anxious to promote the circulation of his newspaper's forthcoming publication of six articles on 'bodyline' by emphasizing its political importance. It is true that there was growing scepticism about certain aspects of Anglo-Australian relations: but once the test matches ended, it had little to do either with bodyline or even with the financial crisis over British capital loans to Australia.

It was now to do with the much broader and even more complex issues arising from Australia's response to the Ottawa Conferences which loomed large especially from 1936 onwards. These aroused deep unease in Australia: when, later – and especially in 1942 – these economic problems, temporarily shelved but still unsolved – merged with the great strategic crisis of wartime; then, and only then, was Australia faced with agonizing decisions regarding her place in the world and how to order the priority of her loyalties. These could no longer be dodged. The ensuing controversies were deeper, longer, more bitter and widespread than anything that had happened earlier. They began with the economic problems of Australia in the Pacific: they continued with her strategic crisis in the Pacific and the Eastern Seas. These in turn raised in acute form the question – inchoate, sloppily articulated, fuzzily answered, yet fundamentally important – how to define 'the Australian identity'? But for the existence in the northern Pacific of Japan, these problems would never have arisen; at least, not in the form which they assumed. It was thus the problems of the Pacific which revived and kept green the memories of bodyline: but for the Japanese War it would have been forgotten.

12

MR CURTIN MOVES OVER

'European history has shown the transference of world power from the Mediterranean to the Atlantic; there are ominous signs of the transference of that power from the Atlantic to the Pacific; in whose hands is that power to be?'

*(Florence Gay)**

On 22 May 1936, Australia announced that it proposed to adopt what the Minister concerned described as 'a trade diversion policy'.†

Trade Diversion

Briefly, 'trade diversion' was an application of the ideas discussed at the Ottawa Conference of 1932, for developing international trade within the Empire; and for adjusting, in the interest of any member of the Conference who might need it, trade relations with any other non-Empire countries dumping goods produced under conditions of unfair trade. Tariff or import licences were to be used to afford preferential treatment to British and other European producers. In general, the grant of licences would be free to countries with whom Australia had, for example, a favourable trade balance; where the trade balance was unfavourable, the position would be open to argument. Motor vehicle chassis would be imported only from Britain: the object being to develop the Australian motor industry, on grounds of the trade balance and the defence needs of the country which the engineering industry represented. Similar measures would apply to textiles.

The country most affected by the 'diversionary' measures was Japan; and Japan had responded immediately with counter-measures. Japanese buyers were forbidden to buy wool, hides and dairy produce in Australia.

---

* *In Praise of Australia: An Anthology of Prose and Verse* (London, 1912), Introduction.
† The details of the moves and counter-moves are set out and analysed in *Australian Commentaries, Select Articles from the Round Table 1911–1942*, L.L. Robson (ed.), (Melbourne, 1975). The editor's discerning introduction and critical commentary makes this a very valuable source for historians.

The graziers and wool traders of Australia – the original export industry of Australia – suffered worst in the interests of a theory of international trade far less advantageous than its attractive paper logic promised. Leo Amery, the leading Conservative exponent, had pointed out that few countries were large enough to provide the market conditions for industrial efficiency and profitability. The answer was to group countries together so as 'to satisfy the technical requirements of modern production and yet retain some common ideal, some permanent cooperative purpose to enlist the forces of economic nationalism.... The British Empire ... provides for us, at least, our natural starting point....'

'But', asked the *rapporteur* of *The Round Table* on behalf of Australia, 'is this sound policy for Australia today?' The answer was that slowly (for Australian opinion was divided, ill-informed and generally in the dark about its Government's objectives) the impression was forming that it was 'neither economically expedient nor politically safe for Australia to adopt towards the countries of the Northern Pacific the attitude which the new policy implies'. Australia found herself on the horns of a dilemma. She had long been trying to obtain a larger share of the British market in meat and dairy produce. Her bargaining counter was to offer to regain – at Japan's expense – a larger share of Australia's imports of textiles for British manufacturers. But, said *The Round Table*, 'the very act of making such an offer impairs the success of Australia's efforts to find in the Northern Pacific an expanding market for meat, flour and wool ... Australia loses, perhaps, whichever way she chooses'.

Meanwhile, contemporary British policy was turning (under threat of war) towards making Britain more self-sufficient in food. Here was little prospect of an expanding market for Australian produce. The East was a different story. But, *The Round Table* concluded,

> the trade diversion policy not only produces immediate dislocation of that market; it threatens contraction of it, in wool especially ... the diversion of trade may help Lancashire rather than Great Britain, and even there, taking a long view, its advantages to Lancashire are dubious.

If reports were correct, what Lancashire needed was 'courageous reorganization and re-equipment'. The present concessions could, therefore, be on the wrong foot altogether.

Within two years, the United States had joined Japan in retaliatory action against the 'trade diversion' policy. There was, accordingly, an inevitable and humiliating retreat by the Australian Government. But already, great harm had been done to her trade (in wool especially); and undoubtedly a feeling lingered, not only in the Labour Party, that the Australian Government had deferred too much to British interests. Worst of all, they had done it behind doors virtually closed to Parliament and the public: Mr Lyons was not good at public relations. His only course was to drop 'trade diversion' – in so far as he could. It was not easy. There was little or no recovery in the damaged trades with Japan or the United States before the outbreak of the Second World War.

The Second World War

Australia responded immediately in 1939, offering help to the West in the shape of military, naval and air power (Japan at this stage was still neutral). By 1942 the whole scene had changed very much for the worse. Hitler had overrun France, Belgium, Holland, Denmark. Mussolini had joined Germany. Sweden was still officially neutral but had shown her total weakness by letting the Germans through her territory to overrun Norway. Worst of all, Japan had entered the war dramatically, wreaking vast damage at Pearl Harbour. There followed the advance by Japanese forces to Malaya, defeating British and Australian forces, inflicting a humiliating capitulation on Singapore – its defences supposedly reinforced by recent improvements – sinking the *Prince of Wales* and *Repulse* (two of Britain's last modern battleships) by air attack of unprecedented violence and accuracy.

Australian opinion was bitterly critical of what seemed the casual attention paid to these Eastern defences of her security. And now it was not merely those described by the Australian *Round Table* correspondent as 'the small minority which expresses a distrust of all things English' who felt that Australia had been let down, their manhood needlessly sacrificed and their interests and opinions neglected in London. Churchill's broadcast after the fall of Singapore evoked sympathy and admiration for its heroic determination: it did nothing to reassure Australian opinion at large that reform of the overall strategy of the war, especially as it affected the Pacific in general and Australia in particular, was at hand.

This was the tense and delicate situation in which Curtin and Evatt came to the top. Neither they nor many others were looking for a way out of the war through any policy of isolation. Both had subscribed to the policy of loyalty to Britain: both, though critical of Britain's apparent neglect of Australia's interests, stood by their declaration. They did, nevertheless, lay claim to a larger say in the direction of the war. In an article printed in the *Sydney Morning Herald* (27 December 1941), Curtin (now Prime Minister) made his famous declaration on 'the Pacific struggle'. He aligned Australia with America as entitled to the 'fullest say' in the direction of the fighting. Then followed the two sentences which put the cat amongst the pigeons:

Without any inhibitions of any kind, I make it quite clear that Australia looks to America free of any pangs as to our traditional links or kinship with the United Kingdom. We know the problems that the United Kingdom faces, we know the constant threat of invasion, we know the dangers of dispersal of strength, but we know, too, that Australia can go and Britain can still hold on.'

His phraseology provoked immediate protests, in Australia as well as in Britain, where the War Cabinet, and Churchill especially, took strong exception to what they read as ingratitude and irresponsibility bordering on disloyalty. Two days later Curtin made a firm disclaimer of any such intent. It ended: 'Our loyalty to the King goes to the very core of our national life.'

Even many who had always disagreed politically with him in Australia accepted his declaration without hesitation. 'It is admitted', wrote the *Round Table* correspondent,

that his choice of language is sometimes unfortunate, his quotations from the poets almost invariably so; but his sincerity and his disinterested desire to serve Australia in her present need have not been doubted.... The reproach of 'squealing' should not be directed against a Dominion which has done everything that Great Britain has asked of it.

Mistrust nevertheless remained, fanned by an inevitable trickle of rumours on both sides. Curtin had pressed for General MacArthur to be appointed Pacific Commander-in-Chief. This did not prevent MacArthur from passing on some indiscreet comments on Anglo-Australian relations to his British Liaison Officer. Curtin (he said) had indicated to him that Australia was ready to shift her loyalties from Britain to the United States. This (added the recipient) 'is probably extravagant, but MacArthur *has* previously told me that Curtin and Co. more or less offered him the country on a platter when he arrived from the Philippines'.*

'Billy' Hughes, former Labour leader and Prime Minister, now leader of a 'United Australian Party' and indefatigably pro-British, cabled Churchill to warn him that Curtin's ministers were anti-British and Curtin himself 'at best cool towards Britain'. Such suspicions and rumours

* Quoted in *Australian Outlook*, vol. 29, No. 1, April 1975, p. 62.

should not be taken too seriously: wartime alliances were always vulnerable to gossip of this kind. All the mistrusts common in peacetime were sharpened and exaggerated amidst the high tensions of war. What did happen, without doubt, was that once it had been recognized that Australia could only be succoured by closer American ties, the application of measures to realize military co-operation inevitably increased Australian reliance on American aid in many forms. Anglo-American agreement itself, with its objective of a joint European strategy against Hitler, insisted on exigently by Stalin, inevitably limited, once again, British aid for Australia.

American aid to Australia grew enormously. By the end of the war, some 60 per cent or more of Australian imports, previously supplied from British sources, came from the United States. American influence over the Australian economy increased as the British inevitably dwindled. Covenanted or uncovenanted, lend-lease beat out the paths for post-war United States investment overseas in allied territories.

This did nothing to slacken the heavy pressure on Australia's contribution to the war against Japan: nor – that other prevalent misconception – did Churchill and his Cabinet and Chiefs of Staff exonerate or exclude Britain from participating in the defeat of Japan, once the German problem was disposed of. Curtin did not need to urge Britain to send warships to the Pacific, as he did in 1944. He was apparently not told that it was already planned – against bitter resistance by the United States naval Chief-of-Staff, Admiral King, and General MacArthur – to send a British fleet, with a 'Fleet Train' to supply it – into the Pacific, once conditions in the West enabled Britain to release the necessary resources.

The United States–Australian liaison, or marriage of convenience, was by no means without its problems. True love or shotgun wedding, the path of the newly-wed couple was strewn with suspicions and misunderstandings, most of them genuine, some contrived. The Americans were 'liked and admired'. Australians, used to blunt speaking themselves, seem not to have taken it amiss when the Americans disclaimed any thanks for coming to Australia's help: 'They tell us laughingly but truly enough that they are here because the best place to defend the United States is on distant territory and in somebody else's air ... the defence of Australia is the defence of the United States.'* But the reporter added, 'of the ultimate political consequences of the present alignments we have not yet begun to think. The first task is to beat back the enemy's assaults upon the postern gate.'

* *The Round Table*, May 1942.

The last desperate battle in the Far Eastern war was fought by the Australian troops in New Guinea. The jungle terrain, still sheltering 90,000 Japanese troops, was appalling; the casualties too. The assault on Balikpapan in July 1945, was the last major Allied landing. President Truman's decision to drop the atomic bomb ended Japanese resistance. Japan surrendered unconditionally on 11 August 1945.

John Curtin died in 1945. He still lacks an adequate biography but it is plain that, in spite of his sometimes clumsy use of language, he stands out from the rank-and-file of Australian politicians as a statesman of rare integrity. He was an old-fashioned kind of socialist-patriot, of Irish blood, like some of his close friends in politics: Scullin, Chifley, Calwell, Forde. As a young man, in 1919, he had suffered a complete breakdown in health, probably because of heavy drinking. He recovered and reformed, though his comparatively early death – he was only fifty – was probably partly due to his early excesses. A lapsed Roman Catholic, he read widely, if erratically. His socialism was of the humanitarian rather than the dogmatic Marxist brand – Morris, O'Dowd, Henry George and the radical poets like Shelley and Walt Whitman, all influenced him. His career was with the trade union movement as organizer and orator; though to judge from those who heard him, his appeal lay in his ability to speak clearly and sincerely to an audience rather than rouse them by political rhetoric. His vision was that of Vance Palmer; 'of founding in our remote seas an ideal republic from which the evils of the old world were removed ...'.*

John Curtin felt it his patriotic duty to part company with Churchill over the role of Australia and the Australian troops in the war. Churchill's unshakeable conviction was that the war would be lost or won in the West: he threw all his own energy and genius into the pursuit of that end. Curtin could not agree. Reluctantly Churchill agreed that Curtin should fill the role he demanded in South-East Asia and the Pacific. In 1942 this cost Churchill dear, and it took him a long time to forgive Curtin. But in the end he did forgive him; essentially magnanimous, he confessed that when he came to meet and know Curtin, he formed a personal friendship with 'this eminent and striking Australian personality'.†

* Norman Lee *John Curtin, Saviour of Australia* (Sydney, 1983) is somewhat hagiographical, but more up-to-date than Lloyd Ross's *John Curtin: A Biography* (Sydney, 1977) – though the latter is more scholarly.
† Winston Churchill *The Second World War* vol. IV (London, 1951), p. 5.

Unfortunately, Churchill's magnanimity is not recognized by Curtin's recent biographer. It is a pity that Churchill did not visit Australia; had he done so, the Australian perception of him might have been different. As Ronald Lewin has said of him, 'the men most close to him, most subjected to his imperious pressures, were those who loved him most'.*

The Aftermath of War

With Curtin's death and the Japanese war over, Australia's traditional aptitude for retreating from international commitments reasserted itself. The original warmth of the relationship with the United States had cooled markedly. When Robert Menzies was returned to power as Prime Minister, his first moves were to reaffirm the old ties with Britain, the Commonwealth and the Monarchy: but it was not possible to turn the clock back. Before the war, British, Dutch and French colonial power in South-East Asia had provided – or seemed to provide – a protective screen for Australian security from attack. When the Japanese forces retreated, the former European masters of this whole area began to de-colonize. Gradually, India and the former European colonies to the east and south achieved independence. Australia, for reasons of convenience, trade, and general liberal democracy, supported the emergent states like Indonesia. This tended to distance her from Britain, the Netherlands and France. But what was to replace the security they had previously afforded to Australia? Would the new states, with growing populations, problems of food and necessities, settle down peacefully? Or would their future be to seek expansion, backed by restive diplomacy and even military aggression?

To this was added the even more threatening possibilities of a Communist alliance between China, newly rising to power under Mao tse Tung, and Russia. Percy Spender, Menzies' Foreign Minister, was haunted by the fear that the defeat of Japan was no panacea for the ills of the world between South-East Asia and the Pacific. Australians had by now tasted American 'imperialism' in action: many of them had not found it to their taste. They looked back nostalgically to the Anglo-Australian relationship, which in retrospect seemed a more natural, easy-going affair than anything they might enjoy with the high-powered, dominant, victorious United States. (The latter now produced over half the world's oil

---

* Lewin Churchill as Warlord (London, 1973), p. 135. As one who was a minor and occasional victim, I readily and warmly endorse this perception.

and nearly half of its total industrial output, and, not unnaturally, was apt to assume that what was good for the United States was good for the rest of mankind.)

Yet, in face of American pressure, reviving markets in Japan, United States loans and the increasing drive of multinational companies (dominated by the United States), anxious and ready to invest in Australian manufacturing industry, the traditional patterns of Australian economic ties with Europe, especially Britain, seemed poor alternatives. By the 1950s a new wave of American and Japanese enterprise was sweeping over the Australian economic scene. British preferential tariffs in favour of Australian exports were reduced. An agreement with Japan gave that country equality with other trading nations in return for a Japanese promise to buy more Australian wool. American manufacturing interests swiftly came to control important sectors of the Australian economy. Many of the new immigrant workers came from refugee camps and Southern Europe as British emigration slackened.

The Anzus Treaty

The changing situation was not only, nor perhaps even predominantly, economic in character. Important sections of Australian opinion – of British opinion too – shared the American fear and hatred of Communism. To many, the brutal overrunning of the former independent nations of Eastern Europe, like the spread of Communism in South-East Asia, portended a world revolution based on a Marxist–Leninist ideology which threatened the future of civilization as it had been known and for which the Second World War had been fought. Britain, drained, exhausted and pauperized by the war, was herself willing to accept American economic and political domination of areas once under her own leadership as the only alternative to their falling to Russia and China. The treaty of peace signed with Japan in 1951 was so lenient that Australia and New Zealand pleaded for an international alliance with America to preserve them from a resurgent Japan. The result was the Anzus Treaty. The omission of Britain from this defensive arrangement simply underlined that Curtin had indeed had no alternative but to turn to the United States a decade earlier.

Few responsible Australians were prepared to envisage the risks that would ensue if the United States suffered another fit of isolationism and withdrew from Asia. In any case there was no definitive breach in relations with Britain. Menzies – largely supported by majority opinion in Australia – gave strong support to the British Government during the

Suez Crisis in 1956. The previous year, Australia had sent troops to help Britain suppress the Communist revolt in Malaya. On this occasion the United States agreed to support the renewed co-operation of Britain and Australia in South-East Asia. Later, however, when Indonesia, in 1961, seized the western half of New Guinea and threatened to take it from the Netherlands by force, America refused to join Australia in supporting the Dutch. Four years later there were further differences over Indonesian–Australian quarrels in Borneo.

The Anzus Alliance was, from the start, fraught with problems, and these were to persist. Australia was involved in the Korean War and, even more deeply, in the Vietnam War. By 1967, there were some 8,000 Australian troops in Vietnam. The 1960s also saw three major American military bases installed in Australia; an important navigation station near Adelaide (1961) of critical value to the United States Navy, especially its submarines; another at North-West Cape (1962), vital to such operations as those of the Polaris nuclear missile submarines; in 1970–1 the Pine Gap group of high-technology communications and intelligence centres. All were (and remain) strictly under the control of the United States, as were bases in a number of other countries, including Britain.

Few of these developments were popular. In some quarters in Australia they aroused fear and anger. By 1984, it could be alleged by a severely critical chronicler that 'Australia was a southern dominion of the United States.'*

Increasingly, the Anzus Alliance came under fire. The American Government had acquired, via that treaty, a chain of bases stretching from Japan to the South Pacific. The Australian forces began to replace British with American weapons. Was the purpose of Anzus the mutual protection of its three signatories? Or of America alone?

The Vietnam War

The Vietnam War seemed to be the test. In July 1966, the Australian Prime Minister (Harold Holt) told the American President that Australia would be 'all the way with L.B.J.'. He won an outright electoral victory in favour of his policy. When President Johnson visited Australia in the same year he was cheered by huge crowds who chanted their welcome: the anti-war demonstrators threw paint at the presidential car; they were swiftly dispersed. Even in 1968 the alliance held – at least half those questioned in a Gallup Poll favouring Australian participation in Vietnam.

* Michael Dunn *Australia and the Empire: From 1788 to the Present* (Sydney, 1984).

1969 saw a profound change of mood. Opposition to the continued war grew: so, equally, did opposition to, and evasion of, conscription. A nation-wide protest movement developed across Australia. In May 1970, 100,000 people demonstrated in a sit-down protest in Melbourne. The war ended, in profound disillusion and bitter mutual recriminations, in 1975.

The experience of the alliance was puzzling to both contracting parties. The Americans tended to regard Australia as a reluctant ally, unenthusiastic and perhaps unreliable. There were too many Australian Communists: the Union movement was especially unreliable.

Australians reacted in different ways. Young and even middle-aged Australians were, like their British, German, Dutch – even French – contemporaries, deeply under the all-persuasive American influences which permeated daily life everywhere, via technology, radio, popular music, films, television, advertising etc. Yet at the same time they also resented these influences precisely because they could not resist them. Those Australians who experienced the war itself and suffered accordingly threw their minds back to compare American with former British influence. Even here, views differed. Older generations found Britain a less exigent, more understanding ally – even if sometimes inefficient, ineffective and casual. Some younger ones, with less practical experience, assumed that British 'imperialism' must have worked in much the same way as American 'imperialism' did. Weren't all 'imperialisms' the same?

Which Imperialism?

This is the prevailing view of a recent book by Michael Dunn: *Australia and the Empire*. From the title, most English-speaking readers would imagine that its subject was Australia and the *British* Empire. In fact, only the first third of the book is about the British Empire; the rest deals with Britain's successor-imperialists, especially the United States. It is a sour and doom-laden story of an Australasian economy and culture borne down under the oppression of British industrial capitalists, whose slippery financial colleagues ground honest colonial faces in the dust of the City of London. It is a book which owes much to the late Brian Fitzpatrick and his Celtic legends of economic imperialism.

Thus it is somewhat disconcerting that, just as one is settling down in familiar company, Michael Dunn faces us with a surprise: his chapter on 'The Soviet Connection' turns out to be scarcely more favourable to Soviet Communism than his chapters on Britain or the United States are to those examples of capitalist imperialism. By 1977–8, he tells us, the Soviet Union was South Australia's second largest customer, lagging only behind Japan. In a piece of investigation (is it intended to be chilling?) he examines the spectacular operations of Australia's Trade Commissions in Moscow. In 1968 Australia's trade with the USSR totalled $42 million a year: by 1978 it had risen to $500 million: most of this was represented by Australian exports to Russia. Yet is not this what the immortal authors of *1066 and All That* would have called a Good Thing? Apparently not. Mr Dunn explains that in the world of international trade nothing, apparently, is what it might seem to be or ought to be. In reality 'the Soviet Union ... wants Australia to remain a strong exporter of primary products while it sends Australia its manufactured goods, its industrial equipment, and other capital goods' – not to mention Russian vodka.*

The socialist age of Soviet Russia, it seems, is no great advance on the age of Victorian capitalism, when Australia exported wool to England to pay for 'great quantities of nails, bolts, paint, lime, plaster, cement and ornate household fittings from British factories'.† Nor do Russian enormities stop at such ambitions. Russian fishing fleets (along with Japanese) threaten Australia's control of her own fishing grounds. The Russian merchant shipping fleet offers frequent rates to Asia 15–20 per cent lower than Australian rates, thus upsetting the Waterside Workers' Federation. From the WWF, Mr Dunn abruptly turns to the even greater threat posed by the United States whose interests Australia is meanwhile defending. And because the United States does not need Australian produce in the quantities that Britain had done (alas! apparently, for those good old days) it cannot 'play the same role in the Australian economy'.

It was, therefore, 'left to Japan to provide the consuming end of the imperial relationship once post-war reconstruction and the Korean War had revived its steel industry. Japanese companies depended on cheap, regular supplies from Australia.' Japan has thus become the industrial rival of the United States, while 'Australians have not had the political will to be independent.' In a couple of paragraphs, Michael Dunn explains what (in his view) needs to be done:

First, the states should keep out of all matters to do with overseas trade. All overseas marketing should be 'co-ordinated' by the Federal Commonwealth so as to prevent foreigners (for example, Japanese steel mills) playing off one Australian coal mining company against another. The 'targeting of investment' in Australia should also be undertaken by government; thus capital locked up in private home ownership could be redirected into 'industrial research and development'. The (Common-

* Michael Dunn *Australia and the Empire*, p. 203.
† Ibid., p. 51.

wealth) Government should also calculate better political and military bargains with, for example, the United States. For America will defend what it owns in Australia only when it is in its primary interests to do so. *'Australia's sole insurance will be its own capacity and will to act independently.'*

Now it is neither unnatural nor stupid for any sovereign state, however small or large, to assert its sovereign rights. Unhappily, as well as illogically, Michael Dunn goes far beyond this in his book, which – in my view regrettably – reflects confused prejudices quite commonly found amongst certain sections of Australian opinions connected with the media, academic or pseudo-academic circles, as well as the more gullible and impressionable members of the public at large.

To return to his title: *Australia and the Empire: From 1788 to the Present.* The confusion is inexcusable – it clearly conveys to the prospective reader a serious study of the Anglo-Australian relationship, yet this is not the major concern of the book. Michael Dunn is really concerned about the importance of an 'independent' Australia. We shall return to this very important problem in our final chapter. Here it is enough to say that not only was the British connection totally different from the other connections he deals with – the United States, Soviet Russia, Japan: it also underwent a total sea-change with the advent of responsible self-government. This came in two instalments: first, 1850 to 1856, when all the states except Western Australia were authorized to prepare written constitutions which reflected, as far as possible, the rules and regulations that made up the unwritten constitution of Britain itself (Western Australia followed more slowly in the 1880s); second, the federation of the independent states in an Australian Commonwealth, completed in 1901. To the new Federal Government the contracting states yielded only the powers they chose to yield: no more.

Before the 1850s, Australia and its people were strictly colonial dependencies of an Imperial Britain. After the 1850s they became increasingly independent. More than that, Britain itself dismantled between 1815 and the 1860s the whole apparatus constituting the legal and administrative basis of the old mercantilist, imperial system which most vividly and concretely reflected the colonial dependence of Australia (and other colonies). This deregulation was viewed by many swept along on the tide of doctrinaire, 'liberal', *laissez-faire*, as only the first step to a *total* separation, economic and political, of Australia from Britain. The 'separatist' movement, as we have seen (chapter 9) lost its momentum by the 1890s. Australia remained, voluntarily, within the British Commonwealth. She remains there still, voluntarily – though free to leave whenever she pleases. Only sentiment, history, convenience and consider-

rations of international trade jointly serve to preserve the present relationship.

It is, though, these factors which distinguish the Australian–British relationship from Australia's relationship with the United States, Japan and Russia. The relationship with the United States, in so far as it is basically economic, is generically the same as that with Japan or Russia. In non-economic, diplomatic and strategic respects, it is marked by a special attachment via the so-called Anzus Treaty which binds the United States, Australia and New Zealand together in a pact for mutual defence. (Its fragility will be examined later.)

There is no warrant whatever (except socialist doctrine) for describing the relationship of either the United States or Japan, or Russia, to Australia as an 'imperial' or 'imperialist' relationship. The mode of conducting the economic relationship differs in every case. It is open to the contracting parties to adopt anything from binding state-to-state contracts for fixed periods (for example, the Soviets) to completely free-market associations, or such associations modified as necessary by membership of other binding international organizations (for example, Britain's membership of the European Economic Community) or by special supply arrangements made in wartime (for example, with the United States, during the Vietnam War or with Britain in the First and Second World Wars).

All in all, it is probably true to say there were few, if any, economic relationships in the history of international trade that were more free of government pressure than the Anglo-Australian relationship from 1860 to 1930. Despite numerous observations to the contrary, both sides were free economic agents. The terms struck were those reached between a willing buyer and willing seller. It was natural that Jack Lang, as premier of temporarily bankrupt New South Wales, should allege that the mess and muddle was the work of Jewish money-lenders in London. This was the standard resort to abuse long used by the *Bulletin*, the Shearers' Union press and similar organs of frustrated opinion. It was no worse and no better than the clamour – from the same quarters – for a 'White Australia and to hell with imported labour whatever its colour, black or yellow'. It was, like Michael Dunn's 'analysis', political rhetoric of a kind (diminishingly important in Europe, still very strong and characteristic in certain circles in Australia) designed to satisfy those who demand that their narrow nationalism should be well-laced with the noises and stimulants of old-fashioned radicalism.

If Michael Dunn's analysis and recommendations for an international trade policy for Australia were to be put into action, her ports would be shut down in a matter of months. Even those economic illiterates (as Michael Dunn might describe them) the 'mercantilists' of the pre-Adam Smith age, realized that not every nation can have a favourable balance of trade with every other, or export only manufactures and not primary products, or wheat or coal.

The former Prime Minister of Singapore, Mr Lee Kuan Yew, has recently given some wise advice to the Australian press. He drew their attention to the economic vulnerability of Australia: to her persistent habit of invoking anti-dumping actions against importers as a substitute for tariff protection; above all, of maintaining the wrong frames of mind on industrial development: 'as long as Australia's industrialisation is primarily based on import substitution, not on export orientation, she will not develop the [necessary] economic ties with her Asian neighbours....' They were still left with mingled feelings of envy and dislike for their imagined Australia and its *dolce vita*.

Until his lessons sink in, there will still be many Australians who fail to realize that we all – even Australians – live in a world where economic, political and cultural nationalism must give way to interdependence between nations. As Michael Dunn's book shows, some Australians are slow to learn. His prescriptions are the prescriptions of the *Bulletin* of the 1890s: a confused compound of domestic radicalism, narrow nationalism, fear and ignorance of the world outside Australia. In the 1980s this will not do.

13

WINDOWS ON THE WORLD

'It is hard to quarrel with men who only wish to be innocently happy. And out of this very wish there is growing a taste for art which in time may come to something considerable.'

(James Anthony Froude)*

'Why should we only toil ...?'

(Tennyson)†

From the sixteenth to the nineteenth century, the nation state was the dominant form of political and strategic organization. Wars between the nation states, conducted for religious, economic, or territorial advantage, occupy much of the space in books on 'modern history'. Yet these centuries were not exclusively governed by nationalist concepts. The arts – painting, sculpture, architecture, music, literature – inherited and expanded the functions of the medieval wandering minstrels and scholars; by a curious and important irony, the ages of nationalist war saw the styles and method of the artists and musicians spreading universally and regardless of national barriers. From Italy, Europe took the sonnet, the madrigal, the notations and forms of music – *sinfonia, sonata, opera*. All musical directions *adagio, nobilmente, vivace, forte, piano* – were Italian down to the present day. Eighteenth-century London's music was dominated by Handel, a German: and Handel employed for the operas and oratorios he wrote (in an Italianate style learnt during seven years in Italy) mainly Italian and German singers and instrumentalists.

Victorian England knew Italian opera mainly through the Carl Rosa touring company, which was founded by a German (who Italianized his name). The company was directed for about seventy-five years by Flemish Belgians from Bruges; the famous Goossens family (see p. 228). While the English carried on three ferocious naval wars against the Dutch in the seventeenth century, Dutch painters came in considerable numbers

* *Oceana* (1886), p. 166.
† Choric Song

to England to paint portraits and landscapes. The 'English' visual arts were dominated by the Dutch. The official English war artist during the second and third Anglo-Dutch wars was the great Vandervelde; he came over from the Dutch side. The classical Georgian style in English architecture was borrowed from Palladio, the Italian genius; but it seems to have come via Netherlandish intermediaries. Two world wars temporarily interrupted the popularity of Wagner; Verdi's reputation never suffered at all; neither did Puccini's.

In Western Europe, the years since the 1940s have seen a revolutionary change in international political attitudes. In the 1960s and 1970s, not only did the attractions of nationalism recede. The ultra-Europeans fighting for a united Europe defined as their top priority the reconstruction of a Europe from which all traces and memories of nationality were to be eliminated. Fortunately the absurdity of this proposition became clear as the force of the historical movements just described became apparent even to the most dedicated 'Europeans'. Better surely to recognise that Shakespeare, Beethoven, Newton, Handel, Verdi, Donizetti were already not just 'European': they were for the world.

In the light of this inherent internationalism of the arts, and the undeniable evidence that grows daily of the economic and social interdependence of the nations, it is puzzling that Australia should in the last two decades have experienced a nationalist resurgence. The weight that should be attached to this is debateable; it is not necessarily to be measured by the volume of noise created by some of its protagonists. The reasons are equally in doubt. Some simpler, salient features may be outlined. Political analysts would mostly agree that Australians generally show a casual indifference to events and developments in the world outside. This is an attitude not limited to Australians. National electorates in most countries remain largely indifferent to foreign affairs, as Britain and France remained indifferent in the 1920s and 1930s to events in Germany, Italy and Czechoslovakia. It is within living memory that American 'isolationism' was perhaps the major factor in world politics.

Indifference to everything beyond the parish pump means ignorance also. Prosperity – and distance – tend to encourage both. The prospect of undisturbed peace, or the absence of any fear of immediately destructive war, is also of assistance. Foreign affairs and national defence recede, to become recondite issues for the specialists. They are rarely the pivots on which elections, or the careers of politicians, turn.

Australians have shown themselves capable, in peace and war, of withstanding the ultimate rigours of life – drought, flood and fire in the bush, shot and shell at Gallipoli, in North Africa, New Guinea, Malaysia, Korea, Vietnam. Yet these are the trials of a relative handful, of bloody memories best forgotten, or left to the film producer to manipulate into popular entertainment. And entertainment is, not unnaturally in the circumstances, what much of Australian life is about.

Froude and Francis Adams both remarked upon the seductive beauties of the land, the bush, the hills and mountains, the coast, the harbours. They shared the sometimes peaceful, sometimes pullulating life and excitement that is Australia. They sensed (as a serious minority of Australians also sense) the lack of any deep seriousness of purpose. The old saw runs ... happy is the land that has no history; old, but true only in part, and positively untrue when the history is false history, as much Australian 'history' is. Has the noble race of shearers and farmers gone (as Santamaria believes), making way for a race of public-service clerks wearing clean white collars.

Was the bush, as Adams believed, the desert repository of nobility of soul and virtue? Is urban life the seductive ruination of the people? As A.D. Hope has written, a rash of draining sores:

> And her five cities, like five teeming Sores,
> Each drains her: a vast parasite robber-state.
> Where second-hand Europeans pullulate
> Timidly on the edge of alien shores.*

For ordinary people in normally prosperous times, there are few places in the world which can equal the quality of life Australia offers. As the Victorian entrepreneur observed, it is the paradise of my-lord-the-working-man: high wages, short hours, leisure for simple amusements – cricket, football, tennis, swimming, surfing, horse-racing, horse-riding, sailing, sunbathing. When times are busy and prosperous, these diversions relieve the dangers of too much work; when times are bad they mollify the humiliations of bankruptcy and unemployment. In America, unemployment sends up the sales of shotguns and the production of gunpowder so that Americans can shoot more rabbits and game birds: the Australian, in times of stress, gives up and goes to the beach until things improve.

What, in practice, does the 'high standard of living' mean for Australians? Today, thanks to a continued and ethnically more varied policy of immigration, it means that they have a generous choice of good restaurants with varied menus: Italian, Greek, French, Lebanese, German, Asiatic, Oriental, and a choice of fine wines from New South Wales, Victoria,

---

* *The Penguin Book of Australian Verse*, H. Heseltine (ed.) (Sydney, 1972), p. 190.

South Australia, Tasmania, etc. They can read – apart from tabloid rubbish well down to American or British standards – three quality newspapers: the *Sydney Morning Herald*, the *Age* and the *Australian*; they may not achieve the accuracy, range or judgement of American, French or British best, but they come pretty near to them. There is a good range of theatre, *avant-garde* and popular, with a handful (but not more) of good actors and producers. The Australian film industry remains provincial, its production and acting stodgy, speech often unintelligible. Too many films underline Max Harris's observation about the recent dive of some elements in Australia 'into narrow, narcissistic nationalism'. *Gallipoli, Breaker Morant, The Last Bastion* and a number of others illustrate the makers' ability to distort history grossly. Television suffers in the same way. It regularly falls to the depths plumbed by its American and British counterparts, but very rarely reaches the heights they occasionally achieve.

The unfailing glory of the country is its natural beauty, the variety of the endless coastline in calm and storm, the strange fascination of bush, rain forest, ancient rock formations, one-street country towns and villages lined sparsely with wooden shops, shacks and a pub; wheatlands, endless pastures, distant flocks of sheep, herds of cattle – and what seems, to a European eye, almost eternal sunlight on the whitening gum trees. All with the blackened burnt-out reminders that all this beauty is liable to violent interruptions that suddenly, disastrously bring Australians back to the terrifying cruelty and ugliness that is the Janus face of nature. Perhaps it is this folk memory of problems that lie beyond human power to solve which has lodged in the Australian psyche a habit of turning away from fundamental problems. In politics it turns into the devious circumlocutions of government by 'consensus'. There is the refusal to acknowledge until the last moment, or later, that Australia's economy is still interdependent with the rest of the world; and the inability to see that sooner or later Australia has to commit herself to a foreign and defence policy. As one of Australia's most perceptive journalists, Greg Sheridan, said recently: 'effusive burblings towards China are demeaning and counter-productive', so long as the real nature of Australia's relationships with the United States, Britain and Europe remain in suspense. Even as this is written the Australian Government has published the results of another enquiry – again, a one-man show – into the future defence of Australia. It appears to be another aspiration to independence – independence particularly from the United States and the Anzus Alliance – while still keeping the costs down to the same level (3 per cent of Gross Domestic Product) as before. Even for AD

1986 (let alone 1996), this does not seem a workable proposition. It has already been attacked as a cheap rationalization of the Defence Department's basic ideal of neutrality, which ignores the real threats to Australia: her far-flung trade routes by sea and air.

Let us turn from popular amusements, pastimes and politics, to what T.S. Eliot once described as the higher forms of amusement: poetry, the visual arts and music. 'Art' is often treated as though it were something abstract; on the contrary it is something very concrete and individual. It has also, undoubtedly, certain 'national' aspects and identifications, but above all, art is essentially universal, not national, and the greater the art the more universal is certain to be its appeal and value.

The Visual Arts: Painting

We have referred elsewhere (p. 110) to James Gleeson's study of Australian painters and its emphasis on the emergence of a specifically 'Australian' school of painting. No one would dispute that many Australian artists, especially in the past half-century or century, have painted specifically Australian scenes in ways that are original, and 'Australian'. This does not warrant the further conclusions about the history and character of painting in Australia, with an unbridgeable gap round about the 1880s which distinguishes a fully-rounded Australian 'national' vision from an earlier vision: 'of great interest from the social and historical point of view ... a high degree of technical skill ... but only a handful ... can stand on their own feet as significant aesthetic achievements'.*
They failed to unlock top secrets of the Australian continent because they did not possess 'the right key'. There was 'nothing in the imported notions about art that fitted it to cope with the particular pictorial problems set up by the appearance and feel of the newly-settled continent'. Thus (Gleeson continues) John Glover's work seems 'tentative and lacking in perception' in 'the light of later achievements'. Conrad Martens remains 'a brilliant outsider'. Philip Gidley King, in spite of his all-absorbing anxieties as third Governor of New South Wales, found time to execute some remarkable drawings of aboriginals at work and play. Gleeson's only comment on what is itself an historical event, as well as an aesthetic achievement of some importance, is that 'King failed to catch the characteristic features of Aboriginal physiognomy'. Similarly, the remarkable achievement of Samuel Thomas Gill 'remains on the level of social documentation – valuable for the information it

* Gleeson *Australian Painters*, p. 17.

contains but incapable of inducing any deep aesthetic satisfaction'.*

To be fair to Gleeson, it should be said that in the end he concedes the risks of 'a kind of national narcissism', which in young countries turns the artists too much to parochial externals, neglecting more profound 'inward', or 'outward' (that is, international) forms of art. Nevertheless, his book as a whole seems to be an ideological eulogy of a specifically 'national vision' as an essential to Australian art. This is misleading and exaggerated.

Mr Gleeson's book was first published in 1971. Perhaps in the late 1980s he would want to take account of the shifts in public taste since the 1970s, as reflected in prices paid at auction. They are admittedly an inadequate, but nevertheless interesting comment on how widely his theory is acceptable. The highest prices for Australian paintings in recent years have been paid for the earlier, rather than later, more modern works. A von Guérard (1811–1901) of Sydney Harbour recently fetched a record price of $A700,000 at Sothebys. An Impressionist painting by Arthur Streeton fetched the top recent price – so far – of $A1.1 million.

Collectors' prices reflect collectors' tastes; these may or may not, in turn, reflect artistic quality. More important is the creative provenance of these 'Australian' works of art. The early artists were either British or Continental by origin. Von Guérard was Austrian, Martens Anglo-German, Buvalot and Chevalier Swiss. Of the Impressionists, Nerli was Italian, Heysen German. Origins were not unimportant but 'European' influences, by inspiration and direct instruction, more so. As 'Australian' painters ceased to be immigrants and were increasingly Australian-born, these influences became more, not less, important. Gleeson himself has pinpointed what he identifies as the direct, immediate influence of Turner, Whistler, Sickert, Corot, Millet, Courbet, Monet, Degas, Manet, Gauguin, van Gogh, Toulouse-Lautrec and Matisse, on twelve out of twenty-three of the eminent Australian painters who lived and worked between 1855 and 1970. They include Arthur Streeton, Frederick McCubbin and Tom Roberts, to take only three of the top Australian Impressionists. But this is only to scratch the surface of the process by which an 'Australian' style came into being. It was a matter of normal habit for aspiring young artists to travel to France, Britain, Italy, Spain and Germany to study at the teaching academies or in the studios of the European masters. No less important, for them to immerse themselves in the European art of the Middle Ages, Renaissance, Enlightenment and after, as it

* Ibid., and *passim*.

hung revealed in the *palazzi*, galleries and country mansions open to public viewing.

Even Norman Lindsay, who subjected himself less to the pedagogics of art than many artists of his time, derived his inspiration for his larger scenic, dramatic canvases from the classics and the work of Rabelais, Casanova, etc.

All this is common knowledge; but, without in any way detracting from the originality and genius of the Australian schools of painting, it needs to be said that they could not have emerged, and certainly could not have reached the heights of artistic creativity they did, without the inspiration and teaching of their European masters. As in the seventeenth century, when the Dutch portraitists and maritime artists helped to create schools of painting in Britain and Northern Europe, the eighteenth and nineteenth century when French painters of pre-Impressionist, Impressionist and post-Impressionists were a dominant, universal force in art, there were no national boundaries containing the artists' vision.

The influence of climate, light, topography, etc., is mainly evident in Australian landscape painting; hardly less evident is the continuing influence of Paris, Rome, Venice, and London. Portraiture, interiors and still-life are universal, local and individual forms. Nationalism comes into them very little.

So far as modern painting is concerned, Australia can show a large, and still growing, body of talent: Nolan, Lloyd Rees, Drysdale, Pugh, Boyd, Dobell, Williams, Whitely, to mention only a few of the best known. If Donald Friend is singled out for special mention it is a purely personal choice. He is a totally cosmopolitan artist, yet no one could be more unmistakably Australian. London (study with Gertler, Mervyn Peake and Meninsky), Nigeria, Italy, Greece, Ceylon, Bali have all been his homes – not merely bus stops. Goya is his god; Gauguin, Hieronymous Bosch, Piero della Francesca his kindred spirits. Friend is certainly one of the most versatile of living Australian artists. As a draughtsman he is unsurpassed. His paintings glow with life and colour. Portraits and drawings have a splendidly simple, masterly line. His cartoons have all the bustle and wit of a Rowlandson. Nor is he only a visual artist; his pen is as powerful as his brush. His *Art in a Classless Society (and Vice-Versa)* (1985) is an uproarious send-up of artists, critics and art dealers; in its way a masterpiece, as is his superbly illustrated book on Bali, *The Cosmic Turtle* (1976).

The aristocratic unrepentance of the bush, whence he came, lives on in Donald Friend. 'When I was a boy, land, wool and cattle were the *real* heart of Australia, and the proletariat were the kind of people who used to ride horses. Now the proletariat wouldn't know what to *do* with a horse.' In the balance of his technique, wisdom of his judgement and generosity of his vision, Friend is unrivalled.

Architecture

The merits of the convict system were not always immediately obvious to the convicts, their contemporaries or, for that matter, later generations. Yet three architects, all of whom had a touch of genius, came to Australia from London as convicts – all three for alleged forgery. They received free pardons, and the cities where they worked bear the marks of their influence. Their work is still something which visitors to New South Wales and Tasmania should make a point of seeing.

The most famous of the trio is Francis Greenway (1777–1837), an artist and entrepreneur of unruly and rumbustious temperament. He came to the notice of Governor Macquarie, who swiftly directed his talents towards the improvement and development of Sydney. A cluster of Greenway's creations – which, but for his fall from grace, would doubtless have formed a fine embellishment to London or some other favoured English city – now form the most important architectural nucleus of the Georgian and Gothic style in Australia. The Barracks, St James's church, the castellated Music Conservatory (originally the stables for a hopelessly over-ambitious Government House, stopped in its tracks by Whitehall) and the Old Lighthouse (now alas! only in replica but at least respectfully exact) all testify to his genius in designing elegantly simple buildings.

Unfortunately, Greenway quarrelled with everybody, even in the end with his patron the Governor. He died relatively poor and lies buried in an unmarked grave in the Hunter Valley. But his example did not die, and his vision lives on in the impressive but simple Victoria Barracks, designed (1842–3) in Paddington by Lieutenant Colonel George Barney (Royal Engineers, Woolwich). Its elegance in turn stood as a standard of excellence for the anonymous crowd of lesser men, builder-developers, who covered the rest of Paddington with pretty terraced houses and shops in the last quarter of the century, giving the whole area a stylish air of civilized comfort, reminiscent of the better parts of Chelsea or Fulham.

Meanwhile, two other ex-convicts were at work in Tasmania, endowing Australia's other oldest cities with touches of Palladian, neo-Norman, neo-Gothic, Greek revival or neo-Egyptian architecture that make Hobart and Launceston such attractive places. Friends in high places had anxiously pleaded James Blackburn's case, but to no effect; he was packed off to Tasmania. Though primarily an engineer (and a good one), he was also an architect of taste and imagination whose public buildings, churches and bridges added much to Hobart's peaceful charm.

James Alexander Thomson (1805–80), transported for alleged burglary, brought with him the reputation of being 'wild but clever'. His neat, tidy and graceful terraced houses, cottages, offices and shops, helped to make Hobart more habitable.

John Lee Archer (1791–1852), pupil of Rennie, and Blackburn, made Hobart the centre of government, law and religion (Parliament House, originally Customs House, Treasury, Ordinance Department, bridges and numerous churches and chapels). Blackburn was promoted to be City Surveyor to the burgeoning city of Melbourne; he was the creator of what have been described as 'monumental works of genius': Archer's Penitentiary Church has been pronounced 'as good as Sir Christopher Wren'.

Sydney was to come to maturity with the Harbour Bridge and its revolutionary Opera House (inspired by the vision of Eugene Goossens and designed to the sound, not of music but of tumult and shindy by the Danish architect, Utzon). Meanwhile, fed by the gold and mining industries, Melbourne grew mighty and majestic, becoming not less but more like a new edition of London City, as banking, investment, specialists, mining, and grazing all called for their services.

All the great Australian cities were ports. They lived by trade in ships. The development of Sydney and Hobart was relatively even and orderly, largely because of governmental planning and administration. But in Victoria, West and South Australia, above all in Queensland, things went much less smoothly. The earliest attempts to plan and settle Perth, Adelaide and Port Phillip produced only disagreement and disaster. Brisbane was slowest of all to throw off its shackles of convictism and poverty. In the end, and not without much travail, all emerged triumphant. In some ways, Adelaide was to prove the most remarkable.

Adelaide is an early example of a modern, forcefully planned city, designed in a single, roasting Christmas week in 1836 by a military engineer as the centre of a new province, different from the former 'convict' provinces and conforming to Wakefield's new financial ideas. William IV named it after his Queen, the gentle Adelaide (whose only other memorial is the smallest and least distinguished hamlet of the English fenland). Colonel William Light knew exactly where this city should sit; on either side of the river he placed two 'grids' of streets round six spacious squares inside a figure-of-eight of parklands.*

Light weathered all arguments, and had the courage to take the blame or credit for his decisions. In his *Brief Journal* (re-published Adelaide 1984) he wrote:

> The reasons that led me to fix Adelaide where it is I do not expect to be generally understood or calmly judged of at present.... My enemies, however, by disputing their validity in every particular, have done me the good service of fixing the whole of the responsibility on me. I am perfectly willing to bear it: and I leave it to posterity and not to them, to decide whether I am entitled to praise or to blame.

Light fully deserved the praise which posterity has in fact accorded him. Adelaide is (even with today's problems of traffic and planning) amongst the world's most agreeable and habitable cities. So Froude pronounced it by the 1880s; so it remains.

Canberra, that other cynosure of Australian planning (the architect, Walter Burly Griffin, was American) made necessary by federation in 1900, aroused as much controversy as did Adelaide. The dust has not yet settled. Australians displayed little natural enthusiasm for their new federal capital. They suggested suitably less complimentary names for it: Swindlesville, Gonebroke, Federata. Even those who believed it had some architectural merit showed little enthusiasm for living in it. Its summer was too hot, its winter too cold. There were too many flies and too many civil servants (73 per cent of its relatively small population of a quarter of a million).

Some were ready to agree that the stark exteriors of its public buildings concealed better things within, for example the High Court Building (held by others to resemble a power station), the War Memorial (containing some fine works of art), the National Gallery, the Mint (hence the decription of Canberra by an English wag as 'The Hole with a Mint in it') or the new Parliament House (known locally as the Fall-out Shelter). It seems odd that the newly-conscious Australian nature should have chosen to celebrate its first national act of worship with a concept manifestly American in spirit. Yet with all its weaknesses, Canberra illustrates Australia's ability to build on its natural advantages – sunlight, space, beautiful stone, decorative facing bricks, trees, shrub, plants, flowers – to embellish a design that in many other settings might have been dull and commonplace. They had done this elsewhere creating fresh, bright cities and designs. In England the new towns would have been

* See Hugh Streeton *Ideas for Australian Cities* (Adelaide, 1970).

drab, sooty buildings in the discoloured, cracked and dirty concrete of a typical Robbins-era university campus.

Outside the cities, in the land of the squattocracy or prosperous farmers, lies a wealth of architectural interest. Georgian England, wrote Horace Walpole, was filled with noble mansions 'dispersed like great rarity plums in a vast pudding'. The infinitely vaster Australian pudding had its own characteristic colonial brand of rarity plum. They were the 'homesteads'; what the castle, manor, hall were in English history and landscape, the homestead was in Australia. Its golden age was the half-century between about 1830 and 1880, when the free grant of lands to officers, settlers and squatters slowly peopled the empty plains.

Elder sons took the lands nearest original settlement. Younger sons and cousins went farther up the valleys, deeper into the interior. In the 1830s and 1840s, it was often men of education, means and social standing who began to build the homesteads. The process was slow. There was an acute shortage of skilled craftsmen: a few sheds, stables and cottages were raised by unskilled or aboriginal labour. Then, slowly, the larger, sometimes very large, homestead, equipped with wrought iron gates and fences, elegant fenestration, roofed verandah to provide shelter from excessive sun (as in India) with decorative cast-ironwork and furnishings imported from England. In places (for example, at Cressbrook in the Brisbane valley) the owners prudently added a curtain wall all round them, just in case the triennial aboriginal festival of song (with boomerang, spear competitions and other warlike games) should turn rough. In 1841 and 1844 the black conference did indeed address itself to matters other than games. 'They were [writes the historian of the homestead] simple and grim ... to ambush and slaughter every white man, with their flocks and herds, until the tribal lands were again freed ...'*

In New South Wales ('the premier state' as its motor car registration plates still proudly proclaim) and Tasmania, then in Victoria, South and Western Australia, finally in Queensland after its detachment from New South Wales, homesteads proliferated. Many survive, sometimes still in private owership, others the responsibility of the Australian National Trust which has done splendid work comparable to that of the National Trust in Britain. Thus have survived such gems as Camden Park, home of the Macarthur family and nursery of the priceless treasure, the Australian merino sheep; Malahide (Tasmania), Bedervale

---

* *Historic Homesteads of Australia* (New South Wales and London, 1976), for Australian Council of National Trusts.

(NSW), Titanga (Victoria), Bungaree (Western Australia), Kelvin (NSW): in varying degrees Palladian, Italianate, Greek revival, Ionic, Victorian or plain, simple Australian, they symbolize the prosperity of Australia's early successful pastoral economy, its squattocracy and settler class. Most often, like the Macarthurs, Campbells, Riddochs, Gordons, Fife, Angas, McCullochs, Tennants, they were Scots. Occasionally they were English, or Manx (Kermode was called 'the richest Manxman in existence' in the mid-century) or Irish – William Talbot of Malahide (Tasmania) was the son of Richard Talbot the Anglo-Irish owner of Malahide Castle, County Dublin.

The Flow of Music

Visitors to Australia in the 1880s noticed the extraordinary role that music played in Australian life, in the bush as well as in the city, and the extraordinary aptitude that Australians showed in performing and, especially, singing.*

By 1948, Isabella Moresby could write, in her account of Australian music and musicians: 'for years, remote Australia was better known, internationally, through her gifted sons and daughters in the realm of music, than by another means'. She listed over sixty individual musicians who were household names in Australia: most were almost as well known in Britain and some were increasingly familiar to Americans through their tours and recordings.

How did music begin and develop in Australia? Surgeon Worgan brought a *fortepiano* (an early version of the modern pianoforte) with him on board HMS *Sirius*. His example was followed by early graziers and farmers; and it was not uncommon to find a piano in their homesteads and farmhouses. The convicts, especially the Irish, brought their Irish folk songs. So too did the Scots, Welsh and English. Reels, ballads, sea shanties were the stuff of Victorian Sunday sing-songs which were at least as popular in the colonists' new home as in their old. The origins of that most wonderful of all 'Australian' tunes, 'Waltzing Matilda', were with Miss Christine MacPherson, daughter of a well-to-do Scottish squatter in Queensland. She passed on to 'Banjo' Paterson, the famous bush balladist, a Scottish tune called *Craigielea*, imperfectly recalled from a version she had heard played by a brass band on the Warranambool Race Course in Victoria. Paterson added words which probably do little more than mystify non-Australians. That has not detracted from the popularity of the tune which is enchanting and moving.

* See pp. 159–60.

It was another girl of Scottish origin, May Brahe, who began writing (at eight years old) her 450-odd ballads – surely a world record. They were sung wherever there was a voice and a piano in Australia and Britain.

The miraculous success of music in Australia owes another great debt – to the choral society. It was based on a well-established British model, and the oratorios of Handel, Mendelssohn, Haydn, Sullivan, Stainer, etc. There were ladies' choruses, male-voice choirs, police choirs, railway choirs, church choirs, chapel choirs, German choirs (Meistersingers) Cambrian choirs, Eisteddfod and Oriana choirs, Bach choirs, commercial travellers' choirs, etc. Over sixty were still in existence in 1948 (when their numbers had actually dwindled). They were associated with music festivals and their membership, as in Britain, was socially and ethnically varied and democratic. 'I get the fiddlers from the Synagogue', an organizer of one English festival remarked to me, 'the singers are mostly Chapel.' It was not very different in Australia.*

The transition from oratorio and chorale to opera would not have been too difficult in Handel's day. It became progressively more difficult as opera itself became more complex, and in a country the size of Australia it never could have been easy. Yet already during the mining booms of the decades of 1850–90, opera companies were playing (two simultaneously in the 1870s) in Melbourne. Whether opera was naturally more popular than other forms of music with Australians is questionable: that once experienced, it took deep roots is not in doubt; and great voices, keen audiences and ultimately a spectacular opera house followed.

Roger Covell, the Australian music critic, has suggested an analogy between the popularity of opera and that of sport with Australians. Opera offers opportunities similar to those offered by sport, 'for the instant exhibition of prowess ... it is the voice that can sing louder and higher and do more death-defying leaps that will bring an audience to its feet and make an international reputation for its owner'. There may well be something in this, but it is certainly not the whole story.

Since Nellie Melba's day at least, the human voice has had a supreme role in the musical development of Australia. The climate, even the Australian manner of speech and voice production, have been adduced to explain the phenomenal success of Australian singers. Yet, especially in opera, a natural voice is not enough. For success in opera a singer needs training, not only in voice production but in language and acting-

* On the Choral Societies of Australia, see Isabella Moresby *Australia Makes Music* (Sydney 1948). The best account of all-round musical development is Roger Covell's *Australia's Music: Themes of a New Society* (Sydney, 1976).

while-singing. This must be crowned by practical experience. Opportunities to gain such experience were not available for many years in Australia. Here we come to a vital fact known to all Australian musicians (but rarely, it seems, to Australian politicians or publicists of the modern myth of 'cultural independence') : Australia's operatic potential was largely 'realized' in Europe.

Nellie Melba, still regarded by many serious judges as the greatest of all operatic sopranos and by all as one of the top few, was born Helen Mitchell, of Scottish parents, in Melbourne on 19 May 1861. She never lost her affection for Australia or Melbourne, as her later decision to adopt the professional name of Melba proved. Apart from her early years, her musical career and eminence was entirely due to European influence. These began with her musical education at the hands of Pietro Cecchi, an immigrant Italian teacher of singing – and by good fortune, an excellent one. It was doubtless on his advice that she set off for Paris. Here the greatest of contemporary teachers, Marchesi, gave her an audition, and predicted with total certainty a great future. Lessons began at once.

Her debut as a diva was at Brussels in 1887 at the Monnaie Opera. She appeared as Gilda in Verdi's *Rigoletto* and scored a great personal triumph. Belgium was itself experiencing a great era of musical eminence in the wake of its national independence and the popularity of Queen Victoria's favourite uncle, King Leopold I. (It had already exported in 1867 the first of the great Goossens dynasty to direct Carl Rosa's highly successful touring opera company in England.)

After Brussels, triumph piled on triumph : at Covent Garden ; La Scala ; Milan ; Rome ; Paris ; New York. Melba reigned supreme. But Covent Garden, above all else, became her operatic home, where grand opera was at its grandest : and that was what she wanted. Her voice had greater body than that of her closest rival, Galli-Curci, just as she herself had much lesser body than the great (in every sense) Tetrazzini. She was therefore able to tackle a wider range of roles in Italian and French opera. She took to German less readily and positively disliked Wagner.

A fellow Melbournian, to whom she showed much unappreciated kindness in London, was Percy Grainger. He wrote :

> I loved her voice as truly as I disliked her person. Her voice always made me mind-see Australia's landscape ... having some kind of peach-fur-like nap on it that made me think of the deep blue that forms on any Australian hill if seen a mile or more off. [She had] ... mastered ... every technique of her art. [He had] ... never heard anything to compare with the beauty of Melba's voice in any branch of singing. ... Her top notes were ... very

ringing and telling ... but the curious thing with Melba was that her lower
... and middle notes were equally telling. They had a quality all their own:
and even when she was singing with a big orchestra, she was never wiped
out. She had tremendous carrying power, tremendous beauty of tone and
a very great refinement of workmanship in everything she did.*

How much of all this was Australia, or Cecchi, or Marchesi, or living
and working in the great opera houses of the world, no one will ever
know. And it would be presumptuous and foolish to try and quantify.
Melba was the product of all combined and of her own determination,
heart and genius.

Melba's love affair with Europe, its opera and music was not unique.
On the contrary, her example was emulated by many Australian musicians, great and less great.

The Carl Rosa Company did more to bring opera to the English provinces than any other organization between the 1870s and the 1970s.
Arthur Hammond, sometime conductor (along with that admirable, and
in Australia little-known, Australian operatic conductor Aylmer Buesst),
of the British National Opera Company and later Artistic Director of
the Carl Rosa Opera Company, wrote the following to me about the
Australian connection in the Carl Rosa Company:

> ... our own influence on Australian music might be found in the fact that
> Florence Austral, Collier, Eda Benny, Joan Hammond, Margarita Elkins,
> Rosina Buckman, Horace Stevens, Arthur Wallington and others all went back
> to Australia after working here and must have contributed something learnt
> in England to the presently flourishing Australian Opera. The Australian
> singers have a very characteristic 'open' quality of voice, derived it may
> be from their soil, their climate or their manner of pronouncing their vowels
> ... I myself have always been happy working with them all, without exception.

Operatic singing was only one facet of the Anglo-Australian musical
exchange. The Australian singers who trained – in some cases ending
up permanently – in Britain, included a number who rarely ventured
on the operatic stages. Most of Ada Crossley's life was spent singing
ballads, *lieder* and oratorio. Like a great many of Australia's musicians,
she came from Victoria. She was probably the greatest contralto before
Clara Butt. Harold Williams was another singer, a baritone, who made
himself known as probably the best oratorio interpreter in Britain.

Peter Dawson became known above all as a ballad singer who familiar-
ized world audiences with Australian Bush Songs (including *The Land*

---

* Quoted by John Bird in his biography, *Percy Grainger* (London, 1976).

of Who Knows Where, Comrades of Mine and the *Stockrider's Song*),
and Australian ballads like McCall's famous *Boots*, Mary Brahe's *Keep
Thou My Heart*, and dozens more. He owed his fame most of all to
the gramophone, and with twelve million records to his credit topped
the charts of his day. His *forte* was the popular song, but without his
discipline, vocal technique and his essentially Australian open tone and
style, the gramophone record would not have got him anywhere. He
was a great artist in his own right.

Amongst the pianists, William Murdoch was one of William Laver's
pupils at Melbourne. He rose to fame as the partner of Albert Sammons,
the greatest English violinist of his day, in a chamber music combination
unequalled for its style, tone and musicianship. Amongst the string instrumentalists was Daisy Kennedy, who was born in 1893 at Burra, South
Australia. She made her way to Prague, when still a girl, and persuaded
Sevcik, the greatest violin teacher of the day, to accept her as a pupil.
Eugene Goossens remembered her as a striking figure in musical circles
in London in the 1920s – tall, slender, beautifully dressed, with shining
auburn hair falling over her shoulders. She was a familiar soloist and,
with her husband, the pianist Benno Moiseivitch, a chamber music
player, had a great following in London, Manchester and other provincial
cities, to say nothing of Vienna. Lauri Kennedy, the cellist – no relation
of Daisy – was a fairly late arrival in England. His talents were recognized
in Australia by Melba. On her recommendation he sought his fortune
for a short time in the United States, but after a debut in London in
1921 he spent most of his life in London, as soloist, principal cellist
with the BBC and other symphony orchestras. He was professor of the
cello at the Royal College of Music.

Percy Grainger
Melbourne by the 1880s was already a notable centre of music. The
flamboyant Marshall Hall presided over concerts in the Great Exhibition
Building. It boasted two of the best pianoforte teachers in Australia,
William Laver and Louis Pabst. Yet it was still an intimate enough society
for the 'musical' people to know one another. For example, Helen Mitchell's parents were friendly with the architect, John Grainger and his
wife Rosa. To this tragically ill-assorted pair was born, on 8 July 1882,
a son. He was christened Percy: he had blue eyes, flaxen hair, very
good Nordic looks, and early showed extraordinary musical talent.*

* John Bird's biography *Percy Grainger* (London, 1976) is indispensable to anyone study-
  ing him.

By the time he was twelve years old he was Pabst's most brilliant pupil and already something of an oddity. His first public recital was an enormous success, enlivened by the prodigy's carting on to the platform a dustbin lid which he found in the street and bowled all the way to the Concert Hall. He was already a polymath, picking up painting and drawing as well as French and German, with ease. He was only thirteen when he enrolled at the Frankfurt Conservatory: Australia was already too small for him.

At Frankfurt he fell in with a gifted group of students – Sandby, a Dane, was his closest friend, later instrumental in introducing him to Grieg. Others were English; Cyril Scott, Roger Quilter, Norman O'Neill and Balfour Gardiner. The first three were all marked by their creative talents and sensitivities which were to secure them a respectable place in Elysium. Balfour Gardiner had much greater potential (demonstrated by his always memorable 'Shepherd Fennel's Dance', inspired by Hardy's character in *Under the Greenwood Tree*). He was also the source of much (and much-needed) common-sense advice to Percy.

The six were united by a loudly professed contempt for Beethoven and a modish penchant for folk-song. Percy's mind teemed with musical originality and pseudo-intellectual nonsense – Nordic race theories, whiffs of anti-semitism, and proto-fascism (in the shape of a leaning towards Houston-Stewart Chamberlain, the early, crackpot ideologist of national socialism). All this was merely an extension of the fashion well-established among English and American liberals (like John Lothrop Motley) of using theories of Teutonic primacy to explain the historic triumphs of democracy and prove the superiority of a virile Northern Europe over a decadent Mediterranean civilization.

Musically, Percy's ideas were paralleled by the harmonic novelty and unusual orchestration of his 'Hill Songs', 'A Youthful Suite' and a piece entitled (characteristically) 'A Lot of Rot for Cello and Piano'. These early compositions he continued to defend in later life as 'truly Nordic, truly British, truly New World, truly Australian'. Percy never quite grew up.

In 1901 he moved to London. He pretended, (like many Australians) to dislike its aristocratic high-life. In reality, he wallowed ecstatically in a round of grand musical parties. He charmed everybody; fashionable hostesses were drawn to him as to a magnet. His piano playing was brilliant. Percy enjoyed himself shamelessly, while piously denouncing his benefactors and their sumptuous entertainments as heartless, goal-less and drivelling. He received, when he felt in need of it, the warmest kindness from the great contralto, Ada Crossley; from Adelina Patti, the doyenne of the great divas. Chelsea Walk yielded a rich patroness, Mrs Lawrey, who presented him with more, highly-placed acquaintances; she also helped him, it seems, to grow up sexually as well as socially.

He played concerts under the batons of the great conductors – Henry Wood, Dan Godfrey and Beecham. Beecham invited him to act as his assistant, but Percy declined because Beecham was neither blue-eyed nor Nordic enough. His playing of Grieg's piano concerto persuaded that most critical of critics, Ernest Newman, that he was a genius of geniuses. Everybody took to Percy – Sir Charles Stanford, Vaughan Williams, Eugene Goossens, Sargent – the great American portraitist, himself a fine amateur pianist. (When Percy aired his Nordic-superiority thesis, Sargent would remind him that Norway smelt of nothing but fish.)

Gradually, some of Percy's rough adolescent edges smoothed away. He rampaged less against Beethoven and Mozart, admitted that Puccini could write a good tune and that there was something to be said for Richard Strauss. But his passion for folk music survived and grew stronger in the company of Vaughan Williams, Gustav Holst, Arnold Bax, Joseph Holbrooke (today almost forgotten, but then prominent – and very long-winded) and, of course, in Norway, Grieg.

His pilgrimage in folk music took him to North Lincolnshire in the company of the Catholic gentry family of Elwes. Here Lady Winifred Elwes, sister of Gervase, a fine tenor, presided over the local music festival. It was held at Brigg, a small market town, mercifully preserved from modernity, since even the local railway line led to nowhere in particular. Lincolnshire, in fact, had enjoyed (or suffered) little immigration since the Danish invasions of the early Middle Ages. Amongst its antiquities was a small group of ancient folk-singers who (surviving a good deal of typical local scepticism) appeared at the 1905 Brigg Festival in company with Percy. The leading member was Joe Taylor; it was he who provided the tune and words of the song 'Brigg Fair' to Percy; the immortal theme was passed on to Frederick Delius by Percy. (A pianola roll survives of Percy playing along with a second pair of hands his own, faithful, version of the Delius orchestral tone poem. It still reflects, brilliantly, the masterful authority and precision of Percy's playing at its best.)

Folk-song was 'in'. The Ark of the Covenant was, in popular belief, in the charge of the English Folk-Song Society; this, in turn, was in the charge of Cecil Sharp. Percy differed from Sharp in the important matter of how folk-song should be recorded, preserved and presented. Sharp wanted to convert the rough-hewn material (collected from people like

Joe Taylor) into an art form. Percy disagreed – vehemently. The material should be recorded by the newly-invented phonograph, complete, undiluted, uncorrected. A row ensued. Much later, Benjamin Britten had no doubt who was right: 'Percy Grainger is my master in everything where folk song is concerned.'

When the war broke out, Percy went to America. It did not, in the end, prove a happy decision. His development as a creative artist seemed to get jammed. More performing and academic lecturing left him more enclosed, depressed and eccentric than before. His 'blue-eyed' English became more peculiar, 'all but the most un-do-withoutable of the French-Latin-Greek-begotten words should be side-stepped and ... the bulk of the put-together words should be wilfully and owned-up-to-by hot-house-grown out of Nordic word-seeds ...'. He was converted to vegetarianism by George Bernard Shaw; but any possible benefit to his health was more than undone by the suicide of his mother, Rosa. His sanity was probably preserved only by his marriage to a beautiful Swedish girl, Ella; characteristically the marriage was solemnized in the Hollywood Bowl. It was attended by some 20,000 spectators. The Union Jack and the Stars and Stripes waved overhead. Percy conducted the largest symphony orchestra ever assembled there.

In spite of Ella's having to face the discovery that Percy's major sexual interest was flagellation, the marriage survived. It was (she said) 'hell to be with him, hell to be without him'. After his return to England, Eugene Goossens found him still experimenting, with undiminished enthusiasm, with a vast collection of oriental gongs, musical tubes, bells and percussion bits and pieces in his King's Road flat. He then moved on to the *theremin*, an electronic edition of a musical saw, and a home-made pianola constructed from pieces of wire, string or anything else useful that came to hand. Ella (Goossens noticed) was employed as a kind of slave, fetching and carrying.

Lame, half-deaf, half-blind, Percy plodded doggedly on, travelling, thinking, listening, even performing in public – though he hated this more than anything. His prejudices remained, if anything, stronger than ever. He reserved his deepest contempt for Italian and French music. Of Verdi, he only remarked, after seeing a film of *Aida*: 'filthy music, loathsome singing'. There is no evidence that he ever heard the *Requiem*, the crowning glory of Italian musical genius.

When he paid his last visit to Australia, he described it as a sad experience. He found (his biographer says) 'a country aping the worst aspects of American culture and flooded with the kind of European immigrants he disliked most'.*

He felt a stranger, alienated and alone. Yet, when his own music was in question his mind and language remained as clear and vivid as ever. His *Instructions* to conductors (reprinted in full by John Bird) are as concise and original as anything he ever wrote. His ideas remained a congeries of inconsistencies. He returned to Australia to die, and be buried, according to the Anglican rites in which, as a declared atheist, he disbelieved. He was interred in his family vault in an Adelaide Christian cemetery. In Melbourne he is commemorated by the Grainger museum which he had founded, with a characteristic flourish, before leaving Australia – on oath never to return.

If Percy Grainger was mad, as his mother, Rosa, asserted he was, this may have been partly due to her influence. His life was twisted and tortured by her obsession for him, and by the Wowserism and cultural poverty of contemporary Melbourne which drove him to Europe and America. His travels brought him great cultural gains; they also saddled him – America especially – with insoluble problems. Percy was a tragic case of a flawed genius. His development as a composer was hampered and disorganized by his own inner contradictions that sprang from a diseased heritage and a crazed, abnormal relationship with his mother. His output: of music, ideas and letters, together with his travels and performances, represent the product of a brilliant but wayward intelligence, of ceaseless energy fired off with undirected zeal. Abandoning the conventional ways forward in musical invention, he became dedicated to his favourite private cult of what he called 'free music'. By this he meant music freed from the baneful cramps of key signatures, established conventions of timing, rhythm, harmony and counterpoint. Music was even to be emancipated from the tyranny of human performers – 'middlemen' (as he called them). Henceforth it would be performed through mechanical instruments offering vast ranges and varieties of tonal colour.

In all this there was always an element of the prophetic. His early years of 'protest against civilization', his 'Marching Song of Democracy', his enthusiasm for Walt Whitman and the energy of the athletic Anglo-Saxon newer nations – all evinced avant-garde ideas, rhythms of unusual complexity, harmonic novelties, unconventional orchestration. In retrospect they seem to foreshadow Stravinsky, Schoenberg, Delius, Stockhausen. Tragically, the embryo never took shape. He is remembered for the sparkling gems, memorable but miniature, that he polished off

* Ibid.

(as he explained) when he felt 'sad or furious': 'Molly on the Shore', 'Shepherd's Hey', 'Handel in the Strand', and 'Country Gardens'.

Australia (say Australians) always cuts down its tall poppies. Percy Grainger never gave it a chance to cut him down. Fate arranged that he cut himself down.

So the international flow of music has continued, down to the present day of Dame Joan Sutherland, the unique combination of voice and operatic presence, and of Charles Mackerras, a conductor of world stature from one of Australia's oldest musical families whose versatility stretches from grand opera to Arthur Sullivan and Janacek. Distinguished conductors from England have regularly visited Sydney and Melbourne, contributing much to raising standards of orchestral performance – Beecham, Sargent and Harty amongst them. One master of music – conductor, composer, teacher – whose unique contribution to Australia's musical evolution seems to be questioned by no one, must be mentioned.

In 1947 Eugene (later Sir Eugene) Goossens accepted an invitation to direct on a permanent basis the Sydney Symphony Orchestra and the Music Conservatorium. Goossens was the third of his family of the same name who had directed the Carl Rosa Opera and co-operated with Beecham in the British National Opera at Covent Garden. Since 1923 he had lived in America, building up a world reputation as director of several great American orchestras. Goossens did more than any of his conductor predecessors to make Sydney a world-renowned centre of great music. Amongst his many claims on the gratitude of Sydney-siders, not least is the inspiration and drive he brought to the project for the Sydney Opera House. He is commemorated by a bust in the Concert Hall. A portrait by Hanke hangs in the Opera House Library.*

Australian Literature

It would be impossible, and absurd, for the present writer to attempt a survey of Australian writing. Fortunately it is not necessary. H.M. Green's *History of Australian Literature*† provides a guide unequalled in the field of such surveys of a nation's literature. Aspiring examiners in Britain over the years will remember an outwardly similar

* Goossens left a lively autobiography of his earlier life and music in Britain: *Overture and Beginners* (London, 1951).

† Revised, in two volumes, by Dorothy Green (London and Sydney, 1984). H.M. Green was Librarian of the University of Sydney and President of the Australian Institute of Librarians. He died in 1964 and his widow has completed and revised the edition of 1984.

survey by M.M. Legouis and Cazamian of British literature: a remarkable enterprise, but for the most part a work of utility rather than of original judgement or creative stimulus. Green, by contrast, demonstrates on almost every page of his massive critique, lucid, often profound and always personal, judgements and insights.

In her introduction (p. xxxi) Mrs Green remarks that her husband was 'a literary citizen of the world, not a simple-minded nationalist'. His loyalty to the Greco-Christian-British heritage was perfectly compatible with an equal loyalty to his Australian heritage. As the most distinguished Australian historian of recent times, Sir Keith Hancock, said in 1930: this was not a problem for Australians of that generation. Why, then, should Mr Allan Ashbolt (described as essayist and broadcaster) feel it necessary, in a review* of Green, to comment that this attitude of mind 'constitutes something of a problem when trying to measure him by today's standards'? He answers: 'For this country, the imperial epoch virtually vanished in early 1942, with the collapse of British naval and military forces through much of Asia. Anglo-Australian culture lingered on in a residual way.' Consequently, (Ashbolt thinks) it is a good thing that Green's original intention to continue his survey to 1960 was abandoned. The proper end is 1950.

It is not easy to understand why an aesthetic judgement should be hung on the strategic accident of a world war. Britain recovered from her disasters sufficiently to play a major role in the defeat of Germany, Italy and Japan. What of his argument that Green was more at home with the prose of the great English essayists than with 'the patterns of speech emerging in Australia during his lifetime'? This is equally absurd. Such new patterns of Australian English as emerged (especially in Mr Ashbolt's world of broadcasting) were miserable emulations of American speech or the rhetoric of politicians whose speeches are written by bureaucrats. No critic knew more about 'real' Australian speech (for example, the parlance of the bush) than Green. He was, moreover, extraordinarily open-minded about new writing. Dorothy Green makes this point very strongly (see her Introduction, p. xxxvii). Kenneth Slessor (after consulting a number of contemporary writers and critics) left A.D. Hope out of his anthology of *Australian Poetry 1945*; at the same time, Green included him.

In this survey Green decisively ranks Hope well above Slessor as a poet; one reason being that Hope 'is modern in that his language is that of prose ... at times more colloquial than that of even the young

* *Sydney Morning Herald*, 23 March 1985.

intellectual of today'.*

Mr Ashbolt is merely relying on the faulty logic and superficial rhetoric common to the media prophets of 'progressive radicalist nationalism' popular in the last decade or two. There were Anglo-Australian problems long before the Second World War. Australia has always had a perfect right to a 'national' literature (as Mrs Green remarks pointedly in her Introduction). The cultural jingoists of the 1980s will simply run into the ground if they fail to recognize that the world is now ill-suited to nationalistic cultural larrikinism.

Green leaves out no branch of verse or prose from his survey. I propose simply to fill in the (astonishingly few) gaps that he has left in his wake.

Students of Australian history owe an incalculable debt to the late Sir Ernest Scott; to his pupil, Sir Keith Hancock; to Professor Geoffrey Blainey, a master in knowledge, style and those personal convictions so necessary to the committed historian. Few public persons have withstood so much biased criticism with so much patience as Blainey. Green was too late in the day to do more than give him passing credit for his classic study of Australian history, *The Tyranny of Distance* (p. 162). A modest, gentle scholar, he speaks out fearlessly on what he believes are great causes: witness his recent declaration that Australia risks being divided into a collection of tribes if governments pursue some of the more misguided attempts to satisfy the supposed collective interests of, for example, ethnic groups, political activists and trendy minorities by granting them special 'rights' while simultaneously ignoring the civic responsibilities of citizens as a whole.

Green passes over another charismatic figure of the historical profession: Professor Manning Clark. To him, all students of Australian history are in debt for his work in making the sources of their past available for research. His own interpretations of that history are likewise valuable, though often ignoring the specialized work of scholars in, for example, economic development. More seriously, he tends to adopt the approach of nationalist prophet to historical issues: for example, his *Introduction* to the National Trust 'Biography' of one of Sydney's most enchanting great houses, 'Lindesay', which is a Regency Gothic gem built (1834) by a wealthy Scottish immigrant merchant, by name of Campbell. In a curiously admonitory sermon, Manning Clark warns Australian visitors not to allow their imaginations to dwell too long on Lindesay. 'Our sphere', he thunders, in the manner of a new-born John Dunmore Lang, 'is not HERE, or with the creators of here, it is out there, in the bare

* Ibid., vol. 2, p. 982.

brown desert, in Australia.' Australians, it seems, are allowed to enjoy only a strictly 'Australian' kind of satisfaction in life. Does this include the deeds of its British or European begetters? Apparently not. I am reminded of Malcolm Muggeridge's comment that 'perhaps Australia owes its very existence to God's having set it up to be His special theatre of the absurd, or, in Blake's idiom, theatre of fearful symmetry'.*

In the sphere of criticism, there is one remarkable Australian scholar–poet–musicologist who receives only a few lines in Green (p. 504). Walter James Turner (1889–1946) deserves more than this cursory recognition. Though primarily a journalist and editor, he was a truly great literary and music critic, lucid, detached, erudite and objective. Few have written with more understanding on Mozart, or on music generally. His judgement was delicate, catholic, yet strict. His devotion to Mozart did not inhibit him from admiring deeply Delius's *Village Romeo and Juliet*. Jacquetta Hawkes wrote of him (in the *Dictionary of National Biography*):

> his poetry is as idiosyncratic as his nature ... his poetry was too rich in imagery and sound, too lyrical and sensuous and unintellectual to belong to the fashionable trends of the inter-war period. Although no believer in the careful polishing of verses, he wrote a few lyrics which may justly be called perfect. The poetic gift never left him....

W.B. Yeats was a close friend and admirer of Turner's work and verse.

Perhaps Norman Lindsay is worth a few more words. He was a critic and thinker as well as a versatile artist equally at home with horses, dogs, nude and nubile ladies, historic panoramas of cavaliers in fancy dress, Pierrots and Harlequins, and luscious full-bosomed beauties languishing in settings reminiscent of Rubens and forecasting the delights of Sir William Russell Flint. The *Bohemian of the Bulletin* (published in 1965 but collected from his writings of the 1890s and 1900s) was also a scourge of humbug in influential places (including the *Bulletin*). 'In the art of biography', he wrote, 'the idolator is just as objectionable as the debunker.' Of his Bohemian colleagues, Lawson ('sodden with self-pity') and Paterson ('the essential autocrat, withdrawn, *racé*') he pronounced:

> Both images epitomize the conflict principles under which a civilization exists or perishes. When the underdog becomes the topdog, as he seeks to do in these days in the character of a Union Boss, he is a supreme threat to this present civilization, for he has millions of underdogs behind him, all simmering with resentment because they *are* underdogs....

* Malcolm Muggeridge in B.A. Santamaria *Against the Tide* (Oxford and Melbourne, 1981), Introduction.

The poet, Bernard O'Dowd he sees 'oozing meekness and docility', but fraudulently 'infected by what his Irish prudery chose to stigmatize as indecency'.

In a natural line of descent from this same anti-wowser parentage was P.R. Stephenson, an earlier Australian manager of the avant-garde press, the Fanfrolico. Later, in the 1920s he took over the Mandrake Press. He printed for D.H. Lawrence, Aleisteir Crowley and Jack Lindsay, and was associated with Philip Heseltine, biographer of Delius who also composed and edited some very important music under the pseudonym 'Peter Warlock'. Stephenson (known as 'the Wild Colonial Boy') repaid in kind by allowing Warlock to be 'the most potent toper in English history and a man of erudition'. Stephenson described Warlock's book, *Merry-Go-Down: A gallery of gorgeous drunkards through the ages** as 'this anthology of the bouse-can'. All this was the tail-end of the Era of New Naughtiness that had begun with Norman Lindsay and Aubrey Beardsley: a strange *mélange* of genius and rubbish.

An intriguing divergence from much popular approval marks Green's verdict on the early work (that is, to 1950) of the Nobel Prize-winning novelist, Patrick White. Green undoubtedly had serious reservations about, for instance, *The Happy Valley* (1939). A footnote (p. 1130) explains that White's later novels, *The Tree of Man* (1956) and *Voss* (1957), fell outside his closing date boundary of 1950. It would have been interesting to know if they modified the verdict of 'affectation' which Green applied to his earlier work.

So far as White's most recent, autobiographical *Flaws in the Glass: a Self Portrait* (1981) may be thought to throw any light on the problem, I should not have been surprised if Green had maintained his earlier opinion. *Flaws in the Glass* is affected, petulant and disagreeable. It sprays sneers and insults on anybody who happens to incur the author's displeasure. This includes the Queen of England, the Duke of Edinburgh, the former Governor-General of Australia (Sir John Kerr), Dame Joan Sutherland and her husband, Richard Bonynge, and Sir Sidney Nolan, the eminent artist. That serious literature may assign a legitimate role to derision, irony and sarcasm, etc. is not in question – witness Dryden, Johnson, Macaulay, Carlyle, Shaw, Waugh, Graham Greene, et al. *Flaws in the Glass*, however, is merely sour, boring and dislikeable. It lacks the basic elements of fact, information or chronology that readers would want to know. I cannot help wondering what H.M. Green would have made of the publishers' claim that it is done '... with such power that

* London, 1929.

it seems no artist can have attempted or executed a self-portrait so life-like before'. Perhaps he would have agreed?

If H.M. Green is right, the average Australian novelist or short story-writer 'is satisfied to display a superficial aspect of character and life'. He is saying – again – what Froude and Adams said. There is a handful of prose writers to whom this criticism does not apply: nor does it apply to the best poets – certainly not to A.D. Hope, Judith Wright or J.P. Macauley.

A.D. Hope stands out as the most powerful of this trio. His thinking is of unique depth and sophistication; he has wit and his technique always matches the problem he sets himself to examine; he uses words to describe, explain and analyse, moving from mood to mood with a natural mastery surpassed by few living writers. He has no contrived philosophy. He is not – as some of his readers and critics have tried to argue – a Malthusian or a feminist, or an anti-feminist, or a nationalist, or an anti-nationalist. His poetry is simply – with that of Donne, Swift and Pope – a timeless expression and analysis of the human predicament. His intellectual power is always present. In his wicked vein he can produce highly entertaining burlesque:

> I sing of the decline of Henry Clay
> Who loved a white girl of uncommon size.
> Although a small man in a little way,
> He had in him some seed of enterprise.

The reader must be left to read *Conquistador* to discover the sad fate of Henry Clay: it is very frightening. Nor can a student of history fail to recognize the shrewdness behind this stroke:

> ... that sly
> Anus of mind the historian.

In Hope, Australia has achieved that high seriousness which analysts have often found absent.

Steve Fairbairn

Finally, there is one autobiography not mentioned by Green which must, even if only out of Collegiate affection, be touched on: *Fairbairn of Jesus.** The author, Stephen ('Steve') Fairbairn was born in Victoria in 1862, one of five sons of George Fairbairn, a Scottish pastoralist. The Fairbairns were all athletes. Steve, with three of his brothers, went to Jesus College, Cambridge: all rowed with distinction in the Jesus

* (London, 1931).

boat club and helped to establish the outstanding reputation it long enjoyed on the Cam and the Thames. Steve became the uncrowned king of world rowing between about 1885 and his death in 1938. He invented a new style of rowing and new attitudes to the sport. His aphorisms, in and out of print, became famous wherever men rowed in boats: 'Enjoy your rowing, win or lose'; 'If you can't do it easy, you can't do it at all.'

His autobiography gives a warm, vivid picture of his family, of himself, of life in the bush, of the development of Australian pastoralism in its most revolutionary stages. It opens as it means to go on (Steve had an eye for the epic): 'My grandfather weighed 22 stone in good condition, and at the Scotch games he did not go in for the wrestling competition but took on the two best together – one in each hand, so to speak.' His narrative continues on a similar key of modesty.

The Fairbairns were Scots to the marrow. Steve went back to England to be brought up by an old aunt who 'suffered from the severe old Scottish religion ... she always flogged me whenever she saw me'. After Cambridge (1881–4) he went back to the Australian station. His father had by now acquired 300,000–400,000 acres of land – first leasehold then freehold. Partly as a defence against the wallabies, he hired a shipful of wire-netting from England and wrote out the detailed instructions for wiring-in the sheep stations. He was a pioneer (Steve claims the first of all) in breaking with shepherding and fencing his property with netting six feet high.

The first effect of the gold rush was to drain away the Fairbairns' labour. George Fairbairn was left with only a Chinaman and a black boy. The Chinaman hanged himself. The black boy drowned himself.

My father had a library consisting of three books – the Bible, Johnson's *Dictionary* and Boswell's *Life of Johnson*. After the black boy had drowned himself, my father read through his library once more and then went to the diggings. Only a few sheep were left.

In the end, gold helped to restore the Fairbairn fortunes. An ancestor, (Sir) William Fairbairn, was partner to Stephenson, inventor of the steam engine. The Fairbairns had a natural aptitude for machinery. Soon George was involved in incubators, egg marketing, meat freezing, windmills, water pumps and the Apollo Candle Company – to use up the surplus tallow: all told, an investment of some three million pounds sterling. For Steve, his father was 'the bone and sinew of Empire'.

Steve applied himself to farming with the same gusto he had brought to rowing and life at Cambridge. Determined, self-confident, shrewd, humorous, he recounts how he outwitted the shearers in the Great Strike, even Higher Powers in the great drought of 1902, solved the problems of bolting ponies, and overcame the great banking crisis in Melbourne. Steve loved life in the bush. He kept a Chinese gardener who worked all night watering the garden in dry weather. He was called Harry King, spoke good English and got drunk: 'It was a very good sign if a Chinaman got drunk ... it showed that he did not take opium.'

He had a great respect and affection for the aboriginals. He praised their skill at tracking and other crafts of bush life. His black boy talked freely and with great interest to Steve. His information was (wrote Steve) very interesting but 'unprintable in our state of false decency'. The black boy thought white men immoral; 'black men very moral'; and he described the curious, sometimes brutal, conventions of aboriginal marriage.

Steve persuaded 'Q' (Sir Arthur Quiller-Couch, the famous Cornish novelist, critic, Professor of English literature and Fellow of Jesus College) to write a preface to his book. 'Q' wrote: 'I enjoyed reading this because it is written by a real man: an extraordinary book ... by an extraordinary man.... Without going further ... *surtout ne parlons pas littérature* – I affirm that these reminiscences possess the first secret of writing, which is to entertain and amuse.'

Steve was (as the *Dictionary of Australian Biography* entry on him remarks) 'masterful, overpowering yet sympathetic'. He was the model Anglo-Australian. He loved his old College just as he loved the bush. The College repaid his affection and his services by two decisions, unique in its history. They hung his portrait along with those of its greatest alumni: Coleridge, Cranmer, Lawrence Sterne, Thomas Malthus, and its Founder, Bishop John Alcock. And they buried him in the Master's garden near the early medieval chapel, after a form of ceremony reserved for Masters and Fellows. Steve is the only non-Fellow ever to be thus honoured. It will be surprising if anybody else ever manages to follow. Steve, as Quiller-Couch observed, was an extraordinary man, and a great Australian.

14

AUSTRALIA TODAY; AUSTRALIA TOMORROW

'Australia is but a corner of the world, and ... has neither beginning nor end within her own boundaries.'

(E.R.Walker)*

'Most of us living on our side of the country value it not because it is superior to other places but because it is familiar, because it is home. That was also the feeling of the Aboriginal tribes and they even more than us saw magic in every creek and crag. ...'

(Geoffrey Blainey)†

Profound changes have overcome Australia since 1788. In this chapter, I shall try to look at some of these changes as they have influenced (and continue to influence) Australia's political system, her role in international affairs and her economy. Finally, I shall turn to the Australian identity: how it has developed in the past and how it may develop in the future. The identity, personality or spirit of a nation is a nebulous concept, but an identity is important, not only in the consciousness of the nation itself, but also in the perceptions of other nations.

Population

When the First Fleet anchored in Botany Bay, Australia had never, so far as is known, had a single white resident. It had only been visited by a handful of (probably) Portuguese, Dutch, French and English. None had stayed for more than a brief period. By the mid-1980s the population was estimated at just under sixteen million. Within this total, aborigines or part-aborigines numbered less than 140,000, about a quarter of these living in the Northern Territory. Estimates of the aboriginal population in 1788 must be largely guesswork. The present total suggests a decline

* *Australia in the World Depression* (London, 1933).
† *Our Side of the Country* (Melbourne, 1984).

since then of somewhere between a half and two-thirds. Within the Northern Territory, and stimulated by an Act of 1976 authorizing enquiries into aboriginal claims, aboriginal land ownership has grown to some 27 per cent of the entire Territory.

Apart from the black population, the whites, until very recently, consisted overwhelmingly of immigrants of British (including Irish) origin, supplemented by a relatively small number of Italians, Germans and Greeks. Lately, by a revolution in the traditional 'white Australia' policy, substantial numbers of immigrants, mainly from Asia, have been introduced. Other peoples from Eastern and Central Europe, the Balkans and the Mediterranean have also joined the immigrant stream. A very high, and increasing proportion of the total population now live in towns, engaged in trade, manufacturing industry or office work. Inevitably, these internal social changes are linked with changes in Australia's economy and her economic relations with the outside world. Similarly, they are at the roots of the Australian political system.

The Australian Political System

For eighty-seven years, Australia has been a Federal Commonwealth within the British Commonwealth of Nations. Executive government is formally vested in the Queen, but she acts through the Governor-General, assisted by a Federal Ministry of (at present) twenty-seven ministers. The relationship of Federal Government and states remains essentially that defined under the Constitution as laid down in 1900, subject now to the abolition of the functions of the Privy Council as a Court of Appeal open to Australians. The Federal Government acquired certain powers and functions surrendered voluntarily by the individual six states. Subject to this, any state may legislate on any matter. The movement towards total independence of Britain has gone a step further with the assumption in recent years that the appointment of the Governor-General will go to an Australian.

Parliament consists of two chambers: the upper being a Senate, the lower a House of Representatives. The upper is approximately half the size of the lower. At present the Australian Labour Party (ALP) has a majority of six over the largest opposition party, the Liberals, in the Senate, and a majority of thirty-seven in the House of Representatives. The organization and functions of the major parties – Labour, Liberal, Country, Democrat – are important and need to be examined, being different in certain respects, not only from British parties bearing similar labels, but also from parties in different Australian states bearing the same labels. Until the 1880s and 1890s, personal associations or personal feuds were the basis of most local state politics. These originated in domestic disagreements; established 'squatters' opposed unestablished 'selectors' over land, landholders fought land-seekers; protectionists (mostly in trade or industry) fought free-traders (mostly landed). But party programmes and adherents varied from state to state and West Australia barely knew a party system before the rise of Labour.

The need to organize wage-earners for their own protection long antedated the rise of the ALP. English, Irish, Scottish and Welsh immigrants brought the idea of trade unions with them; but when the strikes of 1890 misfired, their thoughts turned to parliamentary politics. The new Labour Party obtained control over the balance of power in the NSW Parliament in the first Federal election in 1901, with a programme designed to appeal not only to wage-workers but to traditionalist Australians – old-age pensions, industrial arbitration, a 'white Australia', public enterprise. They drew their principles from all types of socialism: Christian, Fabian, Marxist, and from the old Australian habit of using public enterprise and capital where private would not work.

They accompanied these by stiff rules of party discipline. The British tradition, illustrated most clearly by Burke, that the elected Member was entitled to reasonable freedom to judge difficult situations for himself gave way to clear undertakings to follow party policy, or else. Parliamentary members became delegates rather than representatives. The party 'caucus' formulated policies and took decisions of principle. This rigid discipline in some measure defeated itself. Individual rebels were driven to defect from the party; parties were split, as happened in Queensland in 1905 and 1908. After 1901 the Commonwealth Labour Party was to split on several occasions. After a long period of growth, Labour was in power in all states except Victoria, and in the Commonwealth as a whole. Then, in 1915, tension grew between the party activists who were determined to forge ahead on the road to socialism, and the moderates who were anxious, especially in view of the war, not to rock a boat now steady for the first time. Irish and pacifists opposed conscription in strength. W.M. Hughes, the 'Little Digger', led a pro-conscription minority out of the party. State Labour parties everywhere were divided on the issue. Hughes formed a 'National' Party, composed of Labour and Liberal sympathizers.

A similar split took place in 1931. In the early 1920s the Labour Party left behind by Hughes reached a peak of 'left' radicalism. From this position it retreated in time to win a sweeping victory in the general election of 1929. Labour also had majorities in New South Wales, Victoria and South Australia. Then, as in 1915, external pressures broke the party's unity. This time it was not war but a world depression, and especially Australia's heavy burden of external debt. Labour moderates joined with Liberals and the Country Party to form the United Australian Party. It was pledged to defeat economic depression by 'sound finance' and especially by honouring Australia's financial obligations abroad.

Neither Liberals (middle-of-the-road believers in gradualness, akin to British Liberals and Conservatives) nor the Country Party (representing, since 1911, landed interests and governed by little in the way of economic dogma) possessed the rigid discipline which, in favourable conditions, held Labour together. The 1931 coalition was nevertheless held together by the extraordinary tactical skill of R.G. Menzies for nearly a decade. Then, in 1942, it was Labour's turn to benefit from the Second World War. Curtin replaced Menzies, and Labour ruled until 1948.

A government under Menzies and A.W. Fadden was returned to power for four feverish years. Its programme was strongly anti-Communist and it was opposed by a Labour Party led by Dr H.V. Evatt. Evatt was the first leader of Federal Labour to come from a professional, legal, non-trade union background. Obstinate and tenacious, he fought the anti-Communist movement both outside the Labour Party and inside, where a largely Catholic minority opposed him with equal vigour. Evatt was decisively defeated in the General Election of 1955.

There was a further serious split in Labour's ranks in November 1975. It became apparent that the Labour Government, under Prime Minister Gough Whitlam, was bankrupt through overspending. It had no money to pay its employees and was dismissed by the Governor-General, Sir John Kerr. A Liberal, Malcolm Fraser, became Prime Minister, and the Liberals ruled until 1984.

Furious recriminations followed which have lasted down to the present day. The new crisis – 'The Dismissal', as it came to be known – was unlike earlier Labour crises in that it did not result from any external pressure. The Governor-General who did the dreadful deed was not a Pom or a retired Field Marshal. He, like everybody else in the melo-drama, was Australian born and bred, and – worst of all – an old and devoted Labour supporter. 'The Dismissal' was an exclusively Australian, political punch-up. The Governor-General simply believed he had no alternative but to turn out the Labour Government. He left wrath and fury raging behind him, for Whitlam was a passionate orator, charismatic and unforgiving.

H.G. Wells, visiting Australia in the 1930s, found it 'all so like Britain

... the same living spirit of freedom, mysteriously stifled and frustrated, not by a simple organised tyranny, but by a complex of obscurantisms'.*

There may have been some truth in Well's dictum, but the opposite was, fortunately, also true. What he called 'obscurantisms' included the refusal of a significant proportion of ordinary men and women to accept the philosophers' belief that they could not see beyond the ends of their noses. Australian political freedom owed not a little to what the orthodox thought of as political misfits, nonconformists, Moonies, traitors and scabs. Australia, like other democracies had its 'don't knows', doubters, floating voters. They were (and still are) politically very important people.

It is a cliché that democracy is easier to criticize than to appreciate. For its basic, minimum objective is simply to avoid civil war. When this is forgotten or seems likely not to be achieved, confidence falters. In Britain, parliamentary prestige was in low water in the years before 1914: on the Right, the voices of Chesterton and Belloc; on the Left, of Shaw, the Webbs, the Fabians and the Communists gloomily predicted social disaster. In the 1930s, Mosley found sympathizers not only amongst fascistically-minded Tories; they also came from the ranks of Labourites and Liberal 'intellectuals'. On both occasions, war switched the points. In Australia, similarly, Labour has veered towards Communism: in the 1920s and 1930s, the plunge created traumatic doubts for Roman Catholics, for Labour-unionism was nowhere stronger than amongst the still underprivileged Irish. Yet the democratic system, including the ALP, can claim remarkable social advances. It has provided steadily rising standards of living, through a mixed economy, public and private, economic freedom and economic controls, and social services which improved education, health, pensions and cultural amenities.

The Character of Politics
Australian politics tend to be in strange contrast to the agreeable hedonism of the land. From 1788 the sounds of rough music had rarely been absent. Ross, Bligh, MacArthur, Wentworth, even Parkes had always been ready for a fight. The Ministers, Senators and representatives carried on the lively, contentious traditions of Australian politics. After federation, the ALP had, in the nature of things, to flourish. Wage-earners now accounted for over 70 per cent of the population, self-employed some 16 per cent, employers about 12 per cent. The new Labour Party was not exclusively a working-class party, nor did the working class

* H.G. Wells *Travels of a Republican in Search of Hot Water* (London, 1939).

or the unions in Australia always resemble the British originals from which they mostly emerged. Rural labour, the peripatetic shearers especially, were more militant, their militancy more long-lived, than anything known to Joseph Arch and his agricultural unionism in late nineteenth-century Britain.

From strikes, the workers and their sympathizers turned to politics. From amongst the *melée* of idealists, natural leaders and power-seekers there emerged, from all parties, enough men to keep Australian politics lively, if volatile and sometimes unelevating in the decades after federation. How could politics be dull when such orators as Billy (Little Digger) Hughes, or Jack Lang, Andrew Fisher, E.L. Batchelor, Alfred Deakin, George Higinbotham, W.A. Holman, Samuel Griffith, Sir George Beely, and many others, were on stage?

The new Labour leadership had one thing in common with those of the Liberal and Country parties of the day : it contained an ever-growing proportion of lawyers. Griffith, Holman, H.B. Higgins, Sir George Beely, and later scores of others, including H.V. Evatt and Gough Whitlam, were all lawyers. For, as party aspirations rose, state functions became more important and social legislation more complex, the demand for sharp legal minds capable of drafting, compromising and deciding grew. (Similar forces had created the vital segment in the English parliaments of the seventeenth century and after.)

In the Liberal Party the greatest leaders and spokesmen, Deakin and Menzies, were likewise lawyers. Fraser's successor as leader of the Liberals, Andrew Peacock, and Peacock's successor, John Howard, are both lawyers. Some – not too much – legal knowledge was essential to their political task, as it was to Albert Dunstan, inveterate tactician and intriguer of the Country Party. Greatest of all Australia's politician-lawyers was George Higinbotham, once Premier, later Chief Justice of Victoria. Higinbotham's mixture of oratory and integrity, of contemplation and temperament became a legend. Finally, depressed by politics, this most attractive figure of Australian politics decided for the law, but even on the Bench, and in principle above politics, he could not refrain from contributing to a trade union in difficulty in the middle of a case over which he was presiding. His was a noble and heart-warming personality.

Such qualities of character sometimes shone the more brightly against the sombre, boring or sordid background against which they were placed. As one of the most distinguished of Governor-Generals remarked of the world of Australian politics : 'Its factions, its personal changes, its waste of time and opportunity ... are but humble imitations of the proceedings of London statesmen.'

A major cause of trouble was distance; this has been discussed by Geoffrey Blainey in one of the most illuminating studies of Australian history.* The transport revolution has helped to alleviate the problem of distance, but has not wholly solved it. Ever since federation, Commonwealth governments have found themselves in conflict with state governments. (We have looked at the conflict over external debt between Jack Lang and the Federal Government in the crisis of the early 1930s.) In recent years Tasmania has clashed with Canberra and the federal conservationists over the heavy felling of forest timber. There have been bitter exchanges between the right-wing Premier of Queensland (Joh Bjelke-Petersen) and the Labour Government in Canberra over his anti-union policies. Even the Labour Government of West Australia has had bitter fights with the Hawke Federal Government over aboriginal 'land-rights', when these have appeared to conflict with the mineral development so economically vital to West Australia as a state.

Since federation, the ALP has taken to the established tradition of a mixed economy with relish. The party was closely associated with the trade unions and their objectives. The influence of ideas from Marx, the Fabians and, later, Leninism, were to add force to the belief in the wisdom of state intervention in economic and social affairs. It was the extent, not the principle, of intervention that caused sporadic divisions between the socialist and Lib–Lab elements in the caucus. But, in any case, there was no alternative to Labour's continuing dependence on external (largely British) capital if the tyranny of distance was to be overcome and Australians made less dependent on imported manufactures. Hence the importance of a growing bureaucracy, headed by the Commonwealth Treasury.

The past decade has seen a major reshuffle of men and ideas in the three principal parties. A successful, if abrasive, leader of the Liberal Party and Prime Minister after the Whitlam débâcle, Malcolm Fraser, disappeared in the General Election of 1983. After a short interval, while the Liberals were making up their minds between the colourful Andrew Peacock and the unspectacular but solid John Howard, solidity and financial experience told in Howard's favour. Under his cautious influence, the Liberals have moved somewhat to the Right, and seem poised to move further. Domestic and social problems – welfare, law and order, inflation – are the moving force, but additional urgency came in 1986 with the sharp decline in Australia's export trade, followed by the fall

* Geoffrey Blainey *The Tyranny of Distance* (Melbourne, 1966).

in the dollar. Even more to the Right, the National Party, under the forthright leadership of Ian Sinclair, articulated the discontents of the rural producers, grievously hard-pressed by worldwide agrarian overproduction. Farthest of all to the Right was the Premier of Queensland: Sir Joh Bjelke-Petersen combined an effectively lapidary style of expression with a no-nonsense attitude to trade-union pretensions. It seems unlikely that Federal Australia will follow Sir Joh. More probably he hopes that his example will steel the resolve of the Liberal and moderate Labour voters to follow his lead to the Right, and that the politicians will see which way the wind is blowing.

B.A. Santamaria

Meanwhile, the ALP is not only feeling the strains of office in a time of economic crisis, but also suffering some disillusionment with the orthodox union and socialist programmes of the party. B.A. Santamaria (once described by Malcolm Muggeridge as the 'hardest' thinking mind in Australian politics) is a devout Roman Catholic of Italian origin. Certainly he is literate and articulate to a degree rare in 'practical politics' anywhere. His own major role was as leader of the DLP and of the 'Movement', anti-Communist and designed to meet Catholic (Irish not least) doubts about the ALP.

Santamaria's strength, and to some extent his weakness, lies in his grasp of the political history and movements in Europe, and in his ability to articulate an alternative means of enabling Australia to organize itself so as to achieve better and higher social goals than it can under the present forms of party organization. Santamaria sees the ALP not as a genuine working-class movement but as an opportunist association of bureaucrats and self-styled intellectuals. He quotes the forceful description by the father of the present Labour Minister of Defence (Kim Beazley Senior) of the metamorphosis of Australian Labour politics: 'When I joined the Labor party as a boy, the branches were filled with the cream of the working class. When I leave, they have been replaced by the dregs of the middle class.'

For Santamaria, the ALP has become a party of 'teachers, social workers, reformist lawyers ... planners of various types' all basically on, or hoping to climb on, the government payroll; primarily concerned with getting a government job, with guaranteed high pay and pension. Such people compose between 10 and 15 per cent of the working population. They are – if the evidence of Canberra is anything to go by – in the process of becoming a hereditary caste, like members of the old

British coal miners' unions. The largest contributors to ALP funds are already the teachers' unions.

Other countries provide ample evidence that 'Labour' parties basically similar in social genesis and evolution to the ALP have already lost the dedicated loyalty which the old labour parties automatically enjoyed from the 'workers' of their day. The 'moderate' socialist parties in Britain, France, Germany, and 'middle' democrats of the United States, have to some extent lost those loyalties. At the moment, high wages, relatively low unemployment, plus force of habit, keep the workers inside the ALP corral, but may not do so forever.

The hope, according to Santamaria, lies in a party based on religious belief, patriotism, the virtues of the small unit in industry and agriculture alike. A party on such foundations would accentuate issues of national defence, security and foreign policy. It would drastically reduce the ever-growing army of *petits-fonctionnaires* who operate the Welfare State, and return as many of its functions to the *family* as being not only the most economic and efficient deliverer of welfare services but the organism with the moral duty and right to undertake such functions.*

Santamaria is something of a gadfly: his programme encapsulates many ideas inherent in the Tory, even in Liberal, traditional philosophy. His own political career, however, has been stormy and controversial. He could claim of the Liberals that he and his allies in the DLP kept Sir Robert Menzies and his Liberal Government in power (by the adroit use of the second preference vote) in a period when otherwise they would have been turned out. He could say, like Hughes, that the ALP left him (rather than the other way around), and that his philosophy represents what the ALP once believed in, ought to believe in now, but have betrayed.

In all this there is some truth. As a practising Roman Catholic and close ally of Archbishop Mannix of Melbourne, and as an Italian deeply imbued with the social doctrines of the Medieval Church, Santamaria's distrust of large-scale capitalism is not unlike the 'Christian' Socialism of R.H. Tawney and the 'distributism' of G.K. Chesterton. He is ready to accept religion 'without confessionalism' and stresses the need for stricter discipline and higher standards in education, university education above all.

Undoubtedly, Santamaria's programme of political reform finds a substantial following among certain sections of the Australian public. His

* B.A. Santamaria '1985: Reflections on Australia's political future' in *Quadrant* vol. xxix No. 5, May 1985 (Sydney).

enemies are to be found, naturally, anywhere to the left of centre, amongst professional politicians who distrust his record in practical politics and – perhaps most important – among middle-of-the-road Liberals who fear he would split the Liberal Party.

Foreign Affairs

Foreign relations have long been a stormy region of opinion and policy for Australia. In the years between 1858 and 1863, the rate of immigration of Chinese labour – in the gold rush the numbers of Chinese rose from a couple of thousand to over 33,000 – caused widespread anxiety. Relations with Britain, then Australia's main international preoccupation, worsened when Britain made known its disapproval of the proposed 'White Australia' policy: for Britain had a treaty of mutual responsibility with China. Sir Henry Parkes riposted with vigorous declarations of Australian intention 'to terminate the landing of the Chinese on our shores for ever'.

When the test case finally came to the Privy Council, it decided, in 1891, that no alien had 'a legal right ... to enter a British Colony'. That left Australia free to pursue whatever policy she chose, saved her bacon and Britain's and dispersed the most ominous cloud hanging over Anglo-Australian relations since 1788.

Foreign relations and defence are areas of policy-making which pose the most formidable problems for every government. Unfortunately, Australian politicians have tended to tread along the delicate paths with unsteady and ponderous feet. For most Australians the outside world seems, thank God, a very long way away. Until the Second World War, Australia's defence was assumed to be the business of Britain, and especially of the Royal Navy. Any such assumption was ended by Pearl Harbour. Since 1945, Australia's defence policy has been as opaque as her foreign policy.

Defence

Defence policy tends to follow foreign policy, once the diplomats and politicians have identified the potential friends and potential enemies. With a liberal, right-wing or moderate centre party in power, the 'friends' were not difficult to identify, even if politicians of those colours might stop short of embracing them with unrestricted enthusiasm. The most important, because the most rich and powerful, is the United States. Hence the Anzus alliance contracted between Australia, the United States and New Zealand. Britain, for most white Australians of moderate political opinions, was a power still to be turned to, in spite of differences in the Second World War and the recognition (on both sides) that British power and influence was much reduced below its old levels. France, still a Pacific power in New Caledonia, was problematical; but, by and large, the middle-of-the-road thinkers saw little point in trying to wind up any French colony until France decided in favour of initiating withdrawal.

Labour spokesmen had no clear message to articulate in foreign policy. Some were still shrouded in guilt about traditional 'White Australia' policy. Nowhere had support for that been stronger than in the unions and left-radical thinkers before 1914. Labour's early philosophers had felt more strongly on this than on the classic socialist doctrine that the producers should be assured of the fruits of their labour. Archibald's radical *Bulletin* defined 'Australians' as

> all white residents and immigrants with a clean record free of the class distinctions and religious differences of the Old World ... ready to place the advancement of their adopted country before the interests of imperialism. ... In this regard all men who leave the tyrant-ridden lands of Europe for freedom of speech and right of personal liberty are Australians before they set foot on the ship which brings them thither ... no Nigger, no Chinaman, no Lascar, no Kanaka, no purveyor of cheap coloured labour, is an Australian.

Such opinions have to be decently hidden in times when the author would certainly be liable to heavy penalties for infringing anti-racist laws. Yet beneath the face of liberal tolerance of Australia, as of many Western societies, the old fear of the yellow, and other multi-coloured perils, still simmers uneasily. A radio sports commentator in Australia recently received a letter from a listener who was critical of his remarks on the unsportsmanlike behaviour of a section of the spectators of an international event:

> If you look at the map you will see that we are an island at the end of the line with a population of 15 million white faces. We are surrounded by water. But to our north are islands and continents which show almost 2,000 million brown, black and yellow faces. ... We cannot afford to lose games or sport – we don't have the numbers to smile at defeat. ... We only want to survive, to keep our beautiful country for ourselves. And we can only do this by winning.

The ambiguities of Australian opinions are reflected in the inconsistencies of the foreign policy of Australian governments; Labour governments especially. For the spectrum of opinion, from idealist hopes to blackest fears, is wider in Labour ranks than anywhere. Thus anti-communist aid to the Americans in Vietnam has been followed, after that war, by pleas for a more friendly attitude to Vietnam, mingled with retrospective shame at the role of Australia in helping America during the war against the Vietcong. Conversely, having opposed the Netherlands and supported the Indonesians in their struggle for indepen-dence, Australia changed her tune as soon as a resurgent Indonesia began to show its teeth in Timor and New Guinea (see p. 202).

Policy towards Japan and China is equally ambiguous. Japan today is too important to the Australian economy to be handled with anything less than kid gloves. Unofficially, Japanese attitudes to Australia over the price and delivery of Australian coal – a major export item – are much resented as cavalier and overbearing. But, characteristically, the resentment is not universal. There are exceptions, particularly amongst the radical Left.

1986 saw a rash of troubles break out in foreign affairs. The Anzus Treaty, in particular, began to look shaky. It was threatened by the sharp withdrawal of the new Labour Government in New Zealand from the Treaty. Their Prime Minister (Mr Lange) used blunt language to Washington. The situation was compounded by French security agents deliberately sinking a vessel – the *Rainbow Warrior* – which belonged to the international anti-nuclear organization, Greenpeace. The boat was sunk, with subsequent loss of life, in a New Zealand harbour. Australia's attitude to the nuclear question remained unclear. What would happen if American warships entered Sydney harbour equipped with nuclear arms? Would the Anzus partner-in-arms be required (as had recently happened to a British warship) either to declare itself 'uncontaminated' or else be denied entry? At this unpropitious moment the United States Government made a request for their missiles to be allowed to fly over Australian territory (where American missile-tracking equipment was already installed).

As uproar broke out on the left wing of the ALP, it seemed that a crisis in what remained of Anzus was unavoidable. Fortunately for the Hawke Government, the United States Government backpedalled and handshakes and back-slapping were the order of the day. But frater-nal puffs of goodwill apart, the meaning or lack of meaning of Anzus remains an unanswered problem.

Relations with Indonesia likewise took a dubious turn when the Minis-ter of Defence (Mr Beazley) set off, in February 1986, on a goodwill visit to Indonesia, designed to allay suspicions that Australia's new defence proposals might be aimed at Indonesia.

He had hardly returned home when a leading Sydney newspaper launched a very frank attack on Indonesian corruption in high places. The President and his family were not omitted from criticism. Indonesia immediately banned all Australian press reporters from the country and made a specific target of the imminent 'Summit' of Third World leaders in Jakarta. Mr Hawke responded with an angry speech ostensibly defending press freedom. Relations became unprecedently bitter.

The Australian Minister for Foreign Affairs (Mr Hayden) made himself no less unpopular in New Caledonia. Mr Hayden had criticized the French and their Government for – so it was said – blocking the rightful claims of the native Kanak separatists to independence of France. Unfortunately, his liberal sentiments were equally unacceptable to both sides in the New Caledonian dispute. His attempt at sweet reasonableness at once irritated the Kanaks and upset the French – especially the French President Monsieur Mitterand (like Mr Hayden, a socialist!) What right, demanded Mitterand, had Australia to criticize France as a colonial power? Had not Australia killed off its aborigines?

The Australian Opposition now weighed in. Where, they asked, did Monsieur Mitterand get his version of Australian aboriginal history from? Was it, perhaps, from Mr Hayden's colleague, the Minister for Aboriginal Affairs, whose every second speech contained accusations of Australian brutality to their aborigines? Who could blame the French President for believing what self-styled 'progressive' Australians recounted to him and the rest of the world as Australian history?

A Labour government is admittedly in difficulties over foreign policy. It inherits what it is desperate, for electoral reasons if not more idealistic reasons, to shed: the sense of guilt over any remnants of 'radical' association with racism, the anti-Semitism of Jack Lang or a 'White Australia'. Like most potential sympathizers with the Americans, it suffers the usual temptation to reject the politics of the society from which most of the 'culture' of its followers derives, and to follow the even more ancient habit of biting the hand that feeds (or fed) it. Its good intentions are on display (in the person of Mr Gough Whitlam) in the proceedings of Unesco, and in New York by its Ambassador to the United Nations. But whether good intentions can be translated into successful diplomacy remains to be seen.

For Australian governments (of all political colours) the fundamental problem of foreign policy remains Geoffrey Blainey's 'tyranny of distance', in this case remoteness from the outside world. Bungles over foreign policy or defence seem less important than domestic mishaps, but this is of course a dangerous illusion.

The Economy

The Australian economy has undergone great changes since its early pastoral days, and upheaval continues in the last decades of the twentieth century. Farming, in its various crop-growing and animal husbandry activities, remains a vital part of the economy but no longer dominates the scene as once it did. A vast range of mining and mineral-related industries (to which oilfields have now been added) account for a value-added roughly equal to just over half the gross value of agricultural production. In addition, 28,000 manufacturing establishments employ over a million persons and account for value-added of $A31,074 million.

These changes are reflected in the revolutionary switch in overseas markets for imports and exports. Down to 1914 and later, Britain continued to be the pivot on which Australian overseas trade turned. Today, in terms of value, Australia's largest source of both incoming and outgoing trade is Japan, followed by the United States and the European Community (see Table 2); within the latter Britain is still Australia's most important partner, but her trade is only a fraction of that transacted with Japan or the United States. Other areas of Asian trade (especially Singapore) have grown greatly in importance.

Table 2   Australian Imports and Exports

1983–84	Imports from (A$ billion):	Exports to (A$ billion):
Japan	5.4	6.5
United States	5.2	2.7
EEC	5.1	3.4

The composition of Australia's export trade has likewise been revolutionized. Metal ores, coal, coke, non-ferrous metals and petroleum comprise far the largest proportion of exports by value: they are followed by textile fibres, cereals, meat, dairy produce, etc., in that order.

Compare this group of mainly primary products with the biggest imports by value: machinery, transport equipment, petroleum, yarns and fibres. The difference between the complex sophistication of the motor cars, trucks, buses, electronic, chemical (including man-made fibres), pharmaceutical products etc., and the (relatively) simple character of much of Australia's exports is very striking. The point is not over-looked by politicians and economists, nor by the employers of labour or the trade unions. It has become a matter of increasingly urgent debate as this book has taken shape. Oddly enough, little attention has ever been given in Australia to the urgent debate in Britain in the 1860s and 1870s. The reliance of the Victorian British balance of payments on the massive export of a 'resource' material – coal – shocked W.S. Jevons, one of the most original and powerful Victorian economists. For him *The Coal Question* (1868) – the unavoidable run down of coal supplies and the folly of giving away valuable advantages in the shape of raw material supplies to foreign manufacturers – was 'a question of almost religious importance'.*

The mixed public–private economy has, from 1788 onwards, been a striking feature of Australia's economy. The unavoidable pressures which explain this have not been relieved by the adoption of state initia-tives in the building of an infrastructure of transport, house and office construction, factories and the provision of public and private services and industries. In fact, the import of overseas capital and the immigrant skill and labour to execute the investment programme in Australia has called for state and municipal initiative from start to finish. Tariff protec-tion – was it necessary? Was it beneficial? Or would it simply featherbed industrial inefficiency? These were questions with which only govern-ment could deal. From the 1860s, factory industry made headway. It was specially important in Victoria: when the first fine flurries of the gold rush subsided, the labour that had flooded into that state would begin to ebb away unless alternative employment was found for it. The tariffs with which Victoria broke through orthodox *laissez-faire* barriers were designed to do precisely this. Trade unions, following up behind, organized Australian labour as it had never been organized before: it could be said that the years from 1872 to 1893 were a Golden Age for the wage-earners. But what was the result?

A visiting English capitalist employer from Birmingham in 1886 was shocked by what he took to be the 'scandalous' attitude of Melbourne building workers to their jobs: industrial workers were a disgrace; only on the farms and in the shops did men and women really work. Australia (he wrote in his diary) was 'the land for my lord the working man'. Right or wrong he would, if he returned today, find ample evidence in the press that his views are still widely shared. The belief in high

* W.S. Jevons *The Coal Question* (London, 1868); R.C.K. Ensor *England 1870–1914* (Oxford, 1968), pp. 108–9.

wages is still all-important. Wage-fixing, and the current 'Accord' between the Hawke Government and the unions, have sent wages up and kept them there. Yet a visiting American expert has confessed he could see no alternative to wage-fixing. The broad scope of Australian unionism and the 'entrenched and dynamic power of the leadership of Australian (National) Council of Trade Unions worked against the evolution of collective bargaining'.

Until relatively recently, there was probably a majority belief that Australia had, through sensible and generous attitudes to organized labour, overcome the class divisions and apathy noted by the visitor from Birmingham. Today there is less optimism and deeper unease at the frequency of strikes which are called for trivial reasons, but which have devastating results on output and, especially, on exports. Dock strikes at all the major Australian ports keep ships anchored outside harbour, queueing for their cargoes of coal, for Japan especially, which comprises a sizeable proportion of Australian exports. Similar paralysis afflicts almost every industry in turn. The upward spiral of wages approved by the ACTU (of which Prime Minister Hawke was once secretary) under the 'Accord' is seen as burdening the economy and creating unemployment. Industrialists are hamstrung by holiday and leave provisions for workers. In some industries these are said to total from three to four months out of twelve. Taxes, amenities for workers and payments for government services make for crippling costs in manufacturing industry.

There is a wide perception that the structure of the Australian economy and, even more, the pressures inhibiting essential changes in that structure are likely to bring stagnation, even regression, unless some necessary reforms can be introduced. Australia's major export markets are beset by too many goods and weak prices. Because, at the same time, Australian imports have risen from 12 per cent of the Gross Domestic Product to 15 per cent in the past fifteen years, Australia's 'terms of trade' have sunk to their lowest level in this same period.

This deteriorating situation will not necessarily continue: but it is difficult to see how it can be substantially improved without radical change. The dynamic area of world trade is the trade in manufactures. At present these represent less than one-third of Australia's exports. There is consensus of opinion amongst entrepreneurs and analysts that this can be improved only by more investment, more research, development and new technology, and – perhaps the only improvement realizable in the near future – a more flexible wage structure throughout Australian industry. If this is not forthcoming by, or at least with, a voluntary initiative from the unions – led by the ACTU – the companies that entered the country via the multinational mode of organization will rectify their error by an equally voluntary act: they will leave for greener pastures overseas. And these will not be the old homes of enterprise – America and Europe – but South-East Asia and, of course, Japan.

There are signs that the shortcomings of the present organization of labour as a prime element in the economy are slowly being grasped not only by employers, investors, managers and academic analysts, but by some sections of the trade union movement itself. Just as in present-day Britain, a power struggle is in progress for control of the unions. In both economies, the unions are split.

How does the record of government today stand in regard to *dirigisme*? Economic experts have accepted that Australia's labour problems have not done badly under price and income policies, but equally they have also predicted a limited life for the present 'Accord', and spoken with regret rather than admiration of the 'muscle' demonstrated by the ACTU. A former (and disenchanted) Secretary of the Treasury, Mr John Stone, in 1985 recommended the business community to reduce the shadows of economic uncertainty hanging over the country by

> getting Australian governments out of business – rather than, as heretofore, devoting much of its energies to getting those governments to provide one kind of favour or another.... Until business leaders can truthfully say that they seek nothing from governments other than freedom and a fair wind for their enterprise....

From one who escaped from the bilboes of Canberra, these are strong words.

The Australian Identity

The abrupt changes in the context of Australia's existence – the political, strategic, diplomatic and economic context in particular – goes a long way to explain the frequency with which Australia's 'identity' recurs in the press, in literature and political rhetoric. From time to time the character of every society, and the quality of life in that society, becomes a topic for discussion and controversy; but neither Danes nor French nor Swiss nor any historic European people argue about their 'identity' as Australians do. And surely the principal reason for this is the switch from being a colony of a Western European power to being an independent, though still geographically remote island, so large as to be almost indefensible, placed between the Pacific and Indian Oceans, surrounded by Oriental and Asiatic nations much larger than itself, and living with memories or legends of a convict past, for long in primitive and depressed conditions that in turn produced a rugged and uncompromising race of people.

Marjorie Barnard has dealt with the problem in a way that combines common sense and imaginative insight. In her *Envoi* to her *History of Australia* she writes: 'There comes the inevitable question: is there an Australian people? Have we any identity in the world?' Her answer is, yes.

> Australia's past is negligible – six generations Australian-born at the utmost. Yet there *is* an Australian people, not just a transplanted collection of English, Scots and Irish. The climate, the bush, social differences, different occupations, and many other factors, have combined to produce a different, special and unique society ... a society where success and money speak more loudly than family.... Go to England and you will feel that though you have come 'home' you are yet different: your roots have been fed in a different earth and for the first time you will know your own speech.

Miss Barnard concerns herself with the effects of Australian conditions upon the Australian psychology. Yet, like Ernest Scott, Keith Hancock and the other classic historians of Australia, Marjorie Barnard succeeded in writing good Australian history which recognized that Australia was an integral part of a wider world. The growing obsession with an Australian identity has coincided with another revival of a 'radicalism' based on old guilt complexes about the treatment of the aborigines, the new feminism, and what that highly perceptive Australian journalist–philosopher, Max Harris has called 'the headlong dive into nationalist narcissism ... really synonymous with isolationism, an attitude we deplore when we see it evidenced in American psychology but tend to applaud in ourselves as an achieved virtue'.

This new, introverted, xenophobic isolationism was well illustrated by the former director of the Bicentenary celebrations when he explained his plans. The brutal treatment of the aborigines would be illustrated dramatically: there would be no representation of the landing of the First Fleet. He did not intend, he said in a picturesque phrase, 'that the Bicentenary should be turned into a white wank'.* Fortunately, this proved not to be the majority opinion of the Bicentenary authority on the early history of Australia. The officer concerned has retired.

Elsewhere, however, the prophets of 'multiculturalism' have continued to preach the doctrines they believe essential if Australia is to slot itself

---

* See the *Macquarie Dictionary* (of Australian English, Sydney, 1982). Wank: 'an act or instance of masturbation; behaviour self-indulgent or egotistical'.

into the Asiatic–Pacific basin. Politicians (like Mr Hayden, Minister of Foreign Affairs) and artists (like Mr Brett Whiteley) as well as numerous 'radical' voices in universities and institutions urging 'liberal' social reform, have described their vision of an Australia populated by 'Eurasians'. That this is possible is certainly widely believed, but does it offer a solution to the puzzle of Australia's identity? Or a hope of removing the present obstacles to a tranquil South Pacific?

Surely any such hope is total illusion. Did racial, cultural or linguistic similarity bring peace between North and South Korea? Or North and South Vietnam? Or between Vietnam, Thailand and Cambodia? Did widespread intermarriage between Dutch and Indonesians avert the bitter crises of de-colonization? Has the physical likeness of Japanese and Chinese ever contributed to lessening the age-old hostility between their governments? (Or made Japan more inclined towards socialism or communism? Or China less inclined?) As the history of Europe proves, differences of nationality or language, even of religion, are no bar to the spread of a common culture. Early modern Europe, in times often bloody and vicious, could still enjoy a growing international commerce and the spread of invention. Literary forms, the visual arts and music were everywhere based on Italian, then Dutch, then German, then English models. The European Community, as it finally emerged, was the work of centuries; but its component nations remain culturally separate entities, even today.

There is no simple answer to Australia's problems of foreign affairs, defence, immigration. All call for statesmanship at a high level. They will not be solved simply by catchwords or slogans, debased, prejudiced history or the political dodges of expediency or fanaticism. 'Identity' is not a passport or a bankcard or a title deed to rights and privileges. It is a description of historic tradition and a way of life which includes heavy responsibilities as well as rewards. There is no carefree future for an Australia unfettered by its past, envisaging only an end to colonialism and international responsibilities and with a Eurasian culture as a universal nostrum and panacea for all its possible troubles.

More thoughtful, critical minds are sceptical of such dreams. Charmian Clift (d. 1969) was Australia's most gifted and engaging woman journalist. Her essay on 'Australia Day' describes the difficulties of explaining to her children just what it celebrated. They all agreed the Australians were the best in the world, Australia the finest country there ever was, Australian girls the prettiest, its sportsmen the most sporting, etc. So, 'as we know we're the most enviable people on earth why get out and wave flags about?' In the end, she takes her tongue out of her cheek:

it isn't quite like that. 'We are not yet clearly enough in focus. We do not have the heroes, nor the race memory of resistance, persecution, plunder, glory, unspeakable barbarities and unbelievable heroisms. We do not have the shining belief, the unshakeable conviction out of which the heroes and the songs are made.'*

Buzz Kennedy, who writes a weekly column in the *Australian*, and says many true and witty things, has much the same feeling.

> We need heroes (and heroines, too ...) and the dreary fact is that we haven't got any – except for a few sportspersons who don't count in this context. I'm talking about people whose blazing minds and inspired actions make them heroes ... we need heroes to look up to so we see the sun and the stars ... and all we see are the shadows and the feet of clay.

It is clear that neither of these social critics is thinking simply of 'physical' heroism: there is plenty of that in Australia's history. I believe they – like Froude and Adams (see Chapter 9) – are talking about the *quality of life*: the deficiencies of materialism and hedonism; the need – from time to time – for men and women of high seriousness, for a Queen Victoria, a Napoleon, a Lincoln, a Gandhi. There are, of course, dangers in the cult of heroism. An age of would-be dictators has left many countries besides Australia sceptical of its merits: yet it is one of the most widely quoted, and accepted, clichés of Australia that Australians will always cut down the poppy that threatens to grow too tall, laugh off the problem that threatens to get too serious; leave the Chamber before the Division bell; go down to the beach if life threatens to get too difficult.

When Shiva Paul visited Australia in 1984 to write a book on South-East Asia, he came with a divided mind on the issues of aboriginal land-rights and 'racism' in Australia. His dilemmas were soon solved: he found himself excluded from the Yirrkala Aboriginal Reserve by its guardian, a white minder, who threatened to arrest him if he trespassed on 'aboriginal' territory. The Yirrkala culture, 40,000 years old, was represented by Nashville music played on electric guitars by white pop singers in American T-shirts. His final, disenchanted vote was in favour of old-fashioned assimilation; against new-fangled 'separatism' or 'pluralism' in its novel manifestation.

Peter Coleman, an Australian political philosopher, shares this view, but contends that there is, indeed, an interpretation of pluralism that can be equated with liberalism and tolerance: 'It means acknowledging

* *The World of Charmian Clift*. Introduction by George Johnston (Sydney, 1970).

*diversity within a generally accepted framework of institutions and values.'**

Another distinguished Australian academic, Professor Eugene Kamenka, of the Australian National University, and himself of Russian parentage, has explored this line of thought further. He argues that the 'immigrants' in Australia (especially the non-British ones) came because

> they admire the tolerance and civilisation of Australia; they do not admire the strident, self-conscious 'Australianism' of the nationalists whose attitudes are composed in equal parts of insecurity and aggressiveness. Basically, this kind of Australian nationalism 'is predominantly an economic doctrine' designed to keep out competition and enable people to live without effort. This is nationalism in its mean revelation; in its generous revelation it is an aspect of humanism, the specifically western contribution to the recognition of human worth and human potentialities.†

Britain's own forgotten immigrants might well have agreed; Tennyson's Saxons, Danes, Normans, Teutons, Celts; the Flemings, Dutch, Walloons, Italians, Germans, Huguenots, Spanish Sephardim, Russian, Polish, German Ashkenazim, who, between the 1560s and 1900, made up a sizeable proportion of London, Norwich, Colchester, Manchester, Liverpool, Glasgow and Leeds. For Britain has also opened her doors to hundreds of thousands of foreign immigrants. They – like the Europeans and Asian immigrants to Australia – have made enormous contributions to British prosperity and its many and diverse attractions. For these too, life in their new home was not always easy. It usually took a couple of generations at least before the newcomers merged into the English landscape.

David Kemp‡ still believes that liberty and justice are the foundations of any worthwhile society. In defining rational identity he has written:

> Australia's identity, like the identity of each of us, is our history, our experiences, our failures and our achievements. It grows and develops with time and change, it strengthens with success and weakens with failure. It is not designed by government like a slogan or a trademark and given to us by advertisers. It is there, a reality, in the hearts and minds of Australians and it is ignored by a government at its peril. The Bicentennial of 1988 will not stir the hearts of Australians until it acknowledges this fact, until

---

* Peter Coleman 'A Pluralist Australia: Conservatives and Radicals', *Quadrant*, December 1984. My italics.
† Eugene Kamenka: 'Migrants admire Australia's civilisation, if not its Culture', *The Age*, 26 January 1985.
‡ Professor of Politics at Monash University, in 'How to Reform the Liberal party', *Quadrant*, May 1986.

it is prepared to fly the flag, honour our institutions and British heritage, our history, our religions and our achievements.

A century ago, J.A. Froude wrote, on leaving the shores of Australia: 'The rising Australians are "promising young men". If they mean to be more, they must either be independent, or must be citizens of *Oceana*.'* By '*Oceana*', Froude meant the British Commonwealth. Today his comment sounds intolerably paternal; 'citizens of an inter-dependent world' would be more to the point. Froude's days of 'neutral' Australian childhood, passed 'in obscurity and amusement' have long since gone. Australia has plenty of artists, musicians, sportsmen, athletes, engineers, scientists and technologists. Yet the problems she faces, external and internal, are fundamentally challenges to the intellect and the spirit. The deterioration of the economy is a challenge to science and enterprise. The vulgarization of thought, by substituting cut-price sociology for history, challenges intellectual standards at all levels of education. The imperative need of the day is for Australia to look outwards, not inwards. If the battles against defeatism are not won, the Bicentenary will not be an occasion for rejoicing. It will become the obsequies for a shameful past, the celebration of a spurious martyrdom, a window-dressing memorial in sackcloth and ashes.

This is unlikely. Thus far the Australian character has overcome the problems of its environment. J.D. Pringle has made a shrewd observation:

> Australia bent its British migrants to its will, not *vice-versa*. . . . The character of its people was what eighteenth and nineteenth century foreigners thought of as John Bull ... kindly but not tolerant ... generous, sardonic, sceptical but gullible ... quick to take offence and by no means unwilling to give it ... at worst aggressive, complacent; at best brave and honest.†

It is a shrewd analysis of Australia's greatest men; men who scrutinized their own beliefs as rigorously as they did those of others; who mingled passion with scepticism, weighing each human 'right' against a counter-vailing responsibility. Above all men who combined a local patriotism for their corner of the world with a broader vision that comprehended a wider world. Such were men like Andrew Fisher, most modest and perhaps still the greatest of Australian Labour Prime Ministers; Alfred Deakin, disciple of Higinbotham, three times Liberal Prime Minister; John Anderson, Sydney's stiff-necked philosopher; W.A. Holman, a Labour idealist too human to relish the cramps of party discipline; and towering above them all, George Higinbotham, Chief Justice of Victoria

* Froude, *Oceana*, p. 168.
† J.D.Pringle *Australian Accent* (London, 1958; Adelaide, 1978).

(by origin a Dubliner) – shy, brave, never afraid to confess when he found himself in a fog. He has been called 'the noblest Australian', and his title has not been challenged. All of these represent something unmistakably Australian. There is no reason to suppose they are the end of the line.

It is their successors' task to steer their *terra Australis* – *Australia Felix*, too, let us hope – through its third century into which it has been launched by Cook, Banks, Phillip and the millions who followed them to the great Southland.

TIMOR SEA

Melville I.

Darwin

Arnhem Lan

C. Leveque
Pender Bay

NORT

TERRI

Great Sandy Desert

N.W. Cape

Hamersley
Range

Gibson Desert

Mt Stue

Macdonnell Ran

Alice Spri

Finke R

WESTERN

AUSTRALIA

Shark B.
Dirck Hartog's I.

Great Victoria Desert

S

Nullarbor Plain

AUS

Coolgardie

Eucla

Eyre

Fowlers B.
Nuits Arch.

INDIAN
OCEAN

Perth
Garden I.

Swan R.

Freemantle

Esperance

Great Australian Bight

C. Leeuwin

Albany

King George Sd

0   500   1000 km

CORAL SEA

Gulf of
Carpentaria

Cape
York
Peninsula

C. Turnagain

Torres Strait

Palmer Field

Great

Barrier

Reef

RN

RY

Great

Simpson
Desert

QUEENSLAND

Dividing

L. Eyre

Coopers C.

Sturt
Desert

Darling
Downs

Moreton Bay

Brisbane

TH

ALIA

Yulgilbar

Darling R.

NEW SOUTH

Menindee

WALES

Range

Port Macquarie

Norfolk I.

Eugowra

Lachlan R.

Ophir

Canowindra

Bathurst

Blue Mts

Hunter R.

Newcastle

Parramatta
Port Jackson

L. Lincoln

Spencer Gf.

Murrumbidgee R.

Jenidene

Bowral

Sydney

Howe I.

Pt Adelaide

Adelaide

St. Vincent's Gf.

Alexandrina

Wagga Wagga

Kiandra

CANBERRA

Murray R.

Encounter
Bay

Mt Gambier

Bendigo

Glenrowan

Snowy R.

Mt Kosciusko

C. Northumberland

VICTORIA

Ballarat

Castlemaine

Australian Alps

Portland

Geelong

Melbourne

Pt Phillip

C. Everard

TASMAN
SEA

Bass Strait

TASMANIA

Launceston

Macquarie Harb.

Risdon

Maria I.

Hobart

C. Frederick Henry

Pt Arthur

FURTHER READING

General

Barnard, Marjorie *The History of Australia* (Sydney, 1962–72)
Blainey, G. N. *The Tyranny of Distance* (Melbourne, 1966)
Clark, Manning *Selected Documents in Australian History* (2 vols)
  (Sydney, 1950–5)
Hancock, Sir Keith *Australia* (London, 1930)
Scott, Ernest *A Short History of Australia* (Oxford, 1916–58)
Spate, O. H. K. *Australia* (London, 1968)

The First Fleet and Settlement

Auchmuty, J. J. (ed.) *The Voyage of Governor Phillip to Botany Bay*
  (Royal Australian Historical Society, 1972)
Barnard, Marjorie *Phillip of Australia* (London and Sydney, 1938)
Cobley, J. *Sydney Cove 1788* (London, 1962)
Crittenden, Victor *A Bibliography of the First Fleet* (Canberra, 1981)
Fitzhardinge, L. F. (ed.) *Sydney's First Four Years: Being the diaries
  of Captain Watkin Tench* (Sydney, Melbourne and London, 1961)
Frost, Alan *Convicts and Empire: A naval question* (Melbourne and
  Oxford, 1980)
Lindley, M. F. *The Acquisition and Government of Backward Territory
  in International Law* (London, 1926)
Marchant, Leslie *France Australe* (Perth, 1984)
Mackaness, George *Admiral Arthur Phillip* (Sydney, 1937)
—— *Blue Bloods of Botany Bay: A book of Australian historical
  tales* (London and Sydney, 1953)
O'Connell, D. P. *International Law* (2 vols) (London, 1970)
Radzinowicz, Leon *History of English Criminal Law*, vol. I (Pilgrim
  Trust, 1948)

Articles
Frost, Alan 'New South Wales as *Terra Nullius*: The British Denial of
  Aboriginal Rights' in *Historical Studies*, vol. 19, pp. 513–23 (1981)
Wilson, Charles 'Convicts, Commerce and Sovereignty: the Forces

behind the Settlement of Australia' in *Business Life and Public Policy: Essays in Honour of D.C.Coleman*, ed N. McKendrick and R. B. Outhwaite (Cambridge, 1986)

Social and Economic

Abbott, G. J. and N. B. Nairn (eds) *Economic Growth of Australia 1788–1821* (Melbourne, 1969)

Adams, Francis *The Australians: A social sketch* (London, 1893)

Barnard, Marjorie *Macquarie's World* (Sydney, 1941)

Blainey, G. N. *The Rush that Never Ended* (Melbourne, 1963)

────── *Triumph of the Nomads* (Melbourne, 1967)

────── *Our Side of the Country: The story of Victoria* (Melbourne, 1984)

Butlin, N. G. *Investment in Australian Economic Development 1861–1900* (Cambridge, 1964; Canberra, 1972)

────── *Our Original Aggression* (Sydney, 1983)

Clark Kennedy, A. E. *Cambridge to Botany Bay: A Victorian family tragedy* (Cambridge, 1982)

Coghlan, T. A. *Labour and Industry in Australia* (4 vols) (Oxford, 1918)

Currey, C. H. *The Irish at Eureka* (Melbourne, 1954)

Dunn, Michael *Australia and the Empire: From 1788 to the present* (Sydney, 1984)

Durack, Mary *Kings in Grass Castles* (London, 1959)

Fairbairn, Anne *Shadows of Our Dreaming* (Sydney, 1983)

Fitzpatrick, Brian C. *British Imperialism and Australia 1783–1823* (London and Sydney, 1939–71)

────── *The British Empire in Australia* (Melbourne, 1969)

Froude, J. A. *Oceana* (London, 1886)

Hall, A. R. *The London Capital Market and Australia 1870–1914* (Canberra, 1963)

────── *The Stock Exchange of Melbourne and the Victorian Economy 1852–1900* (Canberra, 1968)

Kiernan, Colm (ed.) *Ireland and Australia* (New South Wales and Ireland, 1984)

Pearl, Cyril *Wild Men of Sydney* (Sydney, 1958)

Prentis, Malcolm D. *The Scots in Australia* (Sydney, 1983)

Reynolds, Henry *The Other Side of the Frontier* (Sydney, 1981)

Richards, Eric *Highland Clearances* (2 vols; vol. 1, 1982; vol. 2, 1985; London)

Roberts, S. H. *History of Australian Land Settlement 1788–1920* (Melbourne, 1924)

—— *The Squatting Age in Australia* (Melbourne, 1935)

Robson, L. L. (ed.) *Australian Commentaries; Select Articles from the Round Table, 1911–42* (Melbourne, 1975)

Rowley, C. D. *The Destruction of Aboriginal Society* (Canberra, 1970)

Schedvin, C. B. *Australia and the Great Depression* (Sydney, 1970)

Shaw, A. G. L. *The Economic Development of Australia* (London and Melbourne, 1946)

—— *Convicts and the Colonies* (London, 1966)

Shann, E. O. G. *An Economic History of Australia* (Cambridge, 1929; Melbourne, 1963)

Sinclair, W. A. *The Process of Economic Development in Australia* (Melbourne, 1980)

Watson, Don *Brian Fitzpatrick – A radical life* (Sydney, 1979)

—— *Caledonia Australis: Scottish highlanders on the frontier of Australia* (Sydney, 1984)

Wakefield, E. G. *A Letter from Sydney* (London, 1829)

Political and Biographical

Anderson, John *Studies in Empirical Philosophy*, ed. John Passmore (Sydney, 1962)

Baker, D. W. (ed.) *John Dunmore Lang: Reminiscences of my life and times* (Sydney, 1972)

Crisp, L. F. *Ben Chifley: A biography* (London/Adelaide, 1960–3)

Deakin, Alfred *Federal Story* (Melbourne, 1944)

Fitzhardinge, L. F. *The Little Digger: A political biography of W.M. Hughes* (Royal Australian Historical Society, 1979)

Fletcher, B. H. *A Governor Maligned* (Oxford, 1985)

Henderson, Gerard *Mr Santamaria and the Bishops* (NSW, 1982–3)

Kerr, Sir John *Matters of Judgment* (Melbourne, 1978)

Larwood, Harold *Bodyline* (Preface by Douglas Jardine) (London, 1933)

Lee, Norman *John Curtin, Saviour of Australia* (Sydney, 1983)

Menzies, Sir Robert *Afternoon Light* (Melbourne, 1967)

Morris, E. E. *Memoirs of George Higinbotham* (Melbourne, 1895)

Parkes, Sir Henry *Fifty Years in the Making of Australian History* (London, 1892)

Ross, Lloyd *John Curtin: A Biography* (Sydney, 1977)

Santamaria, B. A. *Against the Tide* (Oxford and Melbourne, 1981)

Scott, Ernest *The Life of Captain Matthew Flinders, RN* (Sydney, 1914)

Shaw, A. G. L. *Sir George Arthur Bt. 1784–1854* (London, 1984)

Arts and Pastimes

Bird, John *Percy Grainger* (Melbourne and London, 1976)

Covell, Roger *Australia's Music: Themes of a new society* (Sydney, 1976)

Fairbairn, S. *Fairbairn of Jesus* (Introduction by Sir Arthur Quiller-Couch) (London, 1931)

Friend, Donald *The Cosmic Turtle* (Perth, 1976)

—— *Art in a Classless Society (and Vice Versa)* (Sydney, 1985)

Gay, Florence *In Praise of Australia: An anthology in prose and verse* (London, 1912)

Gleeson, James *Australian Painters (1788–1970)* (Sydney, Auckland, London and New York, 1971–81)

Goossens, Eugene *Overture and Beginners* (London, 1951)

Green, H. M. *History of Australian Literature* (2 vols, revised by Dorothy Green) (London, Sydney and Melbourne, 1984)

Heseltine, H. (ed.) *The Penguin Book of Australian Verse* (Sydney, 1972)

Historic Homesteads of Australia (Australian Council of National Trusts) (New South Wales and London, 1976)

Lindsay, Norman *Bohemians of the Bulletin* (Sydney, 1965)

Moresby, Isabella *Australia Makes Music* (Sydney, 1948)

Stevens, Bertram (ed.) *An Anthology of Australian Verse* (Sydney, 1906)

Streeton, Hugh *Ideas for Australian Cities* (Adelaide, 1970)

van Sommers, Tess and Unk White *Sydney Sketchbook* (Adelaide, 1967)

War

Bean, C. E. W. (general editor and author of first six volumes) *The Official History of Australia in the Great War 1914–1918* (Sydney, 1921–42)

Rhodes James, Robert *Gallipoli* (London, 1965)

Reference

Dictionary of National Biography (London, 1895)

Australian Dictionary of Biography (Melbourne, 1966)

Dictionnaire de Biographie Française (Paris, 1933)

Cambridge History of the British Empire vol. VII Part I (Cambridge, 1933)

Australian Encyclopedia (Sydney, 1958)

Evidence and Conclusions
In the case heard before Mr Justice Blackburn in the Supreme Court of the Northern Territory of Australia between (plaintiff) Milirrpum of the Rirratjingu clan etc. and Nabalco Pty. Ltd., and the Commonwealth of Australia (defendants): being No. 341 of 1968 252 pp.

INDEX

aborigines, 73–89
  and land rights controversy, 84–8
  and smallpox, 77–9
  brutality to women, 80–1, 123–4
  culture of, 122–6
  decline of, 75–88, 148–9
  lifestyle of, 20, 74–5
  original instructions about, 19–20
  present-day, 89
  relations with, 26, 41–5, 69; *see also* Phillip, Captain Arthur, and aborigines
Adams, Arthur, 120
Adams, Francis, 112–13, 144, 152–64, 210
Adelaide, 102, 145–6, 216–17
Age, 102, 211
agriculture, 50, 98–9, 169
Albion, R. G., 10
Allen, 'Gubby', 182, 191–2
America, 7, 13, 142, 195–6, 197–8, 200–1, 202–3, 204–5, 206, 209, 210, 211, 245–6, 247, 248, 249
Amery, Leo, 195
Anderson, John, 257
anti-semitism, 185–6
Anzac (Australian and New Zealand Army Corps), 171–4
Anzus Treaty, 201–2, 206, 211, 245–6, 247
Arch, Joseph, 241
Archer, John Lee, 216
Archibald, J. F., 153, 157, 167
architecture, 168, 215–19
Argus, 112
Arndell, Thomas, 40

Arnold, Matthew, 143
Arthur, Sir George, 64–5, 69
Ashbolt, Allan, 229, 230
Asquith, Herbert, 166
Auchmuty, J. J., 29
Australian, 30, 127, 211, 255
Australian Agricultural Co., 68, 100, 157–8
Australian Board of Control, 191
Australian Council of Trade Unions (ACTU), 251, 252
Australian Labour Party (ALP), 237, 238, 240–1, 242, 243–4, 247, 248
Australian National Trust, 218–19
Avebury, Lord, 124

Backhouse, James, 48
Ballarat, 147–8
Bank of New South Wales, 56
Banks, Joseph, 10, 20, 51, 59, 68
Barnard Eldershaw, Marjorie, 29, 32, 35, 46–7, 98, 99, 134–5, 253
Barnet, Nahum, 168
Barney, Lt Col. George, 215
Batman, John, 85–7
Baudin, Nicolas, 21
Bayley, Arthur, 95
Bean, C. E. W., 118, 172, 174
Beazley, Kim Sr, 243, 247–8
Beecham, Sir Thomas, 225
Bennelon, 42, 69, 74, 76, 80
Bergerac, Cyrano de, 15
Berry, Sir Graham, 156
Bicentenary celebrations, 253, 256–7
Biggs, J. T., 66

Bishop, Cap. Charles, 51
Bjelke-Petersen, Sir Joh, 242, 243
Black, George, 167
Blackburn, James, 216
Blainey, Prof. Geoffrey, 11, 81, 91, 94, 230, 236, 242, 248
Blaxland, Gregory, 50
Bligh, William, 54, 58, 59
'bodyline' test matches, 180–3, 190–3
Boldrewood, Rolf (T. A. Browne), 117–18, 124
Bonnie Prince Charlie, 25
Botany Bay, 9, 17, 29, 39, 65
Bougainville, Louis de, 15, 25
Bourke, Sir Richard, 61–2, 85, 86
Bowen, Lt John, 12
Bradley, Lt William, 40
Bradman, Don, 181, 182
Brady, Matthew, 135
Brahe, May, 220
Brisbane, Sir Thomas, 60
British colony, creation of, 1–4, 8–28
Britten, Benjamin, 226
Brosses, Charles de, 15
Bruce, S. M., 189
Buesst, Aylmer, 222
Bulletin, 116, 121, 153, 155–6, 157, 162, 163, 167, 206, 207, 246
Burke, Edmund, 3
bushrangers, 135, 159–61
Butlin, Prof. Noel, 43, 75, 76, 77–9, 80, 84, 90, 103
Butt, Clara, 222

Calvert, Albert I., 123
Cambridge, Ada, 117, 118, 121
Campbell, Dr Judy, 79, 84
Canada, 26
Canberra, 217
cannibalism, 124
Carboni, Raffaelo, 135
Carl Rosa Opera Company, 208, 221, 222
Carlyle, Thomas, 143
Carrington, Charles Robert, Lord, 162–3
Castella, Ethel, 113

Castella, M., 148–9
Cazamian, Louis, 229
Cecchi, Pietro, 221
Century, 186
Chauvel, Gen. Harry, 174–5
Cheyne, Cap. Alexander, 70
China, 14, 200, 211, 247, 254
Chisholm, Caroline, 131
Churchill, Winston, 171, 172, 174, 196, 197, 198, 199–200
Clapham, Sir John, 96, 99
Clarke, Edward Daniel, 92
Clarke, Marcus, 117, 154, 166
Clarke, W. B., 91, 92
Clift, Charmian, 254–5
Cobley, Dr John, 20
Coleman, Peter, 255–6
Collington, James, 36
Collins, Cap. David, 18, 35, 36–7, 38, 40
'convict question', 27–8
convicts, background of, 128–9
Cook, Cap. James, 3, 4, 10, 13, 16, 20, 23, 51–2
Country Party, 239, 241
Covell, Roger, 220
Crick, 'Paddy', 140
cricket, 179–83, 190–3
crime, 5–7, 71
Crossley, Ada, 222, 224
Crowley, Dr F. K., 127
culture, 109–26, 152, 155–6, 208–9, 211, 212–35
Currey, C. H., 136
Curtain, Patrick, 136
Curtin, John, 174, 196–200, 201, 239

Dallas, Prof. K. M., 11
Dalley, W. B., 137, 149–50, 151
Darling, Sir Ralph, 60–1, 85–6
Darwin, Charles, 70, 107–8
Darwin, Erasmus, 107
Davy, Sir Humphry, 92
Dawes, Lt William, 40, 43, 44
Dawson, Peter, 222–3
de Groot, Cap., 188
Deakin, Alfred, 257

defence, 201–3, 211–12, 245–8; *see also* Anzus Treaty; First World War; Second World War
Delius, Frederick, 225
d'Entrecasteaux, Chevalier Bruny, 21
depression, 178–9
Derby, Lord, 137, 142, 146
Dibdin, Charles, 7
Dufresne, Marion, 15, 25
Dunn, Michael, 203–5, 206–7
Dunstan, Albert, 241
Durack, Dame Mary, 83
Durack, John, 138
Durack, Patrick, 138–9

East India Co., 20, 52
economy, 108, 169–70, 177–9, 183–8, 249–52; *see also* investment, British; trade
Egypt, 137
Eliot, T. S., 126, 212
Elkin, Prof. A. P., 73
Elwes, Lady Winifred, 225
English Historical Review, 13
ethnic origins of Australians, 127–41
European Community, 254
Evatt, Dr. H. V., 196, 239
exports *see* trade

Facey, A. B., 172, 173
Fadden, A. W., 239
Fairbairn, Anne, 134
Fairbairn, George, 233, 234
Fairbairn, Sir William, 234
Fairbairn, Steve, 134, 233–5
Fairfax, John, 92
Farrell, John, 107
Farrer, William, 99, 169
Federal Government, 237
Field, Barron, 74–5, 112
film industry, 211
First Fleet, 7–9, 13, 14, 16–20, 22–4, 32–4
First World War, 171–6
Fisher, Andrew, 257
Fitzhardinge, Prof. L. F., 40, 80
Fitzpatrick, Brian, 97, 106, 203

Fitzpatrick, Dr David, 140
Fitzroy, Sir Charles, 63–4, 67
Foch, Marshal Ferdinand, 175
folk music, 225–6
Forbes, Sir Francis, 61
Ford, William, 95
foreign affairs, 200–7, 245–9
France, 10, 13–16, 21–2, 23–5, 26, 28, 51, 105, 246, 248
Franklin, Sir John, 65
Fraser, John Foster, 120, 121
Fraser, Malcolm, 239, 242
French Navy, 10, 13–14, 17
Friend, Donald, 214–15
Frost, Alan, 26, 87, 88
Froude, James Anthony, 115, 117, 121, 137, 138, 142, 143–52, 153–6, 162, 164–5, 208, 210, 257

Galli-Curci, Amelita, 221
Gallipoli, 171–4
Gallipoli (film), 173
Game, Sir Phillip, 187
Garden, J. S., 185
Gardiner, Balfour, 224
Gay, Florence, 119, 120, 126, 194
George III, King, 45
Germany, 142–3, 146, 167, 171, 196
Gill, Samuel Thomas, 212–13
Gipps, Sir George, 62–3, 68, 70, 76–7, 83, 91, 125, 133
Gladstone, William Ewart, 66, 67, 149
Gleeson, James, 212–13
Glover, John, 212
gold/gold rushes, 50, 91–6, 108, 112
Gonner, E. C. K., 12–13
Gonville, B. P. de, 15
Goossens, Eugene, 216, 223, 226, 228
Gordon, Adam Lindsay, 112–13, 115, 152, 154, 155
Gordon, Gen. C. G., 149
Governors, 58–66; *see also* under individual names
Grainger, Ella, 226
Grainger, Percy, 221–2, 223–8

Grainger, Rosa, 226, 227
Granville, Lord, 142
Green, Dorothy, 229, 230
Green, H. M., 90, 107, 228–33
Greenpeace, 247
Greenway, Francis, 103, 128, 129, 215
Gregory, J. W., 117, 118–19
Grey, Earl, 63, 64, 66, 67–8, 131, 166–7
Grey, Sir George, 123
Griffin, Walter Burly, 217
Griffith, Sir Samuel, 153, 156–7
Groom, William Henry, 156
Grotius, Hugo, 16
Guérard, Eugène von, 213
Gumbert, Dr Marc, 84–5, 87
Gunn, Jeannie, 117, 125

Haggard, H. Rider, 117
Hall, A. R., 105
Hamelin, Jacques, 21, 25
Hammond, Arthur, 222
Hancock, Sir Keith, 229, 230
Handel, George Frederick, 208
Hanrahan, Michael, 136
Hardinge, Sir Henry, 61
Hargraves, Edward Hammond, 92–3
Harris, Max, 211, 253
Hastings, Warren, 13
Hawke, Robert, 179, 248
Hawkes, Jacquetta, 231
Hayden, Bill, 248, 254
Herbert, Sir R. W., 160
Heseltine, Philip, 232
Highland 'clearances', 133
Higinbotham, George, 164, 167, 241, 257–8
Hitler, Adolf, 196, 198
Hobart, 52, 216
Holman, W. A., 257
Holt, Harold, 202
Hope, A. D., 210, 229–30, 233
Hopetoun, Lord, 134
horse-racing, 120
Hotham, Sir Charles, 136
Howard, John, 3, 7, 242

Howe, Lord, 31
Howitt, A. W., 117
Hughes, Robert, 4
Hughes, William Morris, 175–6, 197, 238
Hummer, 167
Hunter, Cap. John, 1, 27, 36, 51, 58–9, 135
Huxley, T. H., 122

identity, Australian, 252–8
'imperialism', 203–7
India, 14
Indonesia, 200, 202, 247–8
industrial revolution, 6
industry, 169
investment, Australian, 101–2
investment, British, 56–7, 97, 99–101, 105–6, 170, 184, 185, 187–9
Irish Harp and Farmer's Herald, 2
Italy, 208

James, George, 46
Japan, 194–6, 198–9, 200, 201, 204, 206, 247, 249, 254
Jardine, Douglas, 180, 181–2, 192
Jeavons, W. S., 250
Johnson, Richard, 41
Johnson, Dr Samuel, 1, 130
Johnson, Lyndon B., 202

Kamenka, Prof. Eugene, 256
Kelly, Ned, 135, 139
Kemp, David, 256–7
Kennedy, Buzz, 255
Kennedy, Daisy, 223
Kennedy, Lauri, 223
Kerguelen-Tremarec, Yves, 15, 25
Kermadec, Huon, 12, 21
Kerr, John, 239
Kidman, Sidney, 158
King, Admiral Ernest Joseph, 198
King, Gregory, 5
King, Lt Philip Gidley, 11–12, 18, 21–2, 53–4, 59, 110, 212
Kingsley, Charles, 143

Kipling, Rudyard, 116
Kitchener, H. H., Lord, 171
Korean War, 202

La Pérouse, Comte de, 14, 16, 17, 21, 22, 26
Labor Daily, 185
Labour Parties, 184–6, 238–9, 240; *see also* Australian Labour Party (ALP)
Lalor, Peter, 136–7
Lamb, Charles, 112
land, settlement of, 55–6, 68–9, 86
land rights controversy, 84–8
Lang, Jack T., 106, 183, 185, 186, 187–9, 206, 242
Lang, Rev. John Dunmore, 57, 60, 61, 63–4, 130–2, 133, 135, 166–7
Lange, David, 247
'larrikins', 139–40
Larwood, Harold, 180–2, 183, 192
Laver, William, 223
Lawrey, Mrs, 225
Lawson, Mr, 50
Lawson, Henry, 116, 231
Lee, Norman, 174
Lee Kuan Yew, 207
Legouis, M. M., 229
Lewin, Ronald, 200
Liberal Party, 239, 241, 242–3, 244
Light, William, 216–17
Lindley, M. E., 26
Lindsay, Norman, 214, 231, 232
literature, 111–21, 228–35
living standards, 210–11
Lloyd George, David, 115, 174
Loch, Sir Henry, 146
Loftus, Lord Augustus, 149, 151
Lonsdale, Cap. William, 86
Lord, Simeon, 129
Losier, Bouvet de, 15
Lumholz, Carl, 117, 118, 123, 124, 125
Lycett, Joseph, 110
Lyons, Joseph, 188, 191, 196

Macalister, Lachlan, 132

Macarthur, Elizabeth, 54–5
MacArthur, Gen. Douglas, 197, 198
Macarthur, John, 54, 55, 59
Macauley, J. P., 233
McCubbin, Frederick, 213
McIlwraith, Sir Thomas, 142, 153, 157
McIntyre, Kenneth, 30
Mackaness, George, 32, 46
Mackellar, Dorothea, 109
Mackerras, Charles, 228
McLoughlin, Mr, 140
Macmillan, Angus, 132–3
Maconachie, Cap. John, 70
MacPherson, Christine, 219
Macquarie, Lachlan, 34, 50, 58, 59–60, 66, 129, 215
Malaya, 196, 202
Malthus, T. R., 3
Mann, Daniel, 29–30
Manning Clark, Prof., 230–1
Mannix, Archbishop Daniel, 137, 141, 244
Marchant, Prof. Leslie, 15–16, 21, 22–3, 25
Marchesi, Mathilde, 221
maritime base, need for, 14–15
Marshall, Archibald, 118, 120, 121–2
Martens, Conrad, 212
Martin, Sir James, 115, 150
Matra, James, 13
Matthews, C. H. S., 120–1
Mauritius, 14, 15
May, Phil, 121
MCC, 182, 191
Melba, Dame Nellie, 121–2, 220–2, 223
Melbourne, 50, 67, 94, 102, 103, 104, 114, 146, 168, 216
M'Entire, Mr, 42, 44
Menzies, Sir Robert G., 200, 201–2, 239, 244
Millar, Roger, 81
miners, 135–6
Mitchell, Helen *see* Melba, Dame Nellie
Mitterrand, François, 248

Moiseivitch, Benno, 223
Molony, Patrick, 114, 138
Monash, Gen. John, 174
Montcalm, Louis Antoine, Marquis
    de, 25
Moran, Archbishop Patrick, 137
Moresby, Isabella, 219
Mortlock, John Frederick, 128–9
Mosley, Oswald, 240
Muggeridge, Malcolm, 231, 243
'multiculturalism', 253–4, 255
Mummery, Mr, 129
Murdoch, William, 223
music, 121–2, 160, 208, 219–28

National Party, 243
nationalism, 166–70
nature, 119
naval supplies theory, 9–12
Nepean, Sir Evan, 33
Netherlands, 13, 14
New Guinea, 167, 171, 199, 202
New Zealand, 14, 52, 88, 201, 206,
    247
Newman, Ernest, 225
Niemeyer, Sir Otto, 185, 186–7
Noble, M. A., 182
Nolan, Sir Sidney, 140
Norfolk Island, 11, 36
Norman, Montagu, 186, 188, 189–41
Norway, 196

O'Brien, Elvis, 4
O'Brien, William Smith, 129
occupation of Australia, 16–25, 85,
    87
O'Connell, Daniel, 135
O'Connell, Prof. D. P., 88
O'Dowd, Bernard, 138, 232
Ogilvie, Will, 114
O'Loughlin, Sir Bryan, 140
O'Neill, Norman, 224
opera, 220–2
O'Shanessy, Sir John, 140
Ottawa Conference (1932), 194

Pabst, Louis, 223, 224
painting, 110–11, 208–9, 212–15
Paish, George, 100–1
Palmer, Vance, 199
Pamphlet, Thomas, 69
Parker, Mrs, 41
Parker, Sir Gilbert, 118, 119–20, 121
Parkes, Sir Henry, 5, 14–15, 58, 103,
    131, 137, 142, 149, 156, 165,
    245
parliament, 237
Paterson, Andrew ('Banjo'), 115–16,
    160, 219, 231
Paterson, G., 30
Patti, Adelina, 224–5
Pattison, Sir James, 156
Paul, Shiva, 255
Peacock, Andrew, 242
Pearl, Cyril, 139–40
'Pentonvillian' system, 67
Pepys, Samuel, 10
Péron, François, 5, 21
Perth, 168
Phillip, Captain Arthur, 1, 2, 7, 8, 17,
    29, 53, 58, 107
  and aborigines, 26, 41–5, 69, 75,
    78–9, 82
  and administration of justice, 34–7
  and free settlers, 34, 38, 39, 55
  and occupation of Australia, 17,
    18–20, 85
  as administrator, 32–9
  as explorer, 39–41
  auxiliaries of, 40–1
  background of, 30–1
  character of, 31, 46–7
  last years of, 45–6
  management of First Fleet, 32–4
poetry, 111–16, 229–30, 233
political system, 237–45
population, 236–7
poverty, 5–7
'Premiers' Plan', 178
Prentis, Dr Malcolm D., 127, 139
press, 130, 155–6, 179–80, 192–3,
    211; see also under individual
    names

Pringle, J. D., 257
Prout, J. S., 110

Quiller-Couch, Sir Arthur, 235
Quilter, Roger, 224

racism, 246, 248, 255; *see also*
    aborigines
Radcliffe-Brown, Prof. Alfred, 75, 87
Radzinowicz, Sir Leon, 71, 82, 128
Reynolds, Henry, 81
Rhodes James, Robert, 172, 173, 174
Roberts, Tom, 213
Robinson, George, 69
Rogers, Frederic, 164
Rosa, Carl, 208
Rose, Sir George, 31, 40
Ross, Major Robert, 8, 35, 40, 108
Round Table, 195, 196
Rowley, C. D., 82–3
Royal Navy, 9–10, 11, 16–17
Rusden, George William, 3–4, 30
Russell, Henry, 129
Russell, Lord John, 63, 76–7, 83, 125

Salisbury, Lord, 163
Sammons, Albert, 223
Santamaria, B. A., 243–5
Sargent, John Singer, 225
Scott, Cyril, 224
Scott, Sir Ernest, 25, 47, 68–9, 77,
    163–4, 230
Scottish immigrants, 130–4
Scullin, James Henry, 184
Sea Fencibles, 45–6, 51
sealing, 51–2
seapower, 9–12, 13–14
Second World War, 196–9, 246
Sedgwick, Adam, 92
Select Committee on Transportation
    (1812), 38
'selectors', 158–9
Service, James, 146–7, 153, 156
settlers, free, 34, 38, 39, 55–6, 62, 69,
    70, 86
sexual problems, 37–8, 39
Sharp, Cecil, 225–6

Shaw, George Bernard, 226
Shaw, Prof. A. G. L., 71–2, 105
Shearers' Union, 161, 167, 206
Sheridan, Greg, 211
shipping, 53–4
Sinclair, Ian, 243
Sinclair, Prof. W. A., 49, 101, 104–5,
    179
Singapore, 196, 207
Slessor, Kenneth, 229
Slim, Bill, 174
smallpox, 77–9
Smith, Adam, 108
Soviet Union, 200, 204, 206
speech, Australian, 121
Spender, Percy, 200
'squatters', 68, 69, 157
St Allouarn, François Alesne, Comte
    de, 15–16, 21, 23
St Helena, 14
Stalin, Josef, 198
Stephen, Sir Alfred, 150–1
Stephens, Brunton, 113
Stephenson, P. R., 232
Stevens, Bertram, 111–12, 137
Stone, John, 252
Streeton, Arthur, 213
Strzelecki, Count Paul, 91, 133
Stuart, Alexander, 132
surf-bathing, 120
Sutherland, Dame Joan, 228
Sweden, 196
Sydney, 9, 39–40, 50, 52, 102, 103,
    104, 113, 149–50, 168, 216
Sydney, Lord, 9, 10
Sydney Harbour Bridge, 188–9
Sydney Morning Herald, 63, 92, 167,
    192–3, 196–7, 211
Syme, David, 102, 169

Talbot, Richard, 219
Taylor, Joe, 225
Tench, Watkin, 37, 40, 41–2, 44, 73,
    74, 78, 80
Tenison-Woods, Rev. Julian Edmond,
    2–3, 30
Tennyson, Alfred, Lord, 65, 208

terra nullius, Australia as, 25–7, 85, 87
Tetrazzini, Luisa, 221
Thomas, Jimmy, 183
Thompson, Andrew, 129
Thomson, James Alexander, 216
Thornton, Right Rev. Samuel, 118, 123
trade, 194–6, 249–50, 251; *see also* economy; gold; investment, British; sealing; whaling; wool
trade development theory, 12–14
'trade diversion', 194–6
transportation of convicts, 3–4, 5, 7–8, 9, 27, 38–9, 50–1, 65–8, 70–2
Trevelyan, Sir Charles, 134
Truman, Harry S., 199
Tryon, Admiral Sir George, 150
Turkey, 171–3
Turner, Walter James, 231
Twain, Mark, 117

unemployment, 5, 6
unions, 161, 250–2
urbanization, 102–4
USA *see* America

Van Diemen's Land Co., 100
Van Diemen's Land, 11–12, 22, 67, 69
Vandervelde, Willem, 209
Verdon, Sir George, 148
Victoria, Queen, 167
Vietnam War, 202–3, 247

Voce, Billy, 180

wages, 150, 250–1
Wakefield, Edward Gibbon, 55–6
Walker, E. R., 236
Wallace, A. R., 122–3
Wallace, John, 94
Walpole, Horace, 218
Warner, 'Plum', 191
Watling, Thomas, 110
Watson, Don, 132–4
Watson, Lord, 25
Wells, H. G., 239–40
Wentworth, William Charles, 50, 61, 62–3, 111
whaling, 52–3
Wheatley, Francis, 31
Wheelwright, Prof. E. L., 97–8
White, John, 40
White, Patrick, 232–3
Whiteley, Brett, 254
Whitlam, Gough, 85, 239, 248
Wilberforce, Sam, 150
Wilcox, Dora, 114
Willey, Keith, 81–2
Williams, Harold, 222
Wilmot, Sir John, 64, 66
Wilson, Paul, 80–1
wool, 50, 54–5, 56, 95
Worgan, George Bourchier, 219
Wright, Judith, 233

Yeats, W. B., 231

Zaharoff, Sir Basil, 186–7

Index compiled by Peva Keane